Global Capitalism in Crisis

Global Capitalism in Crisis
Karl Marx & the Decay
of the Profit System

Murray E.G. Smith

Fernwood Publishing
Halifax and Winnipeg

Editing and design: Brenda Conroy
Cover design: John van der Woude
Printed and bound in Canada by Hignell Book Printing

Mixed Sources
Product group from well-managed
forests and other controlled sources
www.fsc.org Cert no. SW-COC-003438
© 1996 Forest Stewardship Council

FSC

Published in Canada by Fernwood Publishing
32 Oceanvista Lane
Black Point, Nova Scotia, B0J 1B0
and #8 - 222 Osborne Street, Winnipeg, Manitoba, R3L 1Z3
www.fernwoodpublishing.ca

Fernwood Publishing Company Limited gratefully acknowledges the financial support of
the Government of Canada through the Canada Book Fund, the Canada Council for the Arts,
the Nova Scotia Department of Tourism and Culture and the Province of Manitoba, through
the Book Publishing Tax Credit, for our publishing program.

Library and Archives Canada Cataloguing in Publication

Smith, Murray E. G. (Murray Edward George)
Global capitalism in crisis: Karl Marx and the decay of
the profit system / Murray Smith.

Includes bibliographical references and index.
ISBN 978-1-55266-353-0

1. Capitalism. 2. Marxian economics. 3. Economic history—21st century.
4. Global Financial Crisis, 2008-2009. I. Title.

HB501.S645 2010   330.12'2   C2009-907405-2

Contents

For Esther

Acknowledgements

Permissions to republish chapter 3 from *Historical Materialism* (Koninklijke Brill), appendix 2 from *Science & Society* (Guilford Press) and most of appendix 1 from *The Canadian Review of Sociology and Anthropology* (Wiley-Blackwell) are gratefully acknowledged. I would like to thank the following individuals for various kinds of assistance, encouragement and useful criticism provided to me in the writing and publication of this book: Brenda Conroy, Jonah Butovsky, Ken Campbell, Alana Chalmers, Josh Dumont, Esther Kelly, John McAmmond, David McNally, Antonio Pagliarone, Bryan Palmer, Beverley Rach, Tom Reid and Errol Sharpe.

Preface

As I write these lines in the fall of 2009, the world capitalist economy remains mired in its worst slump since the Second World War, notwithstanding signs of a temporary (and largely jobless) recovery in the United States and Western Europe that will likely prove short-lived. In the developed and so-called "emerging" countries, business bankruptcies are multiplying, unemployment continues to rise, wages and salaries are being slashed, pension plans are being eviscerated and homes are being foreclosed. Working people, in many cases, have lost all hope for the future. At the same time, in many regions of what used to be called the Third World, the number of people literally starving to death is surpassing by a wide margin the previously all too grotesque "normal" levels. A spike in unemployment in countries lacking even the most rudimentary of safety nets, combined with persistently high food prices, is devastating the lives of untold millions.

A globalized capitalist economy is giving birth to a globalized social and economic crisis of unprecedented intensity and geographical reach, completely vindicating Karl Marx's observation that the capital-labour relation — and the world economy it fashions — must lead to an accumulation of fabulous wealth at one pole and utter misery at the other. Meanwhile, the capitalist mass media are working overtime to conceal this simple truth, while concocting absurd "feel good" messages about how the economic downturn should prompt "everyone" to reconsider what is truly important in life!

In the United States, the Obama administration has exploited its waning popularity among working people to pursue, under the guise of a stimulus program, an agenda that is manifestly pro-business and anti-labour, its plans for the restructuring of the U.S. auto industry and for health care "reform" constituting the latest proofs of its determination to "save the system" on terms agreeable to the financial aristocracy and the corporate elite.

Since March, the New York stock exchange has experienced a significant rally, with the Dow Jones average surging from a low of 6,540 to around 10,000 points (still well below its peak of 14,000 in 2007). Predictably, speculation is rife in the mass media that the bear market is giving way to a bull (although a few commentators are speaking more soberly of a new bubble). Yet this much-touted "surge of confidence" among Wall Street investors has almost nothing to do with what is happening on Main Street, where indications of economic recovery remain few and far between. Instead, it has every-thing to do with a political assessment by leading capitalists, above all, Wall Street bankers, that they will continue to have their way, despite the popular anger aroused by the financial meltdown of 2008 and notwithstanding the election of Obama and a Democratic majority in Congress. Many of these plutocrats had fretted that a Democrat-led federal government might yield to pressure from below and implement policies detrimental to their interests. But such fears have been allayed for two reasons: the non-emergence, to date, of significant working-class struggles in response to the economic crisis; and the determination of the Obama administration and the Democrat-led Congress to demonstrate their complete prostration to capitalist interests — above all through the government-funded Troubled Asset Relief Program and other measures designed to "stabilize" the financial system and "jump start" the economy. It is these factors that explain the recent spike in share values, just as it is the underlying rot of contemporary capitalism that makes a vigorous and sustained recovery of the global economy highly unlikely in the near future.

As the economic crisis continues to unfold, one can only hope that North American workers will soon join the class battles that are now underway and multiplying on other continents and that working people throughout the world will soon find the means to end the crisis in the only progressive way possible: through the expropriation of capital and through a socialist transformation that replaces production for profit with production to meet human needs.

The present volume offers a Marxist analysis of the origins, implications and scope of the global economic slump that began in 2008, but it goes well beyond this. The crisis of global capitalism referred to in the title should be understood in two distinct senses: as a *conjunctural* crisis of overproduction, credit and finance, and as a deep-seated *systemic* crisis. In other words, the current crisis should be viewed against the backdrop of a historical-structural crisis of capitalism — as an extreme conjunctural expression of the decay of the profit system.

Chapter 3 and much of the material contained in appendices 1 and 2 were originally published in the 1990s (Smith 1999; 1991a; 1993 respectively) to make the case that, notwithstanding the collapse of Soviet Bloc "actually existing socialism" and the ascendancy of neoliberal, pro-free market hubris, capitalism had long since "overstayed its historical welcome as a means to furthering the material wealth, the social and cultural development, and the general well-being of humankind." This argument, most fully elaborated in my book *Invisible Leviathan* (Smith 1994a: 11, now out of print), fell on few receptive ears in the 1990s. The present crisis presents an important new opportunity to revive and win a larger audience for it.

The lead essay (chapter 1), which originated as a public lecture delivered in November 2008 at Brock University, provides an overview of the events leading up to the slump and its early phases, an argument as to why Marx's "law of the tendency of the rate of profit to fall" is central to an understanding of the current crisis and a discussion of certain political/programmatic implications from a Marxist-socialist perspective.

Written specifically for this book (but also incorporating some passages from *Invisible Leviathan*), chapter 2 offers an overview of Marx's critical analysis of the capitalist mode of production, focusing on his theories of labour value, exploitation, overproduction and the falling rate of profit. It can be usefully read either before or after the opening chapter.

Taken together, chapters 3 to 5 provide an in-depth defence and elaboration of the principal arguments of chapter 1. Chapter 3 is a slightly modified version of an article previously published in the British journal *Historical Materialism*. Chapter 4 is an edited and minimally updated version of the tenth chapter of *Invisible Leviathan* (1994a). Chapter 5 is a new essay that draws together the principal themes of the book and relates them to some of the major challenges confronting the contemporary anti-capitalist left. The two appendices at the end of the volume, drawn from articles I published in the early 1990s (1991a and 1993 respectively), provide readers with an opportunity to explore in greater depth two issues that are of central importance to the arguments developed in the main body of the book: the controversy surrounding Marx's theory of value, and the theoretical status of unproductive labour in Marx's crisis theory.

The publication of this book will, I hope, contribute to a better understanding of what is now being called "the Great Recession," but which may yet become the most severe economic depression in the history of capitalism. Uniquely among the spate of books that have appeared on the current crisis, it provides not only a theoretical defence but also an empirical investigation of Marx's "law of the falling tendency of the rate of profit" — a law Marx considered essential to a scientific understanding of the historical-structural limits of capitalism. It is above all to a reassertion and revival of Marx's scientific socialism that this book is dedicated.

Murray E.G. Smith

Chapter One

The Global Economic Crisis —
A Marxist Perspective

The financial earthquake that erupted in September 2008 and that massively reinforced a downturn in the U.S. economy that began in 2007 has produced the worst global economic slump since the Great Depression of the 1930s. The U.S. government's $700 billion bailout of the financial industry in late 2008 and early 2009 guaranteed lavish bonus packages for Wall Street executives and provided funds for a new round of buyouts, mergers and accelerated concentration of financial capital, but did little to alleviate the credit squeeze that paralyzed new business investment and dampened consumer spending, generating a wave of bankruptcies across financial, manufacturing and commercial sectors.[1] Similar government infusions of liquidity into the banking systems of other countries, notably the U.K., proved just as ineffective in arresting the downward slide. By early 2009, stock markets in North America and overseas had lost between 30 and 50 percent of their nominal value due to tightening credit markets, declining corporate profitability and shattered "confidence." A growing list of countries, beginning with Ukraine, Hungary and Iceland, had obtained major loans from the International Monetary Fund (IMF) to fend off bankruptcy, while the economies of all the leading capitalist countries had begun to contract. By October 2009, the IMF predicted that the gross output of the world's most advanced economies would shrink by 3.4 percent in 2009 — the first such contraction since 1945 (see table 1.1).

According to the IMF, growth in the volume of international trade fell from 7.3 percent in 2007 to 3.0 percent in 2008 and was projected to be minus 11.9 percent in 2009 — a harbinger of much slower growth for the recently booming economies of South and East Asia. China — the most dynamic of these so-called "emerging economies" — saw its annual growth rate fall from 12 to 8.9 percent, and this was expected to drop to about 8.5 percent for 2009. While robust by global standards and higher than forecast earlier

Table 1.1: IMF Projected Growth Rates for 2009: Selected Economies

U.S.	Japan	U.K.	Eurozone	Canada	Developing	World
-2.7%	-5.4%	-4.4%	-4.2%	-2.5%	+1.7%	-1.1%

Source: IMF 2009.

1

in the year, this projected level of growth is considered barely sufficient to absorb the 24 million people entering China's labour market each year.

The global economy has spiralled down into a very severe and lengthy recession — or depression. But sharp disagreements have emerged over the causes of the crisis, its likely course and the solution to it. Those intent on "Saving the System" — the headline of the October 11, 2008, issue of the *Economist* — insist that there is "no alternative" to global capitalism and try to convince the worst-hit victims of the economic crisis — working people and the poor — that they must quietly accept massive job losses, pay cuts, slashed benefits and a roll-back of public services to help "speed recovery." At the same time, the ideological guardians of the status quo are putting forward various accounts that absolve the capitalist system itself of responsibility. Some focus on the greed and short-sightedness of the Wall Street financial elite and the failure of government agencies to adequately regulate markets. More sophisticated apologists for capitalism blame the excesses of "neoliberal ideology" and urge a retreat from "free market fundamentalism." A few go so far as to advocate a social-democratic "mixed economy," including the nationalization of the banks and a significantly expanded public sector.

At the other end of the mainstream spectrum, aggressively rightwing elements are, true to form, blaming the working class and the socially marginalized. According to these shameless victim-bashers, the deflation in housing prices that precipitated the 2008 financial crisis was triggered by "irresponsible" working people who took advantage of sub-prime mortgage rates between 2002 and 2006 and subsequently defaulted on their mortgages when rates went up. It is, however, a measure of the degree to which "greed" and "reckless irresponsibility" have become exclusively associated with the capitalist class and especially its financial aristocracy that this gambit has (so far) found little popular resonance.

Productivity, Value and Capitalist Crisis

On September 15, 2008, the Lehman Brothers investment bank collapsed, accelerating the financial crisis that began in 2007 and that gained momentum with the Bear Stearns fiasco, the failure of California's IndyMac Bank and the U.S. government takeover of the mortgage giants Freddie Mac and Fannie Mae. Lehman's collapse signaled to investors that the multi-trillion dollar market for securitized loans had no real foundation. The real worth of mortgage-backed securities and other exotic debt-instruments was unknown, and that sparked a global sell-off. As stock markets went into free-fall, Republican presidential candidate John McCain responded with the patently ridiculous assertion that "the fundamentals of our economy are strong." Later, in response to criticism from Barack Obama, an indignant McCain defended his remark by pointing to the high productivity of American workers, declaring "our workers are the most innovative, the hardest working, the best skilled, most productive, most competitive in the world."

As unlikely as it may seem, and as foreign as it must have been to McCain's intent, this observation is actually a useful starting point for developing an interpretation of the current crisis that counters the *Economist's* clarion call to "save the system." For if one thing is clear in the present situation, it is this: *the working class can't be blamed for it*. On the contrary, worker productivity is at an all-time high and wages have lagged badly behind productivity growth for a whole generation. Data furnished by the U.S. Bureau of Labor Statistics reveal that productivity and real hourly wages in the private, non-farm U.S. economy grew in lock step between 1947 and the early 1970s, but diverged significantly over the next thirty years (Capitalism and Economic Crisis website n.d.). Referring to the growing income gap between wage earners and investors, U.S. billionaire Warren Buffett remarked candidly in 2005: "It's class warfare, and my class is winning."

Since the 1970s, labour has indeed lost considerable ground in what has been a decidedly one-sided class war. Capital has had its way, in the U.S. and globally, and yet, despite that, capital has still found a way to shoot itself in the foot — and rather badly at that. With Soviet-style "communism" out of the way, with unions decimated and lacking in strategic vision, with the welfare state a receding memory, with China partially reopened to capitalist exploitation and with most of the world's masses seemingly resigned to the inevitability of free-market economics, the global capitalist order is nevertheless now mired in what is clearly its worst economic crisis since the 1930s. The fact that workers and the oppressed cannot be easily scapegoated for the slump means that capitalism may also be on the verge of its deepest political-ideological crisis ever.

Socialists have a responsibility to say what is: the crisis unfolding before our eyes confirms (yet again) that capitalism has reached its "historical limits." This moribund, irrational and inhumane system cannot be reformed in such a way as to promote human progress and well-being but must be superseded, in Karl Marx's words, by a "higher state of social production" — a rationally planned, collectivized global economy under the democratic administration of those who labour.

In support of this claim, I want to elaborate on why McCain's observation about the productivity of U.S. workers is a useful starting point for a Marxist-socialist perspective on the economic crisis and the current predicament of world capitalism. In my 1994 book, *Invisible Leviathan*, I pointed out that at the very heart of Marx's critique of capitalism is the proposition that an immanent contradiction exists between the drive of capitalist firms to increase productivity through labour-saving technological innovation and the imperative of the capitalist mode of production to measure wealth in terms of labour time. According to Marx, the sole source of all "new value" (including the profits of the capitalist class) is the living labour expended in the capitalist production of commodities; and this new value constitutes a definite magnitude that limits prices, profits and wages on an economy-wide scale. These two postulates are the foundation of the "capitalist law of value."

To be sure, Marx's "labour theory of value" (a phrase never actually used by Marx) has been the subject of a long-standing and often tedious controversy, one that I sought to survey and evaluate in *Invisible Leviathan*. Huge quantities of ink have been spilled addressing a question that was of only secondary interest to Marx: namely, the contribution of labour inputs to the determination of relative prices. Marx's primary concern, however, was with exploring the historical significance and long-term implications of the social practice of measuring (valuing) wealth in terms of labour time, especially in a context (namely, a mature capitalist economy) where living labour is becoming a less and less vital ingredient in the production of material output. For Marx, this historically specific, institutionally based and largely unconscious social practice is by no means an eternal or inevitable feature of the human condition. Rather it is bound up with a particular stage in the development of human society, one dominated by the class-antagonistic social relations — and perverse logic — of the capitalist mode of production.

For Marx, then, the measurement of wealth in terms of labour time is by no means inherent in the metabolic exchange between humanity and nature; it is bound up instead with the capitalist social imperative to perpetuate the class domination of capitalists over wage labourers. It was precisely this consideration that prompted Marx to criticize the notion (advanced in the 1875 Gotha Programme of the German Social Democrats) that "labour is the source of all wealth and all culture":

> Labour is *not the source* of all wealth. *Nature* is just as much the source of use-values (and it is surely of such that material wealth consists!) as labour, which itself is only the manifestation of a force of nature, human labour power.... [A] socialist programme cannot allow such bourgeois phrases to pass over in silence the *conditions* that alone give them meaning. (1970: 13, emphasis in original)

Marx's point here is that it is only the social arrangements specific to a capitalist society that render meaningful the identification of "wealth" (a natural category consisting of use values — that is, of useful things and effects) and "value" (a social relation that is created and sustained by a historically specific form of social labour). By way of contrast, Marx suggests that in the future socialist society, "real wealth is the developed productive power of all individuals. The measure of wealth is then not any longer, in any way, labour time, but rather disposable [free] time" (1973: 708).[2]

In a capitalist society, the material output of the economy-wide division of labour is distributed and consumed in accordance with people's ability to purchase it with money — which serves not only as a means of exchange but, above all, as a claim on abstract social labour. Marx's proposition that money is the necessary "form of appearance" of abstract social labour may not seem immediately obvious. But consider this: apart from those who subsist on state-funded social assistance or private charity, people possess money for two basic reasons — they either earn it through the performance of labour or they obtain it by virtue of their ownership of property. The vast majority of the population immediately sees the connection between their labour and the value represented by the money in their possession. At the same time, however, the origin of the money income of those who do not labour and have never laboured for a living seems more obscure. Even so, it's not difficult to understand that those few who hold significant property assets "earn" their money primarily by getting others to perform labour on their behalf. There can be no money profit, money rents, money dividends or any other form of money income for those who own factories, mines, land, apartment blocks, retail stores or banks unless there are people labouring to create the value that finds expression in corporate profits, ground rent, interest and wages. To put the matter starkly, the class of big capitalist property owners can earn income only by exploiting those who labour for a living — that is to say, by paying workers far less than the total "new value" created through the performance of their labour and by appropriating the difference as "surplus value."[3]

If Marx was right about this, then money is indeed the necessary form of appearance of abstract social labour, which is the "social substance" of economic "value" under capitalism. Money profit results from the appropriation of workers' unpaid (surplus) labour and its conversion into surplus value. Furthermore, it follows that the displacement of living labour from production, through increased investments in labour-saving machinery and technology, must undercut the profitability of the system as a whole — its ability to produce "new value" in general and "social surplus value" in particular in magnitudes large enough to sustain the average rate of profit. Accordingly, improved labour productivity, insofar as it results from labour-saving innovation, will actually lower the average rate of profit, which is the decisive regulator of investment and growth in a capitalist economy. As Marx put it: "The progressive tendency for the general rate of profit to fall is… simply the expression, peculiar to the capitalist mode of production, of the progressive development of the social productivity of labour" (1981b: 319).

Capitalism is a system geared not toward the maximization of material wealth (or use values) in general but toward the maximization of wealth in the socially antagonistic form of private profit — the profits of capitalists, who own and control the major means of production, distribution and exchange. This accounts for the characteristic form of capitalist crisis — overproduction. The capitalist economy enters into periodic crisis not because too few goods are being produced to meet human needs, but because too much is produced in the form of commodities intended for sale at a profit. Too many commodities are produced in relation to the effective, money-backed demand that exists for them. What's more, the fundamental reason the economy enters into crisis is not because of a decline in productivity growth (although this can certainly affect the relative fortunes of competing capitalist firms and even national economies), but because not enough surplus value is being produced and subsequently realized in money form across an increasingly globalized capitalist economy. And an insufficient magnitude of surplus value is being produced because, with the introduction of ever more sophisticated technology, the contribution of living labour as a "technical-natural input" into the production process diminishes, even though living, exploitable labour remains the sole source of all new value within the economy as a whole.

So where exactly did McCain go wrong? McCain implied that a high level of labour productivity ought to mean that the "economic fundamentals" are sound — but this assumption presupposes the existence of a rationally ordered economic system. The problem is that capitalism is not rational in this sense. On the contrary, capitalism is dominated by historically specific laws — the law of value and the law of the tendency of the rate of profit to fall — that involve a deepening structural contradiction between the development of the productive forces and the reproduction of capitalist social relations. These laws inform and give expression to a growing incompatibility between the "technical-natural" and "social" dimensions of capitalism. Without grasping them, it's impossible to understand how real progress in labour productivity — based on labour-saving technical innovation — can result in the turmoil in which global capitalism finds itself. Indeed, these laws are the key to understanding how the application of natural-scientific rationality in production, spurred on by the competition of individual firms, creates the "macro" or "global" social irrationality of wasted capacity, wasted labour power and wasted opportunities for human development — as well as a vast and growing mass of human misery.

Production, Finance and the Falling Rate of Profit

What exactly does all this talk about capitalist production have to do with the current global slump and financial crisis? Certainly the most immediate causes of the current crisis lie in the frenzied and short-sighted efforts of investment bankers to realize profits through more-or-less speculative transactions in the sphere of exchange — above all, through the sale, slicing up, repackaging and reselling of "toxic" mortgages. It's also manifestly true that it was the long-overdue puncturing of "bubbles" (in particular the housing bubble) associated with the growth of highly dubious "financial instruments" (a manifestation of what Marx called "fictitious capital")[4] that sent shock waves through the financial system and contributed, directly or indirectly, to the collapse of asset values in the broader economy. All of this has been dissected and discussed ad nauseam by mainstream journalists, politicians, pundits and economists. The relentless chatter about hedge funds, derivatives, collateralized debt obligations, credit default swaps, Ponzi schemes and financial mismanagement and malfeasance has done little, however, to clarify the most fundamental issues underlying the crisis. If anything, its effect has been to deflect attention from the systemic irrationality of capitalism to the greed, corruption and short-sightedness of particular capitalists — precisely, of course, with a view to "saving the system."

What is crucial to understand is that the ground for the financial bubbles and the associated feeding frenzy that led up to the current slump was prepared by an economic malaise that extends back to the 1970s and that originated in the "real economy." The spectacular rise of financial (especially fictitious) capital (relative to productive capital) over the past three decades was neither an accident nor the result of the ascendancy of "neoliberalism," understood primarily as an ideological phenomenon.[5] Rather an adequate account of the long-term financialization of the economy must focus on the tendency of the rate of profit to fall as a result of changes in the capitalist process of production.

Let's consider a couple of observations from the third volume of Marx's *Capital*. Marx stated that the corporate capitalism that was emerging in his own time (in the form of the "joint-stock company") would produce a "new financial aristocracy, a new kind of parasite in the guise of company promoters, speculators and merely nominal directors; an entire system of swindling and cheating with respect to the promotion of companies, issue of shares and share dealing" (1981b: 569). Furthermore:

> The credit system, which has its focal point in the allegedly national banks and the big money-lenders and usurers that surround them, is one enormous centralization and gives this class of parasites a fabulous power not only to decimate the industrial capitalists periodically but also to interfere in actual production in the most dangerous manner — and this crew know nothing of production and have nothing at all to do with it. (1981b: 678–79)

Elsewhere, in the second volume of *Capital*, Marx noted:

> [To the possessor of money-capital] the production process appears simply as an unavoidable middle term, a necessary evil for the pur-

pose of money-making. This explains why all nations characterized by the capitalist mode of production are periodically seized by fits of giddiness in which they try to accomplish the money-making *without the mediation of the production process.* (1981a: 137, emphasis added)

To understand the significance of such "giddy" and unproductive capitalist behaviour, one needs to consider how the preconditions for it develop, which in turn requires a concrete analysis of how the immanent contradictions of capitalism find expression and unfold in particular historical contexts. The current financial crisis is the outcome of a decades-long effort on the part of the capitalist class, in the U.S. and elsewhere, to arrest and reverse the long-term decline in the average rate of profit that occurred between the 1950s and the 1970s. It is the cumulative and complex result of a series of responses by the capitalist class to an economic malaise that can be traced to the persistent profitability problems of productive capital — the form of capital associated with the so-called "real economy."

Virtually all radical political economists agree that the current debacle has roots in the profitability crisis of the 1970s. In response to that crisis, manifested throughout the advanced capitalist world in falling rates of profit as well as in "stagflation" (high inflation rates combined with slower growth and increased unemployment), the capitalist class abandoned the "capital-labour accord," negotiated in the late 1940s and 1950s. Rendered economically feasible by the high profit rates of the immediate post-war period and prompted by the politico-ideological exigencies of the Cold War (especially the necessity to block the emergence of powerful leftwing forces in Western labour movements), this "class compromise" delivered rising real wages, low unemployment and expanded social-welfare programs for over twenty years. But with the advent of the profitability crisis of the 1970s the capitalist class was compelled to undo much of this. The inflation that fuelled high levels of class conflict in the 1970s was defeated through wage controls and/or high interest rate policies under successive post-Keynesian and monetarist regimes. The deep recession of the early 1980s, engineered by the high interest rate policies of the U.S. Federal Reserve under Paul Volcker, along with cutbacks in social-welfare provision by most major Western governments, replenished the "reserve army" of the unemployed and placed downward pressure on real wage growth. Trade liberalization, corporate globalization and the turn toward "lean production" and "flexible labour markets" further weakened nationally based labour movements and removed obstacles to the international mobility of capital. Taken together, these measures — often referred to as "neoliberalism" — stemmed the fall in the average rate of profit in the leading capitalist countries but failed to restore the much higher rates enjoyed by capital in the earlier post-war period. For a considerable period of time, extending into the 1990s, the average profit rate was stabilized, albeit in a comparatively low range. Far more draconian anti-labour measures might have been tried to restore profitability to higher levels, but such measures would have carried considerable political-ideological risks — particularly during the 1980s, when the capitalist West was facing down a weakening but still formidable Soviet adversary.

This was the background to the long ascendancy of the rate of profit in the U.S. financial sector relative to that of the productive economy (manufacturing, construction, mining and so forth). In the early 1980s, the financial sector accounted for only about 10 percent of total profits; by 2007, this figure had risen to 40 percent. From the 1950s to the 1970s, the ratio of financial assets to GDP averaged approximately 4 to 1; by 2007 it had risen to roughly 10 to 1. In 1980, world financial assets (bank deposits, securities and shareholdings) amounted to 119 percent of global production; by 2007 that figure had risen to 356 percent.

Following the capitalist offensive against labour in the 1970s and early 1980s, crises of overproduction were avoided or attenuated (as in 1991–92 and 2001–02) through an enormous expansion of credit. Between the fourth quarter of 1981 and that of 2008, credit market debt in the U.S. mushroomed from 164 percent to 370 percent of GDP. While real wages stagnated or declined, American working people were encouraged to maintain "effective demand" by plunging ever deeper into debt. Between 1980 and 2007, total household debt mushroomed from about 60 percent of national income to over 120 percent. Meanwhile, between 1973 and 2000, the average real income of the bottom 90 percent of American taxpayers declined by more than 7 percent (Chernomas 2009: 21). Ronald Reagan's massive increase in military spending during the 1980s, which primed the demand pump enormously, ran up government debt to unprecedented levels. Throughout the 1990s, federal government debt continued to steadily expand, before exploding under George W. Bush following the U.S. invasion and occupation of Iraq. In early 2009, it stood at about $11 trillion in a $14 trillion (GDP) economy.

What prompted this massive expansion of debt and the associated financialization of the U.S. economy? To answer this question, we need to consider why the traditional, more production-centred investment strategies

Table 1.2: Growth of U.S. National Debt (in constant 2007 dollars), 1945–2009

1945	1950	1990	2000	2008	2009 (projected)
$3 trillion	$2 trillion	$5 trillion	$7 trillion	$11 trillion	$12 trillion +

of the capitalist class began to falter beginning in the 1970s. For the time being, it's sufficient to note that, over an extended period, investment in finance and commerce became a much more secure and lucrative way to earn profits than investment in industrial production, at least for capitalists operating in the most developed capitalist nations. Many giants of industrial capital acknowledged this new reality by expanding their business operations beyond the production of manufactured goods to the provision of an array of profitable financial services, a notable example being General Motors' GMAC financial services company.

The Malaise of Productive Capital

What is most striking about the past thirty years is the persistently lackluster performance of productive capital operating in the "real economy" — the form of capital that is the source of all new value and thus of all "real wealth" in capitalist terms. (According to Marx, surplus value must be produced by living labour employed by productive capital before it can be shared with unproductive financial and commercial capitals.) Since the 1970s, the ruling elites have been successful both in massively redistributing wealth in their own favour and in ratcheting up the rate of exploitation of wage labour, but the rate of growth of the world capitalist economy (global GDP) has been declining and there have been numerous indications of long-term malaise (see tables 1.3 and 1.4).

Cross-national data compiled by the Organisation for Economic Co-operation and Development (OECD) show that a growing gap developed between average profit rates and growth rates in all the G7 countries (the U.S., Britain, Canada, France, Germany, Italy and Japan) following the deep recession of the early 1980s. Furthermore, the trend for the accumulation rate (that is, average annual percentage growth rates of capital stock) began to decline with the profitability crises of the 1970s and continued to fall even

Table 1.3: Indicators of Economic Malaise, G-7 Nations, 1950–93

Private Business Indicators	1950–73	1973–93
Average annual growth rate of output	4.5%	2.2%
Average annual growth of labour productivity	3.6%	1.3%
Average unemployment rate (overall economy)	3.1%	6.2%

Source: Brenner 1998a: 5.

Table 1.4: Average Growth Rates of World Capitalist Economy, 1960–2004

1960s	1970s	1980s	1990s	2000–2004
4.90%	3.93%	2.95%	2.70%	2.76%

Source: World Bank website.

after a partial recovery of profit rates in the 1980s. The average "all business" accumulation rate for the G7 fell from an average of 5 percent in 1960–73 to 4.1 percent in 1973–79 and 3.9 percent in 1979–89. The corresponding figures for manufacturing were 5.5 percent, 3.6 percent and 2.9 percent (Armstrong, Glyn and Harrison 1991).

To be sure, economic growth has occurred unevenly across the world, and certain regions have fared much better than the G7 countries with respect to GDP growth rates, especially since the mid-1990s. In particular, China has experienced growth rates that have been dramatically higher than the global averages, and this performance has been associated with an explosion of productive capitalist enterprise, especially in light manufacturing and construction. Assuming the role of "workshop of the world," China has attracted an increasing share of the productive-capital investments being made by U.S. and other Western-based transnational corporations. The result has been a further decline of industrial production in the advanced capitalist countries and a corresponding rise of the FIRE (finance/insurance/real estate) and service sectors.

Trends in global GDP growth rates tell only a part of the story. When global growth rates are calculated on a per capita basis, and with the erstwhile "socialist countries" included, the declining performance of the world economy as a whole is even more remarkable, with average growth rates of 3.5 percent in the 1960s, 2.4 percent in the 1970s, 1.4 percent in the 1980s and only 1.1 percent in the 1990s (Harvey 2005: 154).

Apologists for the capitalist system have a hard time accounting for the bleak picture I've just sketched. Even so, while leftist critics of capitalism, and even many mainstream economists, have identified the profitability crisis of the 1970s as a vital factor in shaping subsequent economic trends, controversy abounds as to whether Marx's theory provides a satisfactory explanation of its origins. Does our recent history really confirm Marx's claim that "the real barrier to capitalist production is capital itself" (1981b: 358)?

Marx's Law of the Tendency of the Rate of Profit to Fall

For many years, the favoured explanation for the profitability crisis of the 1970s among radical political economists was the "wage-push/profit-squeeze" or "rising strength of labour" account. According to this approach, the profit share of national income declined because real wages (across private and public sectors) rose faster than the rate of productivity growth — a view shared by most mainstream economists as well. The element of truth in this explanation was that, over a considerable period of time, an increasing share of the aggregate wage bill went to wage and salary earners who were not directly involved in the production of commodities, and "total wages and salaries" as a percentage of national income rose relative to the profit share. As workers were displaced from production due to technological innovations in manufacturing, forestry, mining and construction, they found new jobs in commercial and financial sectors as well as in non-profit state or para-state agencies (public administration, education and so on). While the labour performed by these workers was, to varying degrees, useful and even "socially necessary" from the standpoint of capital, it was by no means directly productive of commodities embodying surplus value — and it therefore constituted "unproductive labour" in Marx's terms. The activity of some of this labour (both commercial and financial) accelerated the turnover of productive capital by hastening the realization of commodity values in the circulation phase of the circuit of capital, while the activity of the growing army of workers in finance laid the foundation for the subsequent expansion of fictitious capital. This growth of "socially necessary unproductive labour" was likely a supplementary cause of the post-war fall in the rate of profit in the advanced capitalist countries, but it was by no means the sole or even the primary cause.

As noted earlier, there is strong evidence, particularly for the U.S. economy, that the growth of real wages for private-sector workers did not outstrip productivity growth in the period leading up to the profitability crisis of the 1970s. Moreover, rigorous empirical studies by the Marxist economist Anwar Shaikh have established that the fall in the average rate of profit in the U.S. economy was significantly correlated with an increase in what Marx called the "organic composition of capital" — the ratio of "dead labour" (accumulated fixed capital, etc.) to living labour in production (Shaikh 1989; see also Shaikh and Tonak 1994). Independent studies by Fred Moseley (1987; 1991) have complemented Shaikh's findings, while giving greater weight to the role of a rising ratio of unproductive to productive labour in the overall fall in the average rate of profit.

Over a decade ago, I tested Marx's theory of the falling rate of profit in regard to the evolution of the Canadian economy between 1947 and 1991. This analysis, co-authored by K.W. Taylor (1996), was later summarized in my article "The Necessity of Value Theory" (1999; reprinted as chapter 3 of this volume).[6] The first major finding of the study was that between 1947 and 1975 the average rate of profit on capital investment exhibited a long-term declining trend — a well-established and uncontroversial fact (see chart 1.1). The second major finding was that, as the rate of profit was declining, the rate of surplus value (that is, the rate of exploitation of productive workers) showed a long-term upward trend (see chart 1.2). But the most interesting finding was that the organic composition of capital (the ratio of fixed-capital values invested in machinery and other physical assets to the total new value created by living labour) displayed a very sharp upward trend during the same period (see chart 1.3).:

12

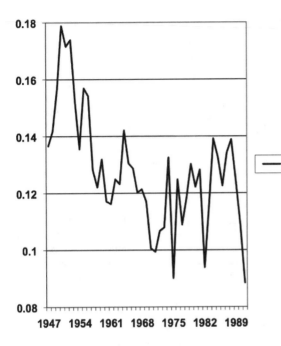

Chart 1.1: The Average Rate of Profit (the Ratio of the Aggregate Surplus Value Flow to the Value of the Fixed Constant Capital Stock: S/C), Canada 1947–1991

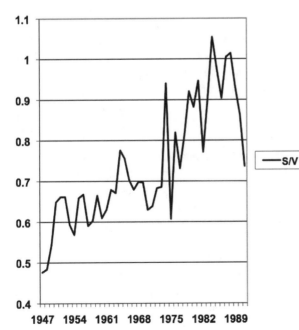

Chart 1.2: The Rate of Surplus Value (the Ratio of Aggregate Surplus Value Flow to Variable Capital Flow: S/V), Canada 1947–1991

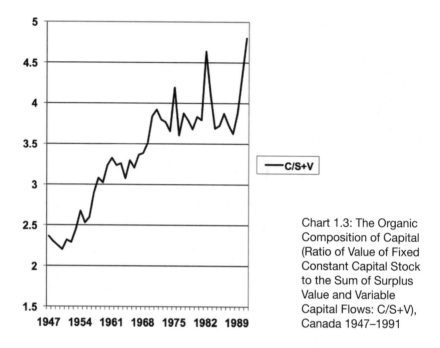

Chart 1.3: The Organic Composition of Capital (Ratio of Value of Fixed Constant Capital Stock to the Sum of Surplus Value and Variable Capital Flows: C/S+V), Canada 1947–1991

From the mid-1970s through the recession of the early 1990s, the trend line for the average rate of profit is relatively flat, while the rate of surplus value increases dramatically and the organic composition of capital levels off.[7] This analysis accords well with established facts about the response of capital and the state to the stagflation of the 1970s: limit wage growth, curtail the strength of the labour movement, improve productivity by intensifying the labour process and lengthening the working day, remove obstacles to international capital mobility, cut back on social programs and reduce corporate taxes, all with a view to restoring conditions of profitability.[8]

The empirical findings of the Smith-Taylor study furnish strong support for the proposition that the profitability crisis of the 1970s in Canada (which paralleled that of the U.S.) resulted from the displacement of living labour from production and its replacement by labour-saving technologies, a process encouraged both by competitive cost-cutting and capital-labour antagonism. Marx's expectations regarding the long-term dynamics of capital accumulation were shown to be fully consistent with the actual performance of the Canadian economy in the mid-twentieth century.

The overall conclusion emerging from this brief survey is that Marx's law of the tendency of the rate of profit to fall holds up remarkably well in light of the empirically verifiable performances of the U.S. and Canadian economies over the course of the second half of the twentieth century. An adequate scientific analysis of the recent trajectory of the world capitalist economy, it would seem, must take into account the phenomenon of a high organic composition of capital in the advanced capitalist countries as a persistent obstacle to global profitability.

Profitability Crisis and Financialization Revisited

Can this analysis contribute to an explanation of the long-term financialization of the advanced capitalist economies — the shift from productive capital investment to financial and, increasingly, fictitious capital in the pursuit of profits? It should be only too obvious that it can. The response of the social capital[9] to the profitability crisis of the 1970s involved a three-fold strategy with regard to investment: restrain new capital formation in industries deemed to be "overcapitalized" and burdened by a high-wage labour force; concentrate investment in technological innovation (such as information technology) in the financial sector with a view to enhancing labour productivity in that sector;[10] and direct an increasing share of productive-capital investment to "newly industrializing" regions (Mexico, Southeast Asia, India and China), where a higher profit rate could be achieved based on much lower wage costs and lower organic composition of capital.

This new investment strategy can be viewed as a determined effort by the dominant fractions of the social capital to mobilize what Marx called the "counteracting tendencies" to the falling rate of profit. The failure of Western labour movements to wage a serious fight-back against the capitalist offensive not only ensured the success of this effort, it also encouraged the capitalist class to overreach in ways that proved to be self-destructive in the longer term. Emboldened by the passivity of the bureaucratic misleaders of labour and exhilarated by the collapse of Soviet Bloc "Communism," the capitalist class (above all in the United States) succumbed to the "giddiness" referred to by Marx. One important consequence was the redirection of a great deal of surplus value into the circuit of capitalist revenue (that is, into the bloated executive pay and bonuses that made possible ever more obscene levels of luxury consumption by the capitalist class) and away from accumulation (that is, new capital formation). But the other major consequence was financialization — significantly increased investment in financial activity, the appearance of new financial instruments like derivatives and hedge funds, frenzied speculation surrounding a growing volume of fictitious capital, a massive overloading of the credit system and a generalized "irrational exuberance," to borrow Alan Greenspan's famous phrase.

Ironically, as dominant fractions of the capitalist class came to believe that money-making was indeed possible without the "mediation of the production process," an increasing share of global production was being concentrated in East Asia, whose balance of trade surpluses served to accelerate the financialization process in the U.S. as well as the massive growth

15

of public and private debt in the Western world. Ken Campbell has written incisively on this process:

> In his memoir, *Age of Turbulence*, former U.S. Federal Reserve chairman Alan Greenspan attributed the lowering of interest rates that occurred during his watch (1987–2006) to a "glut of Asian savings." This explanation suggests that low interest rates were an expression of prevailing market forces rather than central bank and government economic policy. In fact, the "savings glut" that arose in Asia in the 1990s was itself the product of a credit-induced expansion of production and global trade, an effort that was both economic and geo-political in effect and design. The "glut of savings" in such countries as Japan, China, and Korea was the result of the amassing of large trade surpluses with the West, particularly the U.S., surpluses which were then lent back in various ways to the West so that consumers could continue to purchase Asian-made consumables. Consumers in the West, particularly in the U.S., got used to borrowing to feed their consumerist impulses. With easy access to credit, they were all too willing to purchase goods they really didn't need with money they really didn't have.... Low interest rates prompt and privilege consumption over savings. There is little immediate incentive to save when the combined impact of inflation and taxation on savings results in *negative real saving*, as has been the case in the U.S., Canada and the West generally for the last 20 years. The current crisis is a financial crisis, but not just a crisis in the system of finance and credit. It's a crisis of the global economy based on credit. It's a crisis of vast indebtedness, come home to roost. (2009: 4)

The Role of China

Several factors account for the recovery of profitability in the face of slower overall growth rates in the world economy from the mid-1990s on. One was the higher rate of exploitation of labour in the advanced capitalist world, made possible by capital's victory over labour in the class battles that marked the 1970s and 1980s. A second was the proliferation of fictitious capital and the inflation of the huge "debt bubbles" that have already been highlighted. A third, however, was the emergence of significant new sites of capitalist production, surplus value creation and capital accumulation in the "emerging" economies of South and East Asia. In this regard, the contribution of the Peoples Republic of China to the "stabilization" of global capitalism during the heyday of financialization deserves special attention.

A near consensus exists among what currently passes for the socialist left that capitalism has been fully restored to China (see, for example, Hart-

Landsberg and Burkett 2005). To a considerable extent, this assessment echoes the conventional wisdom of the business press that China's rapid growth rates over the past two decades are entirely attributable to the "market reforms" introduced by Deng Xiaoping and his successors and the extraordinary growth of capitalist enterprise in China's "socialist market economy." This view is also often associated with the assumption that China under Mao Zedong had been fully socialist and that the repudiation of Mao's economic policy by his heirs signified a return to the "capitalist road." Thus, leftist defenders of Mao's theoretical legacy and pro-capitalist ideologues often converge in seeing China's recent economic "success story" as the result of an abandonment of socialism and a move toward the full restoration of capitalism by the Chinese leadership.

While such a characterization of post-Maoist China contains some truth (who would deny the massive proliferation of capitalist enterprise in the Chinese economy?), the thesis that China has become fully capitalist is predicated on equating the presence and expansion of capitalist enterprise with the socio-economic dominance of capital. Such an equation presupposes what needs to be demonstrated: that capitalist rule — and, with it, the tyranny of the capitalist law of value — have been re-established in China. Yet a strong case can be made that China is not, or not yet, dominated by capitalist property relations and that it remains a post-capitalist social formation — or, more precisely, a "workers' state," albeit one that is bureaucratically deformed. (This argument draws on the theoretical categories of Leon Trotsky's analysis of the Soviet Union under Stalin and is defended by some, though not all, contemporary Trotskyist groups.)[11]

From this perspective, China is not now and never has been fully socialist. Rather it is best understood as a transitional socio-economic formation, one that has combined elements of capitalism and socialism since the 1950s. To be sure, the balance of these elements has shifted over time, and there is unquestionably a very real possibility that the capitalist elements could soon prevail over the socialist ones. But a convincing case has yet to be made that a "capitalist counter-revolution" has already occurred. The thesis that China has been completely reabsorbed into world capitalism, that the Chinese party-state bureaucracy is now an instrument of capitalist class rule and that the Chinese economy is subordinate to the law of value is simply not credible. What's more, to credit China's recent economic development to the restoration of capitalism is actually to give ground to those who deny that capitalist social relations have become a brake on the development of the productive forces of humankind.[12]

In opposition to the dominant "China is capitalist" perspective, what has been central to China's (highly contradictory) "economic miracle" has been the survival of many socialist elements within its economy. These elements include state ownership of the core of the industrial economy, government control of the financial system, the still significant role of centralized economic planning and, until recently at least, the state monopoly on foreign trade. Indeed, in the absence of these elements, China would likely have been reduced to a semi-colonial status within the world capitalist economy. Furthermore, the specific way in which these elements have been combined and articulated with an export-led strategy of economic development — predicated on an "opening" to the world market and the controlled revival of capitalist enterprise (as well as the suppression of the Chinese working class as an independent force) — accounts for the dynamic but also highly problematic pattern of economic growth that has characterized China over the past three decades.

The fundamental point is that China's "socialist market economy" has remained within the historical ambit of Stalinism — that is, the social phenomenon of bureaucratic rule on the basis of collectivized property forms and the ideological perspective of building "socialism in one country." With its opening to the world market, the Chinese Stalinist bureaucracy has sought to use its monopoly of political power and the surviving elements of "socialist planning" to harness market forces and capitalist enterprise to the essentially nationalist project of modernizing China and transforming it into a "great power." In the process, it has also contributed greatly to a relative stabilization of the world capitalist economy.

China's principal contribution to world capitalism has been its production of cheap consumer goods for the Western working class. Without the influx of these goods into the advanced capitalist countries over the past twenty-five years, it is quite likely — barring the emergence of serious class struggles — that the living standards of Western workers would have declined much more than they have. The super-exploitation of Chinese workers by indigenous Chinese capital, off-shore Chinese capitalists and transnational corporations has allowed not only for the production and sharing out of an enormous volume of surplus value. It has also contributed to a cheapening of "the elements of variable capital" (the commodities purchased by workers' wages), thereby offsetting increases in the cost of living and attenuating the misery associated with job loss in traditional industries and a supine Western labour movement. The combined effect of this super-exploitation has been to mitigate the stagnancy in world economic growth rates, improve global profitability and subdue the class struggle in the advanced capitalist world.

This analysis challenges the conventional understanding of China with respect to its most fundamental premises. In counterpoint to the notion that capitalism "rescued" China from economic stagnation, China's transitional economy is playing a helpful, even crucial role in rescuing Western capitalism from its worst profitability crisis since the 1930s. In pursuit of its nationalistic ambitions, the Chinese bureaucracy placed the resources of the deformed workers' state at the disposal of a badly debilitated world capitalism — which resulted not only in sustained rapid growth for the Chinese economy but also in a temporary restabilization of the global capitalist order.

Mao Zedong was wrong to have labeled Deng Xiaoping a "Khrushchevite capitalist-roader," but he was surely correct (or prescient) to recognize that Deng shared something of Soviet premier Nikita Khrushchev's vision of "peaceful competition" (and co-existence) with the capitalist world. In the late 1950s, Khrushchev proclaimed that the Soviet planned economy would eventually inundate the West with a flood of low-priced consumer goods, thereby striking a decisive blow against the capitalist profit system — a utopian boast that soon rang hollow as the Soviet growth machine faltered a few years later. Deng understood that China was unable to compete with the West in overall productivity (after all, American and Japanese workers set in motion productive apparatuses that are many times more powerful and efficient than the Chinese); but it *could* compete and prosper by attracting productive-capital investment from the West and mobilizing its poorly paid working class to manufacture cheap consumer goods for the capitalist world market.

Thirty years on, however, Deng's vision may turn out to be no less utopian than Khrushchev's. Thanks to the irrepressible contradictions of the capitalist mode of production, some rather diseased chickens have come home to the Chinese roost. As of June 2009, China was the nervous owner of just under $800 billion in U.S. Treasury securities — financial assets whose real value is now very much in doubt. Little wonder then that in March 2009 Chinese premier Wen Jiabao stated: "We have lent a huge amount of money to the U.S. Of course we are concerned about the safety of our assets. To be honest, I am definitely a little worried." This worry has since led the Chinese leadership to openly call into question the role of the U.S. dollar as the pre-eminent world currency and to broach the possibility of an overhaul of the international monetary system.

To date the Chinese government has shown little appetite to use its massive currency reserves to help finance further bailouts of Western banks, despite fears of ongoing financial instability. Instead, it is concentrating its resources on a program of domestic stimulus (suggesting a partial turn toward "market socialism in one country") as well as the buying up of Western assets at bargain-basement prices.

The future of China's deformed workers' state and "socialist market economy" remains very much in doubt and with it China's continuing ability to contribute to the stabilization of world capitalism. But one thing is fairly certain: either the Chinese working class will settle accounts with the Stalinist oligarchy and usher in a revolutionary workers' state committed to socialist democracy and working-class internationalism, or the oligarchy will continue to prepare the ground for a full-scale capitalist counter-revolution. In either case, China will emerge, for better or worse, as the foundry in which the destiny of humankind will be forged for a considerable period to come.

How Much of a Recovery Did the U.S. Rate of Profit Make?

Let's return to what has been called "ground zero" of the financial crisis: the U.S. economy. Chart 1.4 traces the evolution of the "corporate rate of profit" in the U.S. from 1948 to 2007. One of the interesting things about this chart is the overall upward movement in the rate of profit from about 1991–92 to 2006–07. Clearly, the profit rate wasn't restored to the levels that prevailed between 1950 and 1968, but it did show some promise of overcoming the malaise of the late 1960s to the early 1990s.[13] As previously noted, much of this improvement is attributable to the above average returns of the financial sector in the late 1990s and after the 2001 recession. But following that recession, U.S. manufacturing continued its decline while the role of the "housing bubble" in fuelling growth became crucial. Indeed, between 2002 and 2007, as much as half of the growth of U.S. GDP was housing-driven (new home construction, home renovation, home-equity driven consumer spending and other financial activity associated with the high-flying real estate market).[14] David McNally observes: "during this round of credit-driven growth, U.S. household debt more than doubled, increasing from $6.4 trillion in 1999 [to] $13.8 trillion in 2006" (2009a: 14). The rate of profit of the U.S. construction industry also reached heights that were historically unprecedented during this period. The result was not only a huge expansion of credit market debt but also overproduction in the housing sector — a glut of overvalued homes for which there turned out to be insufficient effective demand. The ensuing wave of mortgage foreclosures precipitated a sharp decline in housing prices, igniting the financial crisis and setting the stage for a severe economic downturn with dire implications for the economy-wide rate of profit.

Fred Moseley, who presents a data set for the U.S. profit rate similar to that represented in chart 1.4, comments:

> It has taken a long time, but the rate of profit is now approaching the peaks achieved in the 1960s.... The last several years, especially since the recession of 2001, have seen a very strong recovery of profits, as real wages have not increased at all, and productivity has increased rapidly (4–5 percent a year). And these estimates include only profits from domestic U.S. production, not the profits of U.S. companies from their production abroad. They also do not include the multimillion dollar salaries of top corporate executives. On the

Chart 1.4: Corporate Rate of Profit, U.S. Economy, 1948–2007

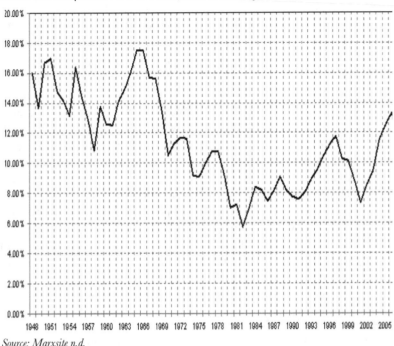

Source: *Marxsite n.d.*

other hand, these estimates do include a large and increasing percentage of profits from the financial sector (approximately one-third of total profit in recent years has been financial profit), much of which will probably turn out to be fictitious (i.e., anticipated future earnings that are "booked" in the current year, but will probably never actually materialize because of the crisis). (2009)

Oddly, Moseley concludes that "there has been a very substantial and *probably almost complete recovery* of the rate of profit in the United States" — despite the fact that "total losses of U.S. banks could reach as high as one-third of the total bank capital" (emphasis added). Contrary to Moseley's assessment, however, it seems likely that the bursting of the financial bubble that sustained the relatively high profits of recent years will bring a definitive end to the recent upward trend in U.S. corporate profitability.

Robert Brenner provides a more concrete and detailed picture of recent profit rate trends than that sketched by Moseley, one that is attentive to longer-term trends not only in the U.S. but also in what are the second and third largest capitalist economies in the world, Japan and Germany:

In Germany, as in Japan, the average rate of profit for the private economy as a whole during the business cycle of [2000–2007] failed to rise above the already very reduced figures of the 1990s, languishing in both places, *as in the US non-financial corporate sector*, at the lowest levels of the postwar epoch. Between 2001 and 2007, in Japan and Germany, like the US, the growth of investment, measured in terms of the growth of the capital stock… was far and away the slowest for any comparable interval during the postwar period. In the same years, in Japan and the Euro 15, as well as Germany and the US, both the growth of real compensation per employee (wages plus benefits) and the increase in employment for the economy as a whole were also the slowest for any comparable interval in the postwar era…. Simply stated, despite the enormous subsidies to purchasing power that were provided by the wealth effect of the historic asset price bubbles, as well as the return just about everywhere to old fashioned Keynesian budget deficits, the struggle to revive profit rates that had sunk to postwar lows left the growth of aggregate demand at postwar lows across the advanced capitalist countries, making for the worst economic performance since the end of the 1940s. (Brenner 2009: 69, emphasis added)[15]

The upshot is clear enough. Thirty years of neoliberalism, corporate globalization and financial chicanery did not succeed in "completely" reversing the profitability crisis that has long plagued the core of the capitalist world economy — a crisis deeply rooted in capital's persistently high organic composition. These class strategies could only postpone the day of reckoning for capital — which is now looking less like a rationally calculating vampire lurking within the sphere of production (to which Marx once compared it) and much more like a rampaging zombie gorging itself at a casino crime scene.

Where Are We Headed?

To date, the responses of capitalist governments to the crisis have included the following:

- a buyout by the federal government of toxic financial "assets" held by U.S. banks (the so-called TARP program) — a gambit destined to fail not only because these "troubled assets" are widely diffused but also because they represent liabilities that exceed the value of the approved bailout package by a few trillion dollars;
- effectively nationalizing and partially recapitalizing some of the worst-hit American and European financial institutions using borrowed money.

While this might temporarily stabilize the banking system, it will do nothing to address the underlying problem of the toxic assets; and

• a "collective effort" by the G-20 countries to stimulate employment and demand through boosts to government spending. How these stimulus packages will be financed in the long term remains something of a mystery. Most banks are illiquid, with many of the ostensible assets on their balance sheets exposed as uncollectible liabilities. Western governments have few significant currency reserves. Both China and Japan have substantial foreign currency reserves, but are likely to use them mainly for domestic purposes. The Arab oil states are still swimming in money-capital, but it's unclear why they would choose to lend it out at low interest rates rather than use it to acquire some of the steeply discounted corporate assets now becoming available.

In the capitalist West, consumer credit cards are maxing out, and delinquency is on the rise. The financial system hasn't been fixed: it's just been put in different (and fewer) hands. Even if central banks can find some way of injecting liquidity into the system (for example, by printing money and risking hyperinflation), it seems unlikely that the relatively small stimulus packages being implemented in the U.S. and elsewhere will be able to kick-start the world economy. Past consumption has borrowed heavily against future demand; in Britain and North America consumers are deep in debt; and the credit system that made it all possible is several trillion dollars in the red. A tsunami of layoffs and bankruptcies has sent the G-20 economies into a tailspin. With declining tax revenues and the credit system in shambles, governments are going to have a hard time financing existing levels of expenditure—much less launch the major "public works" programs proposed by reform-minded leftists who appear to harbour an inexhaustible faith in capitalism's ability to "renew" itself and who are hoping (no doubt with "audacity") that Obama will be the second-coming of Franklin Delano Roosevelt.

In short, it's hard to see where the U.S. and the other advanced capitalist economies will find the means for renewed profitable growth. The depth of the crisis, the massive existing government debt and justified fears of runaway deficits make a "Keynesian fix" highly improbable. Indeed, the last time there was a crisis of this magnitude the profit system was only restored to "health" through the combined effects of a massive devaluation of assets (the Great Depression) and the *physical destruction* of capital stocks during the Second World War. Contrary to liberal opinion, it was the cataclysm of global war, not FDR's "New Deal" or Keynesian economic policy, that finally pulled the U.S. and world economies out of depression and created the conditions for the robust capital accumulation of the post-war era.

Capitalist Crisis and Marxist-Socialist Politics

On that somber note, I shall conclude with a few general remarks concerning the political consequences of what we are now witnessing. From a Marxist-socialist perspective, the current crisis lays bare the fundamental irrationality of capitalism in an era marked by unprecedented global economic integration, profound global inequality and the prevalence of advanced, labour-saving technology within the core of the capitalist world economy. The crisis also confirms Marx's law of the falling tendency of the rate of profit as the harbinger of capitalist decline:

> Beyond a certain point, the development of the powers of production becomes a barrier for capital; hence the capital relation a barrier for the development of the productive powers of labour.... The growing incompatibility between the productive development of society and its hitherto existing relations of production expresses itself in bitter contradictions, crises, spasms. The violent destruction of capital not by relations external to it, but rather as a condition of its self-preservation, is the most striking form in which advice is given to it to be gone and to give room to a higher state of social production. (Marx 1973: 749–50)

But as Marx knew well, capital is a *social relation*, not a thinking entity, and it therefore cannot take such "advice." What's more, the human beings who seek to perpetuate this social relation (above all, the capitalist class) will never accept it. The outcome of the growing contradiction between the "technical-natural" and the "social" imperatives of capitalist production will not depend on the unfolding of immutable historical laws but on the response of conscious human beings to the systemic irrationality manifested by this contradiction. In other words, it will depend on a competition of "programs" and a struggle of social classes.

The agents of capital — its main beneficiaries — will do everything possible to "save the system," regardless of the terrible human costs involved. They will seek to win support for their program from working people and the middle classes — partly through bribery, intimidation and blackmail, partly through the promotion of reformist illusions and partly through the exploitation of irrational and backward prejudices: racism, xenophobia and, above all, nationalism. But the working-class majority is not predestined to swallow the poison offered up by the proponents of "saving the system" — a program that may yet lead to thermonuclear holocaust.

If enough people who understand the "limits" of capitalism devote their energies to building a serious socialist movement, the current crisis can be turned into an opportunity of historic proportions. Seizing this opportunity will require much more than making a moral critique of the depredations

24

and iniquities of capitalism, and more too than elaborating an abstract case for socialism. What is objectively necessary is a revolutionary organization that is rooted in the most politically advanced layers of the working class — among those who recognize that there is nothing inevitable about capitalist rule and who are prepared to fight for the reconstruction of society as a socialist democracy of "the associated producers." A movement capable of successfully challenging capitalism, it bears emphasizing, can only be built as a "tribune" of the oppressed — as a champion of the special needs and interests of women, racial minorities, immigrants and all other victims of the social irrationality engendered by global capitalism.

The looming catastrophe, which threatens to destroy the lives of hundreds of millions of people, starkly illuminates the necessity of forging a new, class-struggle leadership for the labour movement. Such a leadership would campaign for a massive program of much-needed public works and for workers' control of production. And it would fight for a "sliding scale of wages and hours" (a shorter workweek with no loss in pay) to defend living standards and combat layoffs. A struggle for these demands would help mobilize the masses for the conquest of power and the wholesale expropriation of the means of production, communication and transportation, as well as the banks and other financial institutions. A successful mass struggle against capitalist tyranny and decay would culminate in the creation of a government of workers' councils to democratically administer an egalitarian, rationally planned, collectivized economy.

In opposition to such a perspective, the activity of most of the ostensibly socialist left (including many ostensible "revolutionary Marxists") is devoted to promoting various forms of "step at a time" reformism. This gradualism, often involving support of, or collaboration with, putatively "enlightened" elements of the capitalist class, flows from a lack of confidence in the revolutionary capacity of working people, as well as from illusions that capitalism can shed its more inhumane features through a "democratization" of the existing capitalist state. Other putative leftists, in a fashion reminiscent of the utopian socialists of the early nineteenth century, spend much of their time discussing what the "ideal" society should look like — its gender relations, structures of consumption, ecological footprint and so forth — and how this ideal might be prefigured and exemplified through personal "lifestyle choices" within existing society. It was precisely in the service of his programmatic struggle against reformism and utopianism within the workers movement that Marx developed his scientific critique of bourgeois political economy as a guide to a revolutionary political practice.

The time has come for a revival of Marx's scientific socialism. The time has come for a class-struggle, socialist program that appeals boldly to working people's own most fundamental interests. Furthermore, the time has come for a socialist message that declares loudly and clearly that our species can no longer afford an economic system based on class exploitation — a system whose social relations imperiously necessitate the outmoded measurement of wealth in terms of "abstract social labour" and that must, as a consequence, deny humanity the full benefits of scientific rationality while plunging us recurrently into economic depression and war.

The time has come for this great humanity to say: *Enough!*

Notes

1. As of March 2009, according to the *New York Times*, the U.S. government had pledged $9.9 trillion to corporate America in bailouts and loans in response to the financial crisis. That sum did not include the $800 billion stimulus package signed into law by President Obama in February 2009.

2. In asserting this, Marx was not, of course, denying that labour would remain a "cost of production" in a socialist society. But in such a society "concrete labour" will take its place as one among many costs that must enter the economic calculus of the "associated producers." Other costs, which tend to be systematically overlooked within the framework of capitalist social relations, are those associated with the impact of human productive activity on the natural environment and the domestic labour associated with the reproduction of human labour power and care of the young and infirm. The contributions of both "nature" and "domestic labour" to social production and reproduction will enter into the economic calculus of a socialist society in ways that are simply impossible in a society dominated by the capitalist law of value. (That said, domestic labour will likely soon undergo a process of socialization, with massive public investments in quality child-care centres, nursing homes and the like.)

3. For a fuller summary of Marx's own argument regarding the origin of surplus value in the exploitation of wage labour, see chapter 2 of this volume.

4. Suzanne De Brunhoff writes that, for Marx, the "notion of 'fictitious capital' derives from that of loaned money-capital. It suggests a principle of evaluation which is opposed to that which is based on labour-value" (1990: 187). Although "fetishized" on the financial markets, fictitious capital "has some real roots — the necessity of there being money-capital, credit and the means of financial circulation as an expression of the functioning of the capitalist mode of production" (187).

5. The thesis that neoliberalism is an ideologically driven phenomenon — one designed to displace the purportedly more humane capitalism associated with the post-war "Keynesian welfare state" — has been embraced by much of the liberal and social-democratic left over the past twenty years. On the eve of the current crisis, it was championed by the populist journalist Naomi Klein in her best-selling book *The Shock Doctrine: The Rise of Disaster Capitalism*. Despite its veneer of radical critique, the real effect of this thesis is to conceal the fundamental irrationality of contemporary capitalism, to depict the neoliberal class strategy as the product of greed and mean-spiritedness, rather than as a response to the real contradictions of the profit system, and to promote the illusion that "neo-

liberal capitalism" can be replaced by a capitalism that is both more rational and humane.

6. Data sources and methods for Smith and Taylor's (1996) study of the rate of profit:

a) *Constant Capital (stock)*: The current-dollar value of fixed capital in both the sphere of production and the sphere of circulation (inclusive of commercial services, trading and finance, insurance and real estate) in the non-farm, incorporated business sector of the economy. Current-dollar figures on the fixed-capital stock were obtained from the Investment and Capital Stock Division of Statistics Canada. The current-dollar value of the capital stock for the included categories of the economy were reduced by a percentage reflecting the share in Gross Domestic Product of non-farm unincorporated business sector income for each year from 1947 to 1991 (as indicated by figures published in the Statistics Canada series, *National Income and Expenditure Accounts*). Figures on the net capital stock (adjusted for straight-line depreciation) include the value of four components of fixed capital expenditure and investment: building construction, engineering construction, machinery and equipment, and capital items charged to operating expenses.

b) *Variable Capital (annual flow)*: The after-tax income of all workers employed by "productive capital" plus estimated employer and employee contributions to unemployment insurance and pension plans. Current-dollar figures for "v" were obtained from the Statistics Canada series, *National Income and Expenditure Accounts*. Excluded from consideration as variable capital were wages and salaries paid out in agriculture, wholesale and retail trade, the FIRE sector, public administration and defence, and community, business and personal services. All figures from Statistics Canada refer to before-tax income; consequently a comprehensive tax table was constructed to calculate the required after-tax estimates.

c) *Surplus Value (annual flow)*: The sum of profits and other investment income (after tax and net of inventory valuation adjustment), the estimated corporate officer share of "wages, salaries and supplementary labour income," and the estimated amount of surplus value transferred to the state. As with variable capital, the after-tax calculation of surplus value required the use of a comprehensive tax rate table. The ratio of "total taxes" (received by all levels of government) to "net national income at factor cost" was defined as the "effective tax rate on income." The income flows were calculated from data provided in the Statistics Canada series, *National Income and Expenditure Accounts*. For further discussion of methods used, see Smith (1984).

7. Our statistical analysis did not control for the effects of changes in capacity utilization. Consequently, during the years corresponding to the recessions of the mid-1970s, the early 1980s and the early 1990s, the OCC (organic composition of capital) displays a dramatic spike and the rate of surplus value a sharp fall for reasons having to do with lower capacity utilization and associated layoffs in the productive workforce. The secular trends are nevertheless quite clear for each of these ratios following the profitability crisis of the 1970s: a stabilization of the OCC (in a high range) and a sharp increase in the rate of surplus value.

8. A caveat must be introduced at this point. These findings were based on a particular specification of the value categories comprising "gross output" in Marx's theory (constant capital + variable capital + surplus value = total value of gross output). The most controversial question in measuring these value categories concerns the allocation of the wage bill of socially necessary but unproductive workers. We treated this wage bill as a special form of *constant capital*: more precisely, as an element of the *flow* of constant capital — that is to say, as a *special cost* of the reproduction of the "social capital" as a whole. Very briefly, the costs of employing this type of labour were viewed as analogous to the costs associated with maintaining and replenishing the stocks of fixed and circulating constant capital in production, inasmuch as both types of costs involve a transfer of *previously existing values* to the total value of output. If the wages of unproductive workers are added to the wage bill of the productive labour force and thereby treated as "variable capital" (the productive-labour "input" that yields "new value"), the empirical results are much less supportive of Marx's theory. Not only do they reflect theoretical presuppositions at odds with Marx (the presumed irrelevance of the distinction between productive and unproductive labour); they are also much harder to reconcile with many well-established facts about the "real history" of the Canadian economy over the post-war period. Our study also departs from the procedures of Shaikh and Moseley, both of whom argue that "gross surplus value" should include tax revenues and unproductive labour expenditures. However, Shaikh's measure of "net surplus value" in relation to the constant capital stock produces a close approximation to the Marxian rate of profit, as we understand it, for the United States. For a critique of Shaikh and Moseley and for a theoretical defence of the constant-capital specification of unproductive labour, see chapter 3 of this volume, as well as Smith 1994a (chapter 8) and Smith 1993. Portions of the latter article are reprinted as appendix 2 of this volume.

9. In Marxist theory, "the social capital" refers to the totality of capitals, capitalists and capitalist enterprises operating within the economy, as distinct from the "individual capitals" that compete with one another. It is conceptually similar to Marx's notion of "capital in general" — a theoretical category that abstracts from the competitive interactions of individual capitals in order to highlight the relations of exploitation between capital and the class of wage labourers, the latter conceived as the "collective labourer." Thus, the term "the social capital," as used here, does not refer specifically to government-owned "capital goods" or infrastructures as it usually does in mainstream economic theory.

10. David Harvey notes:

> By 2000, [information technologies] accounted for 45 percent of all investment, while the relative shares of investment in production and infrastructure declined. During the 1990s this was thought to betoken the rise of a new information economy. In fact it represented an unfortunate bias in the path of technological change away from production and infrastructure formation into lines required by the market-driven financialization that was the hallmark of neoliberalization. Information technology is the privileged technology of neoliberalism. It is far more useful for speculative activity

and for maximizing the number of short-term market contracts than for improving production. (2005: 157–58)

11. See, for example, IBT 2009. The concept of a "deformed workers state" is an extension of Trotsky's theorization of the Soviet Union as a "degenerated workers' state," in which the working class had been "politically expropriated" by a parasitic state bureaucracy, but in which property forms necessary to socialist development and corresponding to the historical interests of the working class survived. Unlike the Soviet Union, none of the deformed workers' states of Eastern Europe and Asia resulted from an authentic working-class revolution and none had experienced the direct rule of workers' councils. But all had undergone anti-capitalist social transformations or revolutions (either from above, following Soviet military occupation, or from below, through peasant-based insurgencies led by Communist parties) that had established economic and political structures similar to those of the Soviet degenerated workers' state. For further discussion relevant to this issue, see Trotsky 1970a [1937], 1970b [1939–40] and 1998 [1938]; Smith 1996–97; IBT 2009; and chapter 4 of this volume.

12. Conventional discourse on China almost always overlooks that impressive growth and economic progress occurred not only after the introduction of the "market reforms" in the late 1970s and early 1980s but also in the earlier, Maoist period (in spite of disastrous policies like the Great Leap Forward and the major dislocations associated with the intra-bureaucratic struggle of the Cultural Revolution). Writing from a liberal, institutionalist perspective, Cornell University economist Kaushik Basu notes that "the main difference in the periods before 1978 and after is, interestingly, not so much in the average growth rates, as in the volatility…. What I am arguing… is that, even with the market reforms, the Chinese economy continues to be vastly more state-controlled than any industrialized nation and any rapidly growing developing country. It is, therefore, a puzzle that China has grown so fast for such a long period; there are no parallels in history" (Basu 2009: 48). But this "puzzle" is more easily understood once the hybrid, transitional character of China's economy is acknowledged. Even in the midst of the current, deep crisis of world capitalism, the Chinese economy has been able to maintain an impressive level of economic growth (8.5 percent for 2009), and this is undoubtedly attributable to the capacity of China's deformed workers' state to resist domination by the law of value and to insulate itself from the characteristic crisis tendencies of capitalism, despite its increasing reliance on export-led growth. Furthermore, to say that there are "no parallels" in history to China's long-term growth performance is to forget the rapid growth experienced by the Soviet economy over a period of some four decades, despite major problems of bureaucratic mismanagement and the hugely destructive impact of the Second World War on that transitional, centrally planned economy.

13. An even more dramatic upturn in the corporate rate of profit may have occurred in the Canadian economy between 1993 and 2007 (see Baragar 2009: 78–79). Note, though, that Baragar's data set provides less support than the Smith-Taylor study for the claim that the Canadian economy experienced a secular decline in the rate of profit between 1961 and 1975. This discrepancy is due in large part to his representation of the profit rate as "the ratio of busi-

ness sector corporate profits (before taxes) relative to the year-end value of the business sector non-residential capital stock" (78–79, note 7). The inclusion of before-tax profits in the numerator of the rate of profit is unacceptable from my point of view. See chapter 2 and appendix 2 of this volume for an argument as to why only after-tax profits should be included in the calculation of "aggregate surplus value."

14. McNally 2009a: 14. Robert Brenner writes:

> During the first five years of the business cycle, between 2000 and 2005, [U.S. GDP growth] averaged just 2.3 per cent, markedly lower than in any other comparable period during the postwar epoch. Of this increase, moreover, the bubbling housing sector, by way of its effect in raising expenditures on personal consumption and on home construction and home furnishings, accounted, on average, for no less than 0.7 percentage points per year, or about *30 percent of total GDP increase* during the interval. It also accounted for at least *50 per cent of all jobs* created in these years [figures cited from *Economy. com* (Moody's), courtesy of Mark Zandi, and from Merrill Lynch, reported in Bob Willis, "Existing Home Sales Rose 2.0%," *Bloomberg.com*, 26 August 2006]. Had it not been for housing, the average annual increase of GDP between 2000 and 2005 would have been a miniscule 1.6 per cent — even despite the additional shot in the arm provided by soaring federal budget deficits in this period — and employment would have been strongly in the negative. (Brenner 2009: 63)

15. Unfortunately, the strengths of Brenner's empirical analyses of long-term profit trends in the core of the capitalist world economy are not complemented by a fully Marxist understanding of the origins of the profitability crisis. For my critique of the theoretical limitations of Brenner's account, see chapter 3 of this book.

Chapter Two

Marx's Theories of Value, Capital and Crisis

At a certain stage of development, the material productive forces of society come into conflict with the existing relations of production or — this merely expresses the same thing in legal terms — with the property relations within the framework of which they have operated hitherto. From forms of development of the productive forces these relations turn into their fetters. Then begins an era of social revolution.... In broad outline, the Asiatic, ancient, feudal and modern bourgeois modes of production may be designated as epochs marking progress in the economic development of society. The bourgeois mode of production is the last antagonistic form of the social process of production — antagonistic not in the sense of individual antagonism but of an antagonism that emanates from the individuals' social conditions of existence — but the productive forces developing within bourgeois society create also the material conditions for a solution of this antagonism. The prehistory of human society accordingly closes with this social formation. — K. Marx, Preface to *A Contribution to the Critique of Political Economy, 1859*

Capitalism and Human Progress

Karl Marx's vision of the rise and inevitable decline of the capitalist profit system is inseparable from his critical-scientific analysis of labour value, capital and economic crisis in what he considers a historically unique — and impermanent — stage in the "economic development of society." To understand capitalism and its historical limits, he insists, we must get to the bottom of what makes this type of economy and society fundamentally different from those that preceded it — as well as from the one that is likely to succeed it. But this can't be accomplished unless we focus analytically on the social relations of production that characterize capitalist society, something that is done altogether inadequately by those who regard these relations, either explicitly or implicitly, as "eternal" or as simple expressions of a fixed human nature.

What are those social relations of production? They can be described, in broad strokes, under three general headings. The first and most fundamental set of relations pertains to the *exploitation* of wage labour by capital, a process that makes possible the creation, appropriation and accumulation of a rapidly expanding social surplus product and that also embodies and animates definite forms of class cooperation and conflict. Class exploitation is much older than capitalism, but the capitalist form or "mode" of exploitation is historically exceptional in its opacity as well as its dynamism. Exploitation is of the essence of capital (which is itself fundamentally a social relation), shaping and delimiting the ways in which all the other social relations of capitalism find expression over time.

The second set of relations pertains to the *competition* that occurs between capitalist firms and other economic agents in capitalist markets. Capitalists compete with one another for larger market shares and profits, while workers compete for the best available jobs. But it is the competition among capitalist firms that impresses itself most forcefully on the development of the economy, for inter-capitalist competition is the driving force of innovation, determining the concrete forms of the social division of labour, the contours of the occupational structure and the evolution of the labour process.

The third set of relations pertains to the *formal social equality* that exists between commodity producers and commodity-producing labour in the context of "free markets." Unlike the social structures of medieval and ancient times, capitalist markets are indifferent to the origin or social status of individual economic actors (for example, their nationality, social standing, gender, race or creed). The sole concern of the market (conceived as an impersonal ensemble of monetary exchange relations) is with the relative quality and price of what these actors are seeking to buy or sell. This principle underlies the market norm of the "exchange of equivalents," which in turn sponsors the emergence of such historically novel ideological notions as "equal citizenship rights" and "equality before the law."[1]

By examining the ways in which these three sets of social relations interact with each other, as well as with the advancing *forces of production* (that is, with labour-saving technologies, natural-scientific capacities, technical divisions of labour, etc.), Marx was able to discover the long-term dynamics of capitalist society and its mode of production. This landmark achievement, made possible by many years of study in the British Museum, culminated in the publication in 1867 of Marx's great work, *Capital* (volume one). The latter was supplemented after his death with the publication of the second and third volumes of *Capital*, compiled from Marx's manuscripts by his co-thinker and friend Friedrich Engels. The three volumes of *Capital*, along with the *Grundrisse, Theories of Surplus Value* and several other manuscripts concerned with Marx's critique of political economy, comprise over 5000 pages of social and economic analysis, much of it brilliantly written and compelling, but the greater part of it dauntingly dense and intellectually challenging.

Why did Marx — who is now famous for his aphorism that "the philosophers have only interpreted the world in various ways; the point, however, is to change it" — devote so much of his time and energy to the writing of so formidable and difficult a body of work, one that only a relatively small number of his would-be followers in the labour and socialist movements have ever bothered to study seriously? The reason is that he was convinced that the socialist cause to which he devoted his life required not only a moral critique of existing society, but a *scientific* critique of ideas that obscure the historical limits of capitalist society and thereby deflect attention from the need for a social revolution to abolish capitalist private property. Already in *The Communist Manifesto* of 1848, Marx and Engels had declared their opposition to a variety of competing socialist doctrines (reactionary "feudal" and "petty bourgeois" socialism, "bourgeois socialism," "critical-utopian socialism," etc.), insisting that the "theoretical conclusions of the Communists... express, in general terms, actual relations springing from an existing class struggle, from an historical movement going on under our eyes" (Marx and Engels 1998 [1848]: 26). In light of this, Marx's scientific critique of political economy, as elaborated in *Capital* and his other major "economic" works, can be seen as a magisterial intellectual antidote to ideas that deny this historical movement and that seek to contain human agency — including the efforts of working people to change the world — within an essentially capitalist framework.

Marx and Engels understood that such ideas are the stock in trade not only of overtly pro-capitalist political economists but also of would-be social reformers, labour leaders, humanitarians and philanthropists, many of whom present themselves as well-intentioned champions of the downtrodden, but most of whom are also willful defenders of a historically transient and irredeemably unjust social order.

Similar ideas, suitably updated and revised, continue to deceive and disorient the oppressed and exploited in our twenty-first century world. What do Bill Gates (one of the richest men in the world), Bono (a wealthy rock musician) and Jeffrey Sachs (the American architect of Russia's "shock therapy" transition to capitalism and the author of *The End of Poverty*) all have in common as prominent figures in the "campaign to end global poverty"? Above all, it's their commitment to spreading the message that the monumental problem of global poverty can be meaningfully addressed without the abolition of capitalist property. A comment by Ignacio Ramonet, appearing in *Le Monde Diplomatique* in 1998, is relevant in this regard:

> Thirty million people a year die of hunger. And 800 million suffer from chronic malnutrition.... Is this the way it has to be? The answer is no. The U.N. calculates that the whole of the world population's

basic needs for food, drinking water, education and medical care could be covered by a levy of less than 4% on the accumulated wealth of the 225 largest fortunes. (quoted in IBT 2001: 2)

The appeal of this type of argument is that it demolishes the widespread belief that global poverty exists due to inadequate global resources and that therefore "the poor must always be with us." Its deceptive aspect, however, is that it encourages the notion that a 4 percent wealth levy on the global super-rich can be easily exacted. All historical experience suggests otherwise. Such a "reform" would be virtually impossible to implement within capitalism not so much because of the personal greed of the world's billionaires but because it is fundamentally incompatible with the social logic and priorities of a socio-economic system based on capitalist private property and the social relations of production defined above.

Marx's critique of such ideas, suitably updated of course, remains as relevant today as it ever was. But in the spirit of *The Communist Manifesto*, it may be particularly instructive to apply some of the elements of that critique to a cultural product and political message that, unlike the musings of Gates, Bono, Sachs and Ramonet, actually purports to be "anti-capitalist."

Michael Moore on Capitalism
In his 2009 documentary film, *Capitalism: A Love Story*, Michael Moore offers an unremittingly sordid portrait of contemporary American capitalist society. With poignant images and a skilful presentation of numerous damning facts about the prevailing socio-economic order and the financial crisis of 2008–09, the populist filmmaker exposes the pronounced decline in the quality of life of the majority of Americans since the 1970s. At the same time, he links this decline to a striking statistical observation: that the top 1 percent of the U.S. population now possesses more financial wealth than the bottom 95 percent combined.[2]

The story Moore tells is of an America in which the so-called "middle class" is rapidly disappearing, along with traditional manufacturing industries and unionized workforces; in which airline pilots, responsible for the lives of hundreds of passengers, are sometimes paid as little as $16,000 per year; in which corporations secretly take out "dead peasant" life-insurance policies on their employees, profiting from their premature deaths while refusing assistance to their bereaved families; and in which Wall Street investment bankers, insurance executives and other members of the capitalist elite are given massive government assistance at the same time that the working people they have deceived and swindled are evicted from their homes.

And yet as powerful as his narrative often is, Moore's critical portrayal of American capitalism is profoundly flawed. The film's problems begin with its failure to provide even a minimally satisfactory definition of its subject matter. Throughout the film, "capitalism" is talked about and presented in different and even contradictory ways. At one point, capitalism is described as "a system of giving and taking — mostly taking" and is later described as "evil." But at another point, the more production-centred capitalism of pre-1980 America — a form of capitalism that Moore regards as having been tempered by strong labour unions and enlightened tax and regulatory policies — is presented in a much more favourable, even nostalgic, light. Moore provides no real analysis of how this better (if not exactly good) capitalism of yesteryear was transformed into the excessively evil capitalism of post-1980 America — except to imply that political leaders (beginning in the Reagan era) somehow lost sight of their solemn responsibility to restrain rather than encourage the avarice of capitalist elites. Adding to the confusion, he also provides no real explanation for his far more positive estimation of Western European capitalism.

Moore's contradictory assessments and reflections nevertheless lead up to a rather startling conclusion: namely, that capitalism ought to be abolished, if only because it brings out the worst in human nature. But what exactly is it about capitalism that needs to be abolished? Is it the profit motive? Market competition? Private ownership of the means of production? Collusion between capitalists and politicians? Is it only "unregulated" capitalism that needs to be abolished, or is it capitalism root and branch? While Moore remains studiously equivocal on all these issues, he is nevertheless utterly clear on one point (and even more so in his public statements promoting the film): his critique of capitalism is *not* about making the case for socialism. Rather it's about promoting "democracy" as an alternative.

Moore's unwillingness or inability to propose any alternative to capitalism beyond the banal nostrum of "democracy" is stunning and has been widely and justifiably seen as a major dodge on his part. The comedian Bill Maher correctly challenged Moore on this score by observing that democracy is a "political form" and not, in itself, an economic system. We might add that, given the fact that most Americans continue to regard democracy as the identical twin of capitalism, however mistakenly, Moore's proposed alternative to the latter might just as well have been "Mom's apple pie."

To be fair, Moore does suggest that he regards worker-owned cooperatives as an attractive alternative to traditional capitalist businesses. But he doesn't address the fact that such cooperatives have existed within capitalist societies for hundreds of years and have never posed a serious challenge to the dominance of capitalist enterprises or to the fundamental economic logic of the profit system. Elsewhere in the film, Moore endorses the idea of a "second bill of rights" for working people, as advocated by President Franklin Roosevelt in 1944. But he gives no consideration to the historical context in which Roosevelt floated the idea — a context marked by a powerful domestic labour movement, the impending defeat of fascism in Europe and a rising tide of anti-capitalist consciousness throughout the world. Like the New Deal of the 1930s, Roosevelt's proposal was clearly designed to head off the spread of anti-capitalist ideas within the working class — to placate a powerful labour movement and to discourage socialist or communist influence within it. Moore misses all of this, implying that capitalism could be significantly improved, if not abolished, through a simple constitutional amendment championed by a wise leader!

Moore's misplaced nostalgia for Roosevelt is of a piece with his illusions in the Obama administration. Here too his message is strangely contradictory. While excoriating the Democratic-led congress for its bailout of Wall Street and exposing the continuing domination of the Treasury Department by Wall Street insiders like Tim Geithner, he deliberately glosses over the fact that Barack Obama supported the bailout and appointed Geithner as his Treasury Secretary. As for Moore's suggestion that Obama may yet become the standard-bearer of a twenty-first century "economic bill of rights" for working people, one can only marvel at his "audacity of hope." There are few reasons to believe that this Democratic president would ever make such a big concession to populist sentiment, and if he were to do so, it could only be with a view to mollifying an insurgent working class — that is, to legitimizing a crisis-ridden capitalist system in the eyes of its victims.

For all its withering criticisms of modern American capitalism, Moore's film is, at bottom, a case study in confusion. Worse still, the ideas it promotes serve the clear purpose of channelling the political consciousness and activity of working people into reforming rather than abolishing capitalism. The problem is not simply with Moore's continuing support for Obama's Democratic Party — America's main vehicle for tying working people and the oppressed to a purportedly progressive wing of the capitalist class. The more basic problem is that he fails to present capitalism as an inherently class-antagonistic system — one that needs to be subjected to a critical scientific analysis and one that can only be truly abolished through a socialist revolution led by a working class committed to self-emancipation.

It needs to be emphasized that Moore's reformist and class-collaborationist political prescriptions are intimately bound up with a non-scientific and ultimately religious worldview. At bottom, his critique of capitalism is moralistic, and the view of social reality that he champions is naively idealist — that is, one that regards ideas rather than social and material conditions as the basis of human existence. As against Marx's thesis that human nature is nothing other than the "ensemble of the social relations" (and his related view that as social relations are transformed so too is human nature), Moore implies that selfishness and greed are fixed and eternal elements of human nature, while arguing that these tendencies can and should be countered through moral exhortation (of religious inspiration) and institutional safeguards (government regulation, strong unions and unspecified forms of democratic control over the economy). For Moore, then, social reality is the outcome of a fixed human nature (marked, perhaps, by "original sin"), on the one side, and a constantly shifting agglomeration of free-floating ideas, values and beliefs, on the other. Marx's historical-materialist analysis of the interactions and contradictions arising between the forces and the relations of production under capitalism finds no place within such a worldview.

Moore's idealist perspective on history and social reality is most plainly in evidence when he enlists a Catholic priest in support of his idea that capitalism is "evil." It doesn't occur to the filmmaker that the Vatican's purely rhetorical "anti-capitalism" is rooted in the fact that, historically, the Roman Catholic Church was a pillar of European feudalism (the oppressive socio-economic order that preceded capitalism) or that the rise of capitalism significantly reduced the Church's relative share of the economic surplus, as well as its ideological authority, throughout Europe. Nor does Moore choose to question the Vatican's "morality" — for example, its failure to relinquish its own tremendous wealth in order to alleviate human suffering. To the capitalist drive for profit (rooted, it would seem, in sheer human avarice) he simply counterposes Christ's message of charity — and implies that this message is the "idea" upon which the established Christian churches are actually based.

What Moore fails to see — and what sets him apart from Marx quite decisively — is that capitalism is not based on an idea or a particular set of values. Nor is it a way of thinking or acting that has taken the wrong side in an eternal Manichaean war between good and evil. Rather, capitalism is a mode of production that involves definite socio-economic relations (as defined at the beginning of this chapter) and a changing set of human productive capacities. In the early stages of its development, it plays a progressive role in extending those capacities, while in later stages it becomes an obstacle to human progress, transforming the forces of production, all too frequently, into forces of destruction.

To be sure, the capitalist mode of production gives rise to and is supported by an array of ideologies (such as possessive individualism, classical liberalism, social-welfare liberalism, neoliberalism and neoconservatism — not to mention the putatively anti-capitalist "social gospel," to which Moore seems to subscribe). But it owes its historical emergence to none of them. In this vein Marx wrote: "The mode of production of material life conditions the social, political and intellectual life process in general. It is not consciousness that determines being, but, on the contrary, social being that determines consciousness." Marx should have added, however, that consciousness is itself an aspect of social being, and that for a given social reality to change, consciousness must also change. Why else, indeed, would Marx have worked so energetically to challenge the prevailing ideologies of his own time? These observations return us to the question with which we began this chapter: How are we to view capitalism as a definite stage in the economic formation of society? How are we to understand this mode of production in the scientific spirit of Karl Marx?

Capitalism as a Mode of Production

Let's begin with some basic considerations. As a mode of production, capitalism involves a definite set of arrangements for satisfying human needs, in a social context where these needs are perceived in very different ways by the two fundamental classes constituting what Marx calls bourgeois society: the capitalist class and the working class. Within such a society, workers need higher wages/salaries, improved benefits, secure employment and reasonably good working conditions, together with various protections and services provided by government. At the same time, capitalists need higher profits, lower labour costs and ongoing improvements in productivity from their workers, as well as laws and government policies conducive to these goals. While capitalists do all they can to elicit the cooperation of the workers in their employ, these two sets of needs are counterposed and ultimately irreconcilable. Indeed, they contradict each other and lead inevitably to conflict between capitalists and workers. Accordingly, the capitalist mode of production is properly understood as class-antagonistic, for its contradictory dynamics impel working-class people into struggle against capital and (potentially at least) into a fight for a new, socialist/communist mode of production and a classless society.

Like every other class-antagonistic mode of production (for example, ancient chattel slavery or medieval feudalism), capitalism possesses characteristics that are historically specific to it. Only by grasping the features peculiar to it can we uncover its unique "laws of motion" — the laws governing its emergence and consolidation, its structural dynamics and its eventual historical decline. These laws arise out of the encounter between certain natural imperatives, constraints or laws (which are common to all human societies) and the social imperatives of capitalist relations of production (which are at once exploitative, competitive and formally egalitarian). To put the matter slightly differently, capitalist social relations impart a specific and unique form to the human imperative to develop a division of labour, to devise and employ tools to improve the productive powers of human labour and to subdue nature. What's more, capitalism involves a historically unique mode of extracting surplus labour from the direct producers and thus of creating a surplus product that sustains a dominant class of wealthy property owners. While in earlier class-antagonistic modes of production, the social surplus product takes the form of "tribute" (labour service, taxes, rent in kind, tithes, etc.), under capitalism it takes the predominant form of privately appropriated surplus value — money income associated with the ownership of capitalist private property.

Labour Power as a Commodity

Capitalism isn't simply a system of private ownership of the means of production, nor is it just a market economy in which individual economic actors seek to maximize their "utilities" or wealth. Instead, capitalism is a mode of production in which labour power — the capacity to perform physical or intellectual labour, or some combination of the two — has become, on a generalized and expanding scale, a commodity, something sold on a market. Only the widespread availability of labour power as a commodity permits money and other commodities to function as capital.

In pre-capitalist societies, labour power isn't typically a commodity because its possessors — the direct producers — have immediate access to means of production, above all land. Capitalism, however, emerges historically through the separation of the direct producers from their means of production and through the monopolization of these same means of production in the hands of a smaller and smaller segment of society: the capitalist class (or bourgeoisie). As the direct producers lose the ability to secure a livelihood except through the sale of their labour power for a wage or salary, they are transformed into the modern working class (or proletariat). In this way, the system of commodity production becomes generalized.

The "primitive accumulation of capital," which was the historical precondition for this generalization of commodity production, required the widespread application of force: the coercive separation of peasants from their means of subsistence through "enclosures" of what had been common property in land, the plunder of colonial possessions and the super-exploitation of chattel-slave labour, which helped finance the industrial revolution in Europe and America. As Marx evocatively put it, "If money... 'comes into the world with a congenital blood-stain on one cheek,' capital comes dripping from head to toe, from every pore, with blood and dirt" (Marx 1977: 925–26). And yet processes akin to primitive accumulation don't belong exclusively to the early years of the capitalist era. On the contrary, they are ongoing, with new economic sectors and territories subjected (or re-subjected) to capitalist exploitation and plunder over time — a process described by David Harvey as "accumulation by dispossession":

> Some of the mechanisms of primitive accumulation that Marx emphasized have been fine-tuned to play an even stronger role now than in the past. The credit system and finance capital became, as Lenin, Hilferding, and Luxemburg all remarked at the beginning of

the twentieth century, major levers of predation, fraud and thievery.... Above all we have to look at the speculative raiding carried out by hedge-funds and other major institutions of finance capital as the cutting edge of accumulation by dispossession in recent times. (2003: 147)

Accumulation by dispossession, then, is a process that is conceptually distinct from the "normal" processes of accumulation characteristic of a mature capitalist economy. Most of *Capital* is devoted to laying bare the mechanisms through which capital is able to expand itself without resort to theft, fraud and financial chicanery. Indeed, at one point, Marx actually insists that the capitalist doesn't "steal" from the worker, but rather exploits him. So exploitation is by no means synonymous with thievery in Marx's theory. Nevertheless, the conditions for normal processes of exploitation and capital accumulation could only have been established historically through prior processes of accumulation by dispossession. Moreover, even when capitalism is well established, capitalists will continue to resort to "predation, fraud and thievery" as supplementary means of accumulating wealth, above all when the normal processes of accumulation eventuate in periodic crises of overproduction and profitability.

To overlook the latter while obsessing about the former, however, is to turn a blind eye to the intrinsic irrationality of the capitalist profit system — to absolve the system of responsibility for human suffering and to assign blame solely to the bad (abnormal) behaviour of individual capitalists or groups of capitalists (which is exactly what the capitalist mass media has tried to do in response to the current crisis). Marx was determined to show that it is above all the normal operations of the capitalist system — and not just the pathologies that are the predictable by-products of those operations — that render it an obstacle to continued human progress. To follow Marx in this endeavour requires that we give patient and serious consideration to the operations and consequences of the law of value under capitalism.

The Capitalist Law of Value

The law of value is a regulatory principle of an economy in which the products of labour are typically produced for the purpose of private exchange — that is, as commodities. It is also a specific manifestation of the human imperative to distribute the aggregate labour of society in definite proportions to a multitude of different economic tasks. While it is operative to a limited extent in pre-capitalist commodity-producing societies, it rules economic life only in societies where capitalist institutions, property forms and social production relations predominate.

In its fully capitalist incarnation, the law of value regulates the distribution of social labour in accordance with the capitalist imperatives to measure "wealth" in terms of labour performed in the production of marketed goods, to articulate a division of labour through the interplay of market forces and to subordinate social production to the drive for private profit.

Marx's critics often claim that he argued that commodities really do exchange in markets in proportion to the amount of labour they embody. For example, the Nobel laureate Paul Samuelson, writing in the most widely read economics textbook of the mid-twentieth century, attributed to Marx the view that "the price ratios of goods can be predicted from labour costs alone" (1968: 819). In fact, Marx made no such claim. Here is what he did say about the connection between market prices and labour time:

> Whatever the manner in which the prices of various commodities are first mutually fixed or regulated, their movements are always governed by the law of value. If the labour-time required for their production happens to shrink, prices fall; if it increases, prices rise, provided other conditions remain the same. (Marx 1978b: 177)

So formulated, it's hard to imagine how anyone would dispute the actuality of such a law. For Marx, the labour value of an individual commodity is to be understood as a "centre of gravity" around which its market price oscillates.

That said, the substantive content of Marx's law of labour value, which is never explicitly defined by him, is actually much more interesting (and controversial) than the above passage suggests. Its basic postulate is that "the source of the value added of the mass of commodities produced is the labor expended in producing them" (Foley 1986: 14). If we couple this postulate with the idea that value exists as an "objective, quantitatively determined magnitude" (Hilferding 1975: 159), we arrive at the twin propositions that living labour is the sole source of all new value and that value exists as a definite quantitative magnitude at the level of the capitalist division of labour (or economy) as a whole — a magnitude that limits prices, profits and wages. Value, to use a phrase coined by Ernest Mandel, is a "parametric determinant" of the visible economic phenomena of the capitalist socio-economic order.[3]

Much of Marx's critical analysis of the laws of motion of capitalism, including his law of the falling tendency of the rate of profit, stands or falls with these basic postulates of his theory of value, and so it is with respect to them, rather than to the spurious claims of Samuelson and other defenders of the capitalist order, that his theory needs to be evaluated.

Commodities and the Value Form of Social Labour

For Marx, a commodity is a product of labour that is produced in order to be sold in a market. Every commodity has both a use value (a utility or capacity to satisfy some human need or fancy) and an exchange value (the power to command remuneration in exchange; when represented in money, a price). Marx maintains that a commodity's exchange value is a "form of appearance" of its value, which expresses its relationship to all other commodities as a product of the social division of labour existing between commodity producers. The value of a commodity, therefore, represents a definite fraction of the social labour expended in the production of the total mass of commodities produced.

When a commodity is exchanged in the market, it encounters and is compared with other products of a society-wide division of labour. But for just this reason, it isn't the actual "concrete labour" expended in its production that determines the value of the individual commodity, but rather the labour that the social division of labour has established as "necessary" to its production. Consider this example. If two automobile companies produce vehicles that are virtually identical in terms of their use value to prospective consumers, but one company demands a higher price for its vehicle than the other due to higher costs resulting from a greater expenditure of labour on the assembly line (that is, a less efficient use of concrete labour), then the market will deem the "extra" labour performed by this less-efficient company to be socially wasteful and require the price to be lowered to correspond more closely to its "true value."

This example illustrates Marx's point that it is not the "concrete labour" (the actual amount of labour) expended in production that determines a commodity's value, but rather the "abstract labour" necessary for its production. Abstract labour refers to the social labour that is needed — in the here and now — to produce a particular commodity. It constitutes what Marx calls the "social substance" of value. In this sense, the concept of abstract labour is closely related to the "magnitude of value" as determined by "socially necessary labour time" — which is defined by Marx as "the labour-time required to produce any use-value under the conditions of production normal for a given society and with the average degree of skill and intensity of labour prevalent in that society" (Marx 1977: 129).

The dialectical interplay of concrete labour and abstract labour comes into its own fully only under conditions of generalized (that is, capitalist) commodity production and exchange. Anwar Shaikh notes that, once goods are produced solely for exchange,

> the particular labours involved are *aimed* at producing exchangeable goods, and the valorization of these labours is an intrinsic part of their reproduction. As producers of commodities, these labours create not only bundles of useful properties (use-values), but also amounts of abstract quantitative worth. In the former aspect, they are of course concrete labours; but in the latter, they are *value creating*

activities whose content as social labour is manifest only in-and-through the abstract quantitative worth of their products. (1990: 43, emphasis in original)

This abstract quantitative worth finds expression in the money price of the commodity product. And it is for this reason that Marx calls money "the necessary form of appearance" of the abstract labour represented in commodities.

Marx's Theory of Capital and Surplus Value

Capitalist commodity production must be distinguished from the simple or independent forms of commodity production that existed within pre-capitalist social formations for thousands of years, and that still survive, in altered form and on a limited scale, in the capitalist era. Marx describes the "economic circuit" of simple commodity production with the schema: C - M - C. Here a particular commodity (C) — for example, potatoes — is produced by an independent commodity producer, largely through the application of his or her own labour, and is then sold for money (M), which is subsequently used to purchase other commodities — for example, farm implements or clothing.

In this economic circuit, the commodity producer is unable to realize a profit as such. Equivalent is exchanged for equivalent, and no exploitation of the labour of others need occur. The money received by the independent commodity producers may increase or decrease in accordance with how vigorously and efficiently they work, but so long as they perform most of the work on their own account, they are unlikely to accumulate much wealth. At best, only a very gradual accretion of wealth is possible; at worst, the producer loses ground and is forced to find a new livelihood.

In capitalist commodity production, by contrast, we encounter what Marx calls the circuit of capital: M - C - M'. Here the economic process begins with an investment of value (the money-capital, M), which is then used to purchase specific commodities (C) that allow for the realization of an enlarged magnitude of money value (M'). The difference between M' and M is what Marx calls surplus value — an accretion of new value that constitutes the "social substance" of profit of enterprise as well as ground-rent and interest.

On the basis of these considerations, Marx defines capital as both a historically specific type of wealth and as a definite social relation of production — as "the means of production monopolized by a particular section of society" (Marx 1981b: 953–54) and as "value in process, money in process" (Marx 1977: 256). Capital is value seeking to expand itself — money in search of an increment. The different forms of capital (industrial, interest-bearing, commercial) seek expansion through a variety of mechanisms — but, as we shall soon see, all of these mechanisms ultimately depend on the creation of surplus value through the exploitation of wage labour that is directly involved in the process of producing commodities.

Impelled by competition, capital is driven to accumulate — and this process of accumulation necessarily engenders an economic dynamic of "expanded reproduction." This means that, as an economic system, capitalism is utterly incompatible with any steady state. On the contrary, it requires growth for growth's sake — that anathema of the ecologically responsible! Marx's suggested motto for capital — "Accumulate, accumulate! That is Moses and the Prophets!" — speaks to this inexorable if unsustainable logic.

At first glance, the circuit M - C - M' appears to violate the principle of the "exchange of equivalents," which is the normative rule governing exchange in a free market; but, on closer examination, this turns out not to be the case. To be sure, some economic agents are able to realize a profit by buying cheap and selling dear. But such profits result from equivalent losses elsewhere in the market, so profits and losses tend eventually to cancel each other out. The question is therefore posed: how are profits generated on an economy-wide basis under conditions where total values and total prices are equalized?

Marx says that this question can't be answered so long as we remain fixated on the "sphere of exchange" — the vaunted marketplace of bourgeois economics. To answer it we must consider what occurs in *the sphere of production.* Accordingly, he reformulates the circuit of capital as follows:

$$/> MP$$
$$M - C \ldots P \ldots C' - M'$$
$$\backslash > LP$$

In this expanded formula for the circuit of capital, a capitalist invests a definite amount of money-capital (M) in two distinct kinds of commodities, each of which constitutes an input to a capitalist production process (P). The first is "means of production" (MP), consisting of tools, physical plant, machinery, raw materials and so forth — what might be called the objective elements of the production process. The second kind of commodity is "labour power" (LP) — which is the capacity for labour and which is always embodied in living workers. When means of production and living labour power are brought together in production, the result is an output commodity (C') — for example, an automobile — that represents a greater amount of value than the original inputs. If and when this output commodity is sold at its value, a magnitude of value (M') is realized in money form that is greater than the original money-capital investment.

Surplus value, like all value, is created solely by living labour — by that unique commodity known as labour power. No matter how technologically sophisticated they may be, the means of production are unable to create any new value. As the use values of these "objective" elements of the production process are consumed in production, they can only transfer to the new commodity product "previously existing values." Labour power, on the other hand, can produce more value than it "represents." The value of labour power is determined by its cost of reproduction (simply put, the wage), but the physical activity of labouring — its use value — is variable (or elastic) in its contribution to the creation of new value. So surplus value is not only the difference between M' and M, it is also the difference between what living labour creates in the way of new value and the value represented by the wages of productive workers.

The upshot is that surplus value results from exploitation: from the appropriation of surplus (effectively unpaid) labour in production, which is made possible by capitalist ownership of the means of production and by capital's increasing control over the labour process. As Marx puts it:

> Capital is dead labour that, vampire-like, only lives by sucking living labour, and lives the more, the more labour it sucks. The time during which the labourer works is the time during which the capitalist consumes the labour-power he has purchased from him. (Marx 1977: 342)

It was in order to illuminate this process that Marx posited his much misunderstood assumption in the first volume of *Capital* that "commodities exchange at their values." The purpose of this assumption was not to suggest that "prices are determined by labour costs alone" (to quote Samuelson again) but rather to demonstrate that even when labour power is exchanged with capital at its value (that is, even when workers receive what is deemed to be a "fair day's pay for a fair day's work") the exploitation of wage labour still takes place. The exploitation of wage labour is not an anomaly but the norm in capitalist production.

Marx's fundamental point is that the creation of surplus value depends not on "unfair" or "unequal" exchanges in the labour market (or any other market), but on the subordination of labour to capital within the sphere of production — that is, on social conditions that make possible the exploitation of wage labour. It depends on paying the productive worker a wage that corresponds to the value of his or her labour power (as determined by its cost of reproduction) while also commanding the worker to perform labour that creates more value than is represented in the wage.

Marx demonstrates this in detail in his famous chapter in *Capital* (Volume I) on "the working day," which he sees as divided into two components: the hours during which workers perform "necessary labour" and those during which they perform "surplus labour." The necessary labour performed produces the value equivalent of the wage (the price of labour power as a commodity) while the surplus labour performed produces the extra value that ends up in the pockets of capitalists — and to some extent the capitalist state — in the form of profit, interest, ground rent and new tax revenues.

Marx considered the distinction between labour power and labour performed to be one of his proudest scientific achievements, and rightly so. It is crucial to understanding the specific way in which surplus labour is "pumped out" of the direct producers in the capitalist mode of production — the secret of its mode of exploitation. Nevertheless it should be noted that three important questions are skirted (or abstracted from) in his discussion of the two components of the working day. The first is how precisely the value of labour power is determined. To say that it is determined by the labour time required to produce the goods and services needed by workers to sustain themselves (and some dependents) may be abstractly true, but this requires further elaboration — including some attention to the contribution of domestic labour to the "reproduction of labour power." The second question pertains to the contribution of the state to the reproduction of labour power and the extent to which we can speak of workers receiving a "social wage" above and beyond their nominal wage. Marx failed to delve into this question because, in *Capital* (Volume 1), he deliberately abstracts from the role of the state in the reproduction of the capitalist mode of production. What's more, in his day, the state played a much more modest role in the reproduction of labour power than it does in today's advanced capitalist societies. This leads us directly to a third issue that Marx elides: the question of tax revenues. How are taxes to be understood in value-theoretical terms? Does the value/ price of labour power refer to the before-tax wage or to the after-tax wage? These and related questions— which Marx may have intended to address in his planned but never written volumes on wage labour and the state — continue to generate considerable controversy amongst Marxists.[4] (My own answers to some of them are found in the next section of this chapter, as well as in chapters 3 and 4 and appendix 2.)

Commodity Value and Its Constituents

At the level of both the individual commodity and the gross (economy-wide) product, total value can be divided into three fundamental components or categories: constant capital, variable capital and surplus value.

Constant capital represents the value of the means of production (tools, equipment, raw materials, fuel and energy, etc.) along with what Marx called the "*faux frais*" (incidental costs) of capitalist production. As already indicated in chapter 1, many of the "overhead costs" of capitalist reproduction — including the costs of circulation and the costs of maintaining the capitalist state — should also be subsumed under the category of constant capital, even though Marx is far from clear on this issue. Foremost among the incidental and overhead costs of the overall process of capitalist reproduction are the wages of unproductive workers. The wage bill of "socially necessary unproductive labour" — in industry, commerce, finance and the state — represents a vitally important investment on the part of the social capital as a whole in maintaining the institutional framework of capitalist society. If the physical means of production find a value expression as constant capital, it is arguable that so too does the "social machinery" needed to perpetuate the capitalist mode of production (Mage 1963; Smith 1991b, 1993, 1994a).

Constant capital has a stock as well as a flow expression. The flow of constant capital refers to the values that are preserved and transferred over a given period through fixed capital depreciation as well as the physical consumption of raw materials, fuel and energy and unproductive labour. The stock of constant capital refers to the total value of the fixed capital as well as the inventories maintained by private capitalist firms over that same period.

Variable capital refers to the value represented by the wages of those productive workers who are directly involved in commodity production. Its elements include the nominal after-tax wages and benefits of these workers and deductions to the nominal wage that constitute a deferral of the wage, above all pension contributions.[5] Variable capital is usually measured only as a flow, not as a stock.

Surplus value is the value created by the unpaid "surplus labour" of productive workers. It encompasses after-tax profits, ground rents, technological rents, interest and new state revenues resulting from a real increase in taxes received by the capitalist state. The mass of tax revenues, however, is best viewed as an element of the flow of constant capital — as previously existing values that are conserved and transferred in the reproduction process, and that continuously reappear in the total value of the gross output in much the same way that the values of means of production do.[6] Like variable capital, it is measured only as a flow.

We thus arrive at $C + V + S = P$, where the total value of the commodity product or gross product (P) is conceived as the sum of three flows of value. The relationships that exist among these components of the total value of output, along with the value of the constant capital stock, define the key quantitative ratios of Marx's theoretical system.

The average rate of profit, expressed as S/C, is the ratio of surplus value to the value of the constant capital stock and constitutes the fundamental regulator of capital accumulation and growth.[7] The organic composition of capital, represented as $C/S+V$, is the ratio of the constant capital stock to all newly created value: in other words, the ratio of dead to living labour in production expressed as magnitudes of value. Finally, the rate of surplus value, S/V, is the ratio of surplus value to variable capital (the wage bill of the productive labour force) and expresses the rate of exploitation of productive workers. The movements of these fundamental ratios, Marx argues, determine the long-term dynamics and historical trajectory of the capitalist mode of production.

The Equalization of Profit Rates and the Metamorphoses of Value

If living labour is the sole source of all new value, including surplus value, how can we explain that firms relying much more on expensive technology than on living labourers are frequently more profitable than those that are more labour intensive? Marx's answer is that social surplus value is the result of the exploitation of the working class by "capital in general." Exploitation occurs on an economy-wide scale, with surplus value entering the market through a multitude of commodities. The surplus value represented within these commodities is realized and distributed as profit through 1) a competitive process that pits individual capitalist firms against one another, and 2) a division of labour that allocates definite shares of surplus value to industrial, commercial and financial capitals.

The ability of capital to move from relatively less to relatively more profitable firms and sectors enforces a tendency toward the equalization of profit rates and the formation of a "general rate of profit." The profitability of a given firm or sector is therefore not dependent on the degree to which it invests in living labour (V) as opposed to means of production (C). Rather, it is dependent on 1) the mass of its capital investment calculated on the general rate of profit, as modified by 2) the soundness of the investment decisions, business practices and competitive footing of that firm. Firms that invest in state-of-the-art technology are in a better position to lower costs per unit of output than those that rely on more labour-intensive methods. This enables them to cut prices and increase market share while at the same time maintain or even increase their profit margins. Thus, by out-performing and out-competing their less efficient rivals, these "high organic composition" firms are able to capture surplus value that is actually being produced elsewhere in the economy (and not only in the national economy, but in the world economy).

The tendency toward the formation of a general rate of profit underlies a crucial metamorphosis of the value form: the transformation of commodity values (conceived as "direct prices" determined solely by the commodity's socially necessary labour content) into "prices of production." The latter are not market prices — and so we are not considering the metamorphosis of value into a final money exchange value but into an intermediate form. The specific character of this form stems from the influence of a single mechanism on price formation: the redistribution of surplus value that is brought about by the equalization of profit rates through competition.

The individual capitalist firm, other things being equal, will realize a profit that is consistent with the magnitude of its invested capital calculated on the general rate of profit — but this will not necessarily correspond to the amount of surplus value produced by its own workers. As Marx puts it in his theoretical formula for the transformation of values into prices of production: "When a capitalist sells his commodities at their prices of production, he recovers money in proportion to the value of the capital consumed in their production and secures profit in proportion to his advanced capital as the aliquot part of the total social capital" (1978b: 159).

Labour Value and Price Formation

The individual value of a commodity is determined by the amount of socially necessary labour time required for its production, but its exchange value will generally deviate from this value as a result of other factors bearing on price formation — most importantly, the tendency for rates of profit to equalize, but also a range of factors affecting demand. Even so, as mentioned, the labour value of a commodity is the centre of gravity around which its market price will tend to oscillate. Recent empirical work by a number of Marxist economists has shown that 90 percent or more of the individual price of a commodity is determined by its value — that is, by the socially necessary labour time that it represents. But the main purpose of Marx's theory of value is by no means the explanation of price ratios, but rather the illumination of the capitalist economy's macro-economic laws of motion. Regardless of the degree to which individual commodity values and prices diverge (owing to transfers and redistributions of value resulting from market processes), total prices must still equal total values.

Just as value is the social substance of price, the social substance of profit is surplus value: the increment of value created by living labour beyond the value represented in the wages of productive workers. Thus, total profits will equal total surplus value. Each of these propositions is consistent with the key postulate of Marx's law of value: that living labour alone is the sole source of new value.

Overproduction as the Form of Capitalist Crisis

The law of labour value underlies a peculiar characteristic of capitalism: it is the only mode of production in human history to generate crises of overproduction. In pre-capitalist societies, economic crisis is associated with underproduction — the failure to produce enough use values (material output) to meet social needs. But underproduction of use values is rarely a problem in capitalist societies (although some socially needed use values may not be produced in sufficient quantities owing to the fact that their production is deemed unprofitable). Periodically, however, too many commodities are produced in relation to the "effective demand" that exists for them.

Effective demand is demand backed by purchasing power — that is, by money in the hands of the would-be purchaser. The characteristic form of capitalist economic crisis, namely overproduction, is therefore a result of insufficient demand (backed by money, the expression of abstract social labour) for commodities representing a definite amount of value (abstract socially necessary labour time). Under conditions of overproduction, commodities cannot be sold (or markets cleared) at prices that permit an adequate profit margin; and since profit drives capitalist production, economic growth slows, throwing large numbers out of work, bankrupting many firms and rendering productive plant idle.

The phenomenon of overproduction was a prominent feature of the recession that began in the United States in December 2007, contributing significantly to the financial crisis of 2008. Overproduction manifested itself in several sectors of the American economy, but most notably in the crucial housing and automobile sectors. Demand collapsed for "overpriced" homes in many markets as inventories swelled in the wake of a construction boom and a rising wave of mortgage foreclosures. In the automobile market, demand for gas-guzzling vehicles declined sharply as oil prices climbed in 2007 and well into 2008, squeezing the profit margins of many automakers, particularly General Motors and Chrysler.

According to Marx, a number of factors can trigger crises of overproduction; however, the most important cause is the tendency of the rate of profit to fall due to an overaccumulation of capital and an inadequate production of surplus value. If overproduction involves the social capital's inability to realize the full value of the total commodity output, this "crisis of realization" is ultimately the surface manifestation of a crisis of valorization — a crisis in the production of new value and in particular surplus value.

Marx on the Falling Rate of Profit and Capitalist Crisis

Marx's theory of labour value has profound implications for a scientific assessment of the stability and rationality of the capitalist economy, for it leads to the conclusion that capitalism is not only beset by contradictions but that its laws of motion render it prone to severe crisis. Since the principal goal of capitalist production is the private appropriation of profit, the rate of return on invested capital (the average rate of profit) is the key regulator of capitalist accumulation, investment and economic growth. If the average rate of profit falls sharply (regardless of the immediate causes), investment declines and credit is adversely affected. A crisis then ensues and the economy contracts, resulting in a recession or depression.

A conjunctural crisis of capital accumulation, however, may not always be preceded by a sharp fall in the average rate of profit. The current U.S. recession, for example, had multiple causes — some certainly related to the declining profitability and insolvency of key financial institutions and industrial corporations — but some also related to market saturations, overcapacity, rising energy costs and declining consumer confidence. Furthermore, while the rate of profit did fall slightly from 2007 to 2008, this decline wasn't the immediate precipitant of the financial crisis that gathered momentum over the course of 2008. On the contrary, it was the financial crisis that precipitated the pronounced conjunctural decline in the average rate of profit (reflected in plunging stock markets) in 2008–2009.

Nevertheless, the law of the falling tendency of the rate of profit is of central importance to explaining the origins of the current crisis. Marx argues that there is a tendency for the rate of profit to fall in the long term under capitalism — a tendency rooted in the competitive and class-antagonistic social relations of the capitalist economy. This secular (as distinct from conjunctural) fall in the rate of profit sets the stage for other long-term destabilizing tendencies to come to the fore, including, as we saw in chapter 1, the phenomenon of financialization. What then are the main factors that account for the long-term decline in the rate of profit?

The competitive interaction of individual capitalist firms forces each of them to reduce costs of production per unit of output (with a view to preserving or enlarging market share). However, given the antagonism between capital and labour, the favoured strategy for reducing costs is to increase productivity through the introduction of labour-saving and labour-displacing technologies. This is an eminently rational strategy from the point of view of the individual capitalist firm seeking to meet the challenges of competition. But the unintended consequence of this strategy — when it is pursued by all the competing capitals — is to reduce the total social surplus value produced in relation to the total capital investment. In other words, the consequence is a fall in the average rate of profit. By striving to enlarge their own shares of the pie, the competing capitalists unwittingly shrink the pie as a whole!

Marx's argument is predicated on the distinction between the micro rationality of the individual capitalist firm and the macro requirements of capital in general. Individual firms don't behave irrationally when they try to lessen their dependence on living labour. Indeed, in the context of inter-capitalist competition, it is entirely rational for a firm to seek higher profit margins through a reduction of unit labour costs. But it is only because an individual capitalist firm can realize (that is, capture) the surplus value produced by workers employed in other firms (through processes of surplus value redistribution) that the displacement of living labour from production can result in a higher rate of return on the firm's capital investment. (One of the great advantages of labour-saving over so-called "capital-saving" innovation is that it allows the individual capitalist firm to cut unit costs while also reducing its dependency on what Marx called the "limited basis" of capitalist expansion: the working population.) In the end, however, the effect of expelling living labour from production on an economy-wide basis is to reduce the amount of surplus labour performed and therefore the amount of surplus value produced relative to the value invested in the capital stock. The average rate of profit therefore falls, affecting the profitability of all firms (albeit to differing degrees).

The upshot is this: the fundamental social production relations that define capital push inexorably toward an enhancement of labour productivity at the level of the individual capitalist firm. But the resulting fall in the average rate of profit prepares the ground for crises that have a negative long-term impact on the global productivity of the capitalist mode of production. For this reason, the falling tendency of the rate of profit reveals the historical limits to capital's ability to develop the forces of production on a global scale.

Absolute and Relative Surplus Value

The essential condition for the production of surplus value is what Marx termed the "formal subsumption" of labour by capital. Formal subsumption involves the separation of the direct producer from ownership of the means of production, the widespread commodification of labour power and the intervention of capital into the production process as its director or manager. In contrast to formal subsumption, Marx defines the "real subsumption" of labour by capital as an ongoing feature of the developed form of the capitalist mode of production. This involves not only a change in the situation of the agents of production but also a revolution in the "actual mode of labour and the real nature of the labour process as a whole" (Marx 1977: 1021). With every improvement in labour productivity comes a change in the parameters of socially necessary labour time and therefore in the social-structural properties of abstract labour and value. To keep pace with these changes — which create competitive challenges for individual capitalist firms as well as a diminishing magnitude of surplus labour for the social capital as a whole — capitalists must repeatedly revolutionize the labour processes under their direction.

Marx's distinction between the formal and the real subsumption of labour by capital is closely related to the distinction he draws between the production of absolute and relative surplus value. The former corresponds to a form of capitalist exploitation that relies on a lengthening of the working day in order to reduce the proportion of necessary labour time required for the social reproduction of the labourer in relation to the surplus labour time expended. Accordingly, absolute surplus value may be conceived as an extensive magnitude, an expansion of which depends upon increasing the total quantity of labour time performed. Relative surplus value on the other hand is an intensive magnitude, which arises from "the curtailment of the necessary labour-time and from the corresponding alteration in the respective lengths of the two components of the working day" (Marx 1977: 432). Since work time cannot be indefinitely extended, absolute surplus value faces a clear limit in the length of the working day and in the maximal intensity of the labour process. Relative surplus value, on the other hand, faces limits set only by the level of development of labour-saving technology. Consequently, relative surplus value techniques become an increasingly important method of raising the rate of surplus value over the course of capitalist development — especially in the face of successful struggles by working people for a reduced workweek with no loss in pay.

Precisely because relative surplus value techniques allow individual capitalist firms to produce more output with less labour, productivity improvements are sought through increases in the technical composition of capital. The problem is that such increases find a value expression in the diminishing relative role of living labour in the overall process of production. Living labour is displaced by labour-saving machinery, representing a proportionally expanding magnitude of invested constant-capital values, and this signifies a relative diminution in the role of living labour in the process of production. At the level of the social capital as a whole, this displacement must entail a fall in the average rate of profit, since what is involved in the increased value or organic composition of capital is an overaccumulation of constant capital in relation to the volume of surplus value being produced by living labour. This argument is based squarely on what is the key postulate of Marx's theory of value: that living labour and living labour alone generates the new value from which surplus value arises.

As the ratio of dead to living labour in production $(C/S+V)$ rises, the rate of profit is depressed, and this, other things being equal, will tend to slow the rate of capital accumulation and economic growth. In this way, "the barrier to capitalist production" reveals itself to be "capital itself" (Marx 1981b: 358). The system shoots itself in the foot, a crisis ensues and the crisis creates conditions (through what Marx calls the "slaughtering of the values of capitals") for at least a partial recovery in the rate of profit and renewed accumulation and growth.

However, the crisis also calls forth new strategies from capital to ratchet up the rate of exploitation of workers *without* investing in expensive new labour-saving technologies. In this connection, capital may resort to increasingly harsh methods to increase absolute surplus value — such as the lengthening of the working day (or week) and the intensification of the labour process.

In response to the deepening profitability crisis, such methods were embraced by many capitalist firms beginning in the 1970s. For example, workers were encouraged or forced to work longer or more shifts during periods of peak production so that the bosses would not have to hire new workers and assume the additional costs associated with new benefit plans. Under the rubric of "lean production" (Smith 2000), the labour process was also massively intensified in order to increase absolute surplus value. In Fremont, California, for example, workers in the General Motors plant had historically been fully occupied with work tasks for 45 seconds out of every minute. After the plant's closure and its reopening with a lean-production system in place, workers were kept busy "57 of every 60 seconds" (Rinehart 2006: 161). Enforced overtime and intensified labour processes are ways of augmenting productivity and the rate of surplus value without resorting to additional investments in the constant capital stock. They constitute instances of what Marx calls counteracting tendencies to the rate of profit to fall.

Tendencies Counteracting the Fall in the Rate of Profit

The trajectory of the rate of profit can be influenced by a range of factors that serve to counter a rise in the organic composition of capital. Short of a full-blown crisis and a devalorization of capital stocks, the fall in the rate of profit can be attenuated and even arrested by what Marx calls the "counteracting tendencies." In evaluating these counteracting tendencies, it's useful to distinguish between factors that can have only a short-term (conjunctural) impact and those that have a long-term (secular) positive influence on the average rate of profit. It's also necessary to distinguish between factors that may contribute to an increase in the rate of surplus value and those that affect the organic composition of capital (OCC). Under the former we can list increases in the intensity of exploitation, reduction of wages below their value and relative overpopulation, while under the latter we can list the cheapening of the elements of constant capital and foreign trade (Marx 1981b: Ch. 14).

An increase in the intensity of exploitation can only counteract the falling tendency of the rate of profit if it doesn't involve an increase in the OCC. Thus, Marx looks to those methods typically employed by capitalists to increase labour productivity (and therewith the rate of exploitation) without investment in labour-saving, productivity-enhancing technology. These methods include speed-up (which has definite physiological limits and tends to push up the wage rate), prolonging the work day (which likewise faces physiological limits as well as eventual worker resistance), and productivity-enhancing technical innovations as these are applied by individual capitalists "before they are universally applied" and, presumably, before they have an impact on the economy-wide OCC.

Like the tactics employed to increase the intensity of labour exploitation, the reduction of wages below their value should be seen as an ephemeral factor in countering the fall in the rate of profit because a sustained reduction of wages below their value would amount to a change in the value of the commodity of labour power, albeit one requiring far harsher methods (union-busting, suspension of collective-bargaining rights, etc.) than are normally employed to depress wages. Nevertheless, such a change is entirely possible if the labour movement is unsuccessful in fending off a major offensive by capital. (While most workers have seen a decline in their real wages in the U.S. and most other advanced capitalist countries over the past thirty years, the decline has not yet been so great as to constitute a clear reduction in the value of labour power.)

Relative overpopulation can also contribute to an increase in the rate of exploitation by forcing down wages. But this faces a precise limit in the size of the working population. Only where capitalism is in the process of uprooting non-capitalist modes of production and constantly replenishing a massive "reserve army" of the unemployed can this factor have anything more than a short-term effect in counteracting the fall in the rate of profit.

On a purely conjunctural basis, all three of the above factors can play a more or less important role in increasing the rate of surplus value without inducing an increase in the OCC. Yet Marx's apparent expectation that the rate of surplus value would display a secular tendency to rise was inseparable from his view that it would increase as a result of a rising technical composition of capital (TCC); and such an increase in the TCC, Marx assumed, would find a value expression in a falling rate of profit.

Only to the extent that a rising TCC can occur without an accompanying increase in the OCC would it be possible for a rising rate of surplus value to coincide with a stable (or rising) rate of profit. It is precisely in this connection that the cheapening of the elements of constant capital derives its special importance as a counteracting factor:

> [The] same development that raises the mass of constant capital in comparison with variable reduces the value of its elements, as a result of the higher productivity of labour, and hence prevents the value of the constant capital, even though this grows steadily, from growing in the same degree as its material volume, i.e. the material volume of the means of production that are set in motion by the same amount of labour-power. (Marx 1981b: 343)

This passage suggests that the OCC need not rise as impetuously as the TCC; but it doesn't imply that a rise in the OCC will be prevented as a result of a higher productivity of labour. For a rise in the OCC to be prevented, the elements of constant capital must "increase [in mass] while their total value remains the same or even falls" (343). Marx is clearly alluding here to a range of possible capital-saving innovations and techniques: for example, fixed capital of greater durability, increased efficiency in fuel and energy consumption or the discovery and application of inexpensive substitutes for specific fuels or raw materials currently in use. As he suggests, however, such capital-saving is only possible in certain cases.

The limitation of constant capital saving as a factor inhibiting the fall in the profit rate is not very well specified by Marx, but it can be assumed that he regarded labour-saving innovation as a greater priority for individual capitalists for reasons rooted in the totality of social production relations in which individual capitals are enmeshed — relations that impel them not only to cut costs but to cut them in ways that simultaneously strengthen their position in relation to labour.

Marx's fifth counteracting tendency is foreign trade and investment. This factor can play a role in elevating the rate of profit only to the degree that either the terms of trade continue to improve and/or the rate of return on capital invested abroad continues to rise from the standpoint of a given (national) social capital. Yet foreign trade and investment must be considered a two-edged sword, capable of depressing as well as raising the rate of profit.

This survey of the tendencies counteracting the law of the falling rate of profit shows, above all, that the law as such and the counteracting tendencies to the law do not enjoy equal status. All of the counteracting tendencies cited by Marx, with the possible exception of the cheapening of the elements of constant capital, have clearly defined limits as means to checking the tendency of the rate of profit to fall as a result of a rising OCC. The law itself, on the other hand, has no such limits. It is capitalist crisis alone that creates the conditions for conjunctural recoveries of the rate of profit and resumed accumulation. Importantly, however, it is also the recurrence of capitalist crises that induces the capitalist class and its state to deploy historically ever-changing methods to shore up the average rate of profit, to guarantee the conditions of accumulation and to mitigate the destabilizing influences of severe economic dislocations on the class equilibrium of capitalist society.[8]

Underconsumption and Capitalist Crisis

Some critics of the law of the falling tendency of the rate of profit have counterposed to it an underconsumption theory of capitalist crisis, supposedly inspired by Marx himself. In this connection the following passage has been frequently cited:

> The ultimate reason for all real crises always remains the poverty and restricted consumption of the masses, in the face of the drive of capitalist production to develop the productive forces as if only the absolute consumption capacity of society set a limit to them. (Marx 1981b: 615)

What Marx is not saying here is that consumption necessarily lags behind production because of the poverty and exploitation of the working masses under capitalism. Rather, he is saying that the "restricted consumption of the masses" is an immanent barrier to capitalist production — a kind of structural constant, the dimensions of which might exacerbate capitalist crises while not necessarily causing them. Far from contradicting Marx's theory of a rising OCC/falling rate of profit, the above passage can be easily reconciled with it.

Regardless of the concrete events that may trigger a particular crisis (and, again, these are many and varied), there is no doubt that its manifestations can be contained and its consequences attenuated through an expansion of effective demand, making possible the sale of commodities at prices that might otherwise not be realized. As Marx suggests, the overproduction of commodities associated with capitalist crises can be mitigated to the extent that their sale is not wholly dependent on the "narrow basis on which the relations of consumption rest." The massive expansion of consumer credit in the Western world since the 1970s should be viewed, above all, in this light. But the more important long-term factor that is highlighted by Marx is the expansion of the world market. In this connection he asserts that the "internal contradiction seeks resolution by extending the external field of production" (1981b: 353).

The sale of commodities on the world market and the investment of capital in foreign countries become increasingly important strategies for curbing crisis tendencies as these find expression in national capitalist contexts. The same thesis is suggested in Marx's discussion of foreign trade and investment as influences that may counteract the falling rate of profit. Yet, as already noted, all of this is very much a two-edged sword. The social capital of every capitalist country seeks to use such strategies to curb its locally manifested crisis tendencies, even though it is only too obvious that not all of them can succeed in any given conjuncture. The condition for resolving the internal contradiction through an extension of the external field of production (and realization) for the social capital of one country is precisely that the social capitals of other countries *fail* in this same stratagem. Furthermore, as all capitalist countries become increasingly interdependent, as the weakest of them reach the limits of their capacity to absorb the global effects of these tendencies, and as capital exerts itself more and more as an international social power, unhampered by national loyalties or nation-state regulation, such strategies become less effective and even counterproductive.

The Historical-Structural Crisis of Capitalism

As suggested above, the law of the falling tendency of the rate of profit is not only an important element in explaining cyclical interruptions of the capitalist accumulation process, it is also fundamental to a satisfactory account of the growing and irresolvable incompatibility between the social relations and forces of production of capitalism: the chronic "historical-structural crisis" of the capitalist mode of production. This idea is clearly expressed in the following passages from Marx's *Grundrisse*:

[The declining profit rate] is in every respect the most important law of modern political economy, and the most essential for understanding the most difficult relations. It is the most important law from the *historical* standpoint.... Beyond a certain point, the development of the powers of production become a barrier for capital; hence the capital relation a barrier for the development of the productive powers of labour. When it has reached this point, capital, i.e. wage labour, enters into the same relation towards the development of the social wealth and of the forces of production as the guild system, serfdom, slavery, and is necessarily stripped off as a fetter. The last form of servitude assumed by human activity, that of wage-labour on one side, capital on the other, is thereby cast off like a skin, and this casting-off itself is the *result* of the mode of production corresponding to capital; the material and mental conditions of the negation of wage labour and of capital, themselves already the negation of earlier forms of unfree social production, are themselves results of its production process. The growing incompatibility between the productive development of society and its hitherto existing relations of production expresses itself in bitter contradictions, crises, spasms. The *violent destruction* of capital not by relations external to it, but rather as a condition of its self-preservation, is the most striking form in which advice is given it to be gone and to give room to a higher state of social production. (1973: 748–49, emphasis added)

Several points in these passages should be especially noted. First, Marx refers to the "development of the powers of production" as a barrier to capital, and to the capital relation as a "barrier for the development of the productive powers of labour." This suggests a dialectical interaction between the material forces and the social relations of production in which, increasingly, each stands as a barrier to the other. As long as capitalism survives, this destructive interaction must persist. The material forces of production can register real, qualitative progress only in a "higher state of social production."

Second, Marx refers to the "growing incompatibility between the productive development of society and its hitherto existing relations of production." This point is crucial to the historical significance of the law of the falling rate of profit. A falling rate of profit resulting from an overaccumulation of capital is a feature of both the period of capitalist ascent and the period of capitalist decline. But if this law is also the harbinger of capitalist decline — the expression of an irremediable contradiction fatal to capital's continuing ability to systematically promote the development of labour productivity and with it human culture — then it must have a somewhat different significance and expression during the era of capitalist decline and decay than it had when capital was still playing a historically progressive role. This seems to be the burden of Marx's reference to a "growing incompatibility" — and yet the expression of this incompatibility is left unspecified by Marx, except for a reference to "bitter contradictions, crises, spasms" — that is, to phenomena that have been recurrent features of capitalism since its birth.

This brings us to a third point. Marx also implies that the growing incompatibility between the forces and relations of production will find expression in the "violent destruction of capital not by relations external to it, but rather as a condition of its self-preservation." Here Marx proved to be remarkably prescient — for it has been the quite literal physical destruction of capital in world wars (themselves interpretable as products of the growing incompatibility) that led many twentieth-century Marxists to conclude that capitalism had finally entered into historical-structural crisis. In Lenin's terms, capitalism reached its "highest stage" with the advent of imperialism, a phenomenon that expresses, above all, the attempt of the most developed capitalist countries to resolve their internal contradictions not only at the expense of their less-developed colonies and semi-colonies (as they had done throughout the era of colonialism) but at the expense of each other as well.

Under conditions of capitalist decay, the profitability crises of the system tend to become more acute and more protracted, eventually requiring far-reaching "solutions." These may include aggressive attempts to raise the rate of exploitation of living labour by driving down working-class living standards; trade liberalization (or trade wars and colonial adventures) permitting a displacement of the internal contradiction to the external field of production and exchange; fascism, involving the complete destruction of the organized labour movement and the mobilization of the nation to solve its problems at the expense of other nation-states; and full-scale war between nations and the physical destruction of capital, permitting a "new start" — a new material and social basis for capital accumulation — such as emerged after the Second World War. For Marxists, such extreme manifestations of capitalist crisis provide compelling reasons to conclude that the capitalist system has ceased to play any sort of progressive historical role, that its irrational aspects have occluded and triumphed over its rational ones and that it must therefore give way to a more consistently rational as well as cooperative and humane form of social production: socialism.

A Note on the "Value Controversy"

It would be foolish, even religious, to think that Marx resolved all of the theoretical problems associated with a scientific analysis of capitalism. His own original plan for a comprehensive analysis of capitalist society (which was to include not only the three volumes of *Capital* but specific volumes on wage labour, the state and the world market) was interrupted by a relatively early death. Moreover, he can be faulted, with some justification, for leaving doors open to facile misinterpretations of his ideas. Even so, a century of controversy surrounding his theories has failed to establish that they are either logically inconsistent or empirically wrong. Regardless of what one may think about the "skilled labour reduction problem" or the "transformation problem" (or the variety of "solutions" presented to these problems by Marx and his heirs), the fact remains that Marx's analysis of capitalism, as informed by his theories of value, capital and crisis, has had an excellent track record in forecasting the actual historical trajectory of the capitalist mode of production.

"The proof of the pudding," as Friedrich Engels liked to say, "is in the eating." Or, as Marx put it in *Theses on Feuerbach*: "The question whether objective truth can be attributed to human thinking is not a question of theory but is a practical question. Man must prove the truth — i.e. the reality and power, the this-sidedness of his thinking in practice." My point here is that Marx's theories, notwithstanding their incompleteness, have provided a much sounder foundation for understanding capitalist development than have any of the theories advanced by pro-capitalist economists writing either before or after him. In terms of their predictive power, they have outperformed the theories of Smith, Ricardo, Mill, Menger, Marshall, Hayek, Friedman, Galbraith, Samuelson, Schumpeter — and, yes, even those of John Maynard Keynes.

The test of history — of practice — has turned out to be a much more reliable arbiter of the "truth" of Marx's theories of value, capital and crisis than all the esoteric theoretical disputations that have absorbed the energies of so many Marxist intellectuals over the past century. This is not to say that the "value controversy" has been entirely pointless; I would not have produced my own survey of it had I thought that (see Smith 1991a, 1994a; also appendix 1 of this volume). However, to believe that it is possible to win the war for Marx's ideas within the disciplinary domains of academic economics or public policy by solving specific theoretical problems, or that such a victory is in any sense an important condition for building a mass socialist movement, would be foolishly naive. The struggle to bring down capitalism and achieve socialism depends instead on the ability of Marxists to demonstrate the reality and power of Marx's theories to those social forces (above all, the organized working class) that have both an interest in achieving socialism and the capacity to do so. The experience and demise of Soviet Bloc Stalinism (which was falsely linked to Marx's theories for over sixty years) poisoned that effort terribly for several generations. Yet the real history and recent troubles of world capitalism provide a potent antidote.

However we choose to evaluate Marx's prediction of proletarian socialist revolution in the core of world capitalism or to judge the "actually existing socialism" constructed in his name in the "Communist world," we can only be astonished at how well his main predictions concerning the course of capitalist development have held up. It is with respect to these predictions that Marx's theories will need to be popularized to a broad audience of working people, students and intellectuals — most of whom are unlikely to take much interest in the finer points of dispute in the value controversy.

Marx's Predictions in Light of the Historical Record

What follows are six of Marx's more important predictions, together with some commentary and evidence in support of each of them. According to Marx, the rise and spread of capitalism will involve the following:

1) The remorseless separation of the great mass of the population from the ownership or effective possession of the means of production, at first within the pioneering nations of capitalist civilization and ultimately on a world scale, such that humanity will be increasingly divided between a small class of capitalists and a majority class of wage and salary earners compelled to sell their labour power on pain of destitution.

Commentary and Evidence

In just five hundred years, the capitalist mode of production has spread out from its cradles in Northwestern Europe to dominate the entire planet. At times it has swiftly uprooted non-capitalist forms of economy, while at other times it has co-existed with them, all the while pressing them into the service of an expanding capitalist world market.

Prior to the industrial revolution, the leading capitalist nations resurrected and massively expanded the ancient institution of chattel slavery as a means to more effectively exploit and pillage the natural resources of the Western Hemisphere. The profits earned from the slave trade (involving the transport of tens of millions of enslaved Africans to the Americas) as well as from the ruthless exploitation of slave labour on colonial plantations, were of decisive importance to the "industrial take-off" of Western Europe — Britain in particular. Ernest Mandel has estimated that the total capital accumulated between 1700 and 1800 through the slave trade, the colonial plundering of India and Indonesia, and the exploitation of slave labour in the British West Indies amounted to over one billion pounds sterling — a sum exceeding the value of "all the industrial enterprises operated by steam which existed in Europe around 1800!" (1968: 444).

Once consolidated, the capitalist mode of production has everywhere brought about a division of populations between capitalist property owners, on one side, and a mass of workers dependent on the sale of their labour power, on the other. Peasants, self-employed farmers and other petty commodity producers, who once constituted the vast majority of the world's population, have been reduced to a dwindling minority. By 2005, the self-employed represented a small and declining percentage of the workforce in all of the developed capitalist countries: 7.5 percent in the United States, 15.7 percent in the European Union and 14.7 percent in Japan. Even in more backward, late-developing capitalist nations (that is, countries burdened with a legacy of colonial or semi-colonial subjugation and underdevelopment), the self-employed middle class (including poor peasants) often constitutes less than half of the population: 35.7 percent in Mexico, 45.8 percent in Turkey and 34.9 percent in Brazil (Smith 2008).

In the most developed regions of world capitalism, the dream of so many working people to become their own boss is now almost impossible to realize. The overwhelming majority of working people (whether they work in industry or agriculture, in commerce or in government) are obliged to sell their labour power in order to secure a living. While a relatively small middle class of self-employed professionals, independent commodity producers, contractors, restaurateurs and shop-keepers continues to survive in the interstices of the system, the great majority of the population are now members of the wage-earning "proletariat," notwithstanding the subjective proclivity of many workers to identify themselves as "middle class" (see chapter 4 of this volume, and Smith 1997).

2) The increasing concentration and centralization of capital, such that more and more of the assets and activity of the world economy will fall into the hands of a shrinking fraction of the capitalist class itself. The upshot: concentrated wealth at one pole of the world economy; extreme poverty and misery at the other.

Commentary and Evidence

According to a study published by the Institute for Policy Studies, the annual sales earnings of the world's 200 largest corporations were only slightly less than half the total earned by the poorest 4.5 billion people on earth (Anderson and Cavanagh 1997). According to a report issued by the United Nations Development Program, "more than 85 percent of the world's population received only 15 percent of its income" in 1996, and "the net worth of the 358 richest people, the dollar billionaires, is equal to the combined income of the poorest 45 percent of the world's population — 2.3 billion people" (UNDP 1996: 94).

By the end of the twentieth century, the top 200 companies accounted for more than 60 percent of all manufacturing assets in the United States. The comparable figures for 1929 and 1959 were 46 and 55 percent respectively. By 1988, less than 1 percent of all corporations controlled two-thirds of all corporate assets. Corporate concentration is even more pronounced in

Canada. In 1987, the top 1 percent of companies controlled 86 percent of all assets and realized 75 percent of all profits, while the top one-hundredth of 1 percent of all enterprises (about a hundred companies) controlled 56 percent of all assets (Blackwell, Smith and Sorenson 2003: 128).

The concentration of assets and profits in the hands of a relatively small number of huge transnational corporations has dire implications for the masses of people worldwide who depend on the sale of their labour power for a livelihood. While the sales of the top 200 corporations account for a quarter to a third of the world's marketed output, these corporations employ less than 1 percent of the global labour force (only about 19 million in 1995). This means that the great majority of workers must seek employment with small and medium-sized companies, which are often poorly capitalized and not nearly as profitable as the top 200. Little wonder, then, that these workers typically endure low wages and meagre benefits, not to mention poor working conditions and job insecurity.

3) The tendency of capitalist industry to displace living labour from the production process through the introduction of increasingly sophisticated labour-saving and labour-displacing technologies — that is, an increase in the technical composition of capital — and a concomitant expansion in the global "surplus population" of chronically unemployed or underemployed people.

Commentary and Evidence

The technical composition of capital (TCC) can be designated as the ratio of means of production (in use-value terms) to the total number of production workers, or, better still, as constant-dollar value of capital stock employed per hour worked. Wassily Leontieff (1982), a well-known mainstream economist, has furnished data on the long-term trend of this ratio for the U.S. economy from 1949 to 1977. His data show that the TCC ratio almost *doubled* over this twenty-eight-year period, indicating that technological change under capitalism displays a pronounced labour-saving bias. Similar results have been reported by Marxist economists examining trends for the TCC throughout the advanced capitalist world (Shaikh and Tonak 1994; Webber and Rigby 1996).

Setting aside its impact on the organic composition of capital, the rising TCC in manufacturing and other productive sectors of the economy has had a two-fold effect: a) to make available an increasing volume of workers for "socially necessary unproductive labour" in commerce, finance and government services; and b) to massively augment the global "surplus population" or "reserve army of labour." The first effect is discussed at length in chapter 3 and appendix 2 of this volume and will not be addressed here. The second, however, calls for some immediate comment.

Even during the mid- to late 1990s, a period of modest but real economic growth, it is estimated that 20 percent or more of the world's labour force was either unemployed (meaning ready and willing to work, but unable to find a job) or underemployed (meaning employed on a part-time basis, even though seeking full-time work). However this estimate is based on official, government-released unemployment figures, which, while measured in a variety of ways across the world, almost always fail to include either "discouraged workers" or people incarcerated in prisons (or mental institutions) for reasons often related to their unemployment.

The existence of so large a surplus population — one that is now growing rapidly as a result of the current economic slump — is unmistakable evidence of a significant immiseration of much of the world's population, as predicted by Marx. But it is also compelling evidence for the proposition that capitalism has reached a point in its development where it is now restraining the growth of the productive forces. Why should the labour power and talents of over a billion working-age human beings be squandered in this way? Why should so large a segment of humanity be disqualified from making a productive contribution to the satisfaction of human needs — in the first place their own? Clearly, this can be logical only from the point of view of an economic system that has reached an advanced stage of decay.

4)   The transformation of capital — understood as "self-expanding value" — into an international social power that seeks to burst through the confines and constraints of the nation-state even as it continues to rely on the nation-state as the political-institutional form through which its irrepressible contradictions are addressed and managed.

Commentary and Evidence

The facts about "economic globalization" (as promoted by major transnational corporations and the policy-makers of the leading capitalist states) are so well known as to scarcely require rehearsal here. However, in a recent (and otherwise unconvincing) "manifesto" devoted to the defence of the capitalist economic system as the best possible engine of wealth creation, Fareed Zakaria, editor of *Newsweek International*, makes an important argument that unwittingly echoes Marx's nineteenth-century predictions about the increasing international reach of capital and the growing contradiction between the development of the capitalist world economy and the continued pre-eminence of the nation-state:

> [The] fundamental crisis we face is of globalization itself. We have globalized the economies of nations. Trade, travel and tourism are bringing people together. Technology has created worldwide supply chains, companies and customers. But our politics remains resolutely national. This tension is at the heart of the many crashes

of this era—a mismatch between interconnected economies that are producing global problems but no matching political process that can effect global solutions. (Zakaria 2009)

As Zakaria suggests, the current global slump has brought this tension — this fundamental contradiction of a globalizing capitalism — into sharp relief. The question is: can it be overcome? Marx's implicit answer is that the only progressive resolution to this intensifying contradiction is global socialism — a planned, collectivized world economy under the democratic control of a world socialist government. The capitalist alternative will almost certainly involve a retreat (of indefinite duration) into national economic protectionism — something to which most governments are now succumbing in response to the current slump, despite the stern warnings of most mainstream economists. The deeper and longer-lasting the slump turns out to be, the greater will be the dangers of rising protectionism, trade wars and, eventually, shooting wars. The history of capitalism is unequivocal on this score.

5) The persistence of periodic crises of overproduction rooted in the competitive interactions of capitalist firms and in the antagonistic relations between capital and labour — that is, in the fundamental social production relations of capitalism itself.

Commentary and Evidence
Although pro-capitalist ideologues and policy-makers (not to mention financial advisers and stock brokers) perennially express the optimistic view that the capitalist economy will eventually overcome its tendencies toward severe crisis (with or without the "right mix" of macro-economic policies), capitalism has repeatedly given the lie to such optimism. The history of capitalism has been a history of economic cycles involving the recurring sequence: economic recovery — boom/prosperity — overproduction/crisis — slump/depression. Ernest Mandel identified seventeen such cycles between 1816 and 1958, each with a boom featuring a particular type of "extension of the basis of production" (1968: 359). Over the past fifty years, we have seen another half dozen such cycles. But contrary to the hopeful expectations of mainstream economists writing in the 1950s and 1960s (in the wake of the so-called Keynesian revolution in economics), four of these more recent cycles have been punctuated by rather severe conjunctural downturns: the slump of the mid-1970s (which affected virtually the whole of the capitalist world economy, but which was of relatively short duration); the deep recession of the early 1980s (which was partly induced by a high-interest-rate, monetarist policy as a means to expanding unemployment and arresting inflation); the recession of the early 1990s (which was felt unevenly across the world

economy, but which hit many countries quite severely); and the current slump (which is universally recognized to be the deepest and longest-lasting downturn since the Great Depression).

To deflect criticism from an economic system with so impressive a record of fomenting crises, large and small, is no easy task. For this reason the ideological guardians of capitalism bend every effort to convince the working-class public that capitalist crises are the result, above all, of mistaken government economic policies (high taxes, bad trade policy, excessive government spending, ineffective monetary policy, etc.). Failing that, working people are encouraged to see them as something akin to "natural catastrophes" — as episodic "storms" that must be accepted as inevitable, regardless of the many hardships they exact. Of course, to further forestall any consideration of the inherent contradictions of the capitalist system, working people are also encouraged to think that crises result from "too many immigrants," "too much union power," "too many people on welfare," "too many women in the workforce" or even "natural limits to growth."

Blaming politicians and encouraging finger-pointing among the exploited and the oppressed serves to drown out the few voices prepared to indict the capitalist system itself. Sadly, this gambit is reinforced by many would-be progressives, and even ostensible socialists, who, eager to be heard, put their own spin on the idea that economic dislocations stem from "bad policy choices" or, even worse, the "greedy behaviour" of individual capitalists and workers.

6) A long-term tendency for the average rate of profit to fall as a result of a rise in the organic composition of capital — that is, an increase in the ratio of dead to living labour in the sphere of production and in the economy as a whole (the ratio of the value of fixed constant capital stock to the sum of variable capital and surplus-value flows).

Commentary

As this prediction is central to the subject matter of this book, the evidence supporting it need not be reviewed here. But let's consider the implications of this prediction for the future of the profit system. Assuming the actuality of Marx's law of the falling tendency of the rate of profit, capitalism is clearly doomed to recurrent crises. To avoid these increasingly destructive crises, the productive forces must be liberated from the capitalist imperative to subordinate production to profit making. The only way this can be accomplished, however, is through the abolition of capitalist property and the establishment of a socialist economy in which production is geared toward meeting human needs rather than private profit. Such a socialist economy would not only be collectively owned and democratically administered by the associated producers, it would also be free from the tyranny of the law of value (that is, the measurement of wealth in terms of labour time).

The reason that Marx considered the law of the falling tendency of the rate of profit to be the most important law of political economy from the "historical standpoint" is that it provides an extremely powerful but also essentially simple argument in support of the proposition that the development of the forces of production under capitalism points with inexorable logic toward socialism. The following "thought experiment" illuminates this point.

Imagine a society in which living wage labour is entirely displaced by advanced machinery and automatons endowed with artificial intelligence. No living labour, either manual or intellectual, is any longer needed to produce the material output that sustains the population. The capitalist owners of these advanced machines have guaranteed access to this material output by virtue of their ownership. But those with no ownership share in these machines — the former wage-earning working class — have become an idle surplus population and lack any source of income.

Now imagine that instead of fighting for a share of the material output of this entirely automated economy, the non-owners simply accept the argument that they have no legal or moral claim on it. Since they no longer have a wage or a salary to purchase their means of subsistence, they have no choice but to depend on the charity and goodwill of the owners. At a certain point, however, the owners decide to withhold their charity, and the non-owners then choose to voluntarily "disappear" — that is, to perish.

What kind of society would remain? Assuming that the owners decide to cooperate with each other and pool their resources to meet their common needs, what would remain would be a collectively owned and cooperatively run economy in which the private pursuit of profit would be replaced by the principle: "From each according to his or her ability, to each according to his or her need." What we would have, in other words, would be "the higher stage of communism," as Marx called it in his 1875 work, *The Critique of the Gotha Programme*.

Of course, such a scenario is impossible to imagine outside of science-fiction. But its implausibility stems not so much from the futuristic idea of an entirely automated economy as from the truly bizarre notion that the working-class majority of a capitalist society would simply accept its own transformation into an increasingly impoverished surplus population and then agree to die off.

Was Marx wrong to believe — to predict — that the working class would struggle against such a fate, at first defensively, to be sure, but also, in due course, with a conscious plan to reconstruct society on new foundations? That plan — the socialist program — aims to establish a world in which the masses of working people, and not a handful of capitalists, would be the final beneficiaries of the advanced productive forces that workers have laboured so hard to create and that constitute the capitalist system's most enduring contribution to human progress.

Summing Up

In the end, Marx's analysis compels us to consider a few simple questions that flow inexorably from his theories of labour value, capital and crisis. How can the capitalist mode of production survive indefinitely when it promotes the displacement of living labour from the production of social wealth even while continuing to demand that this wealth be measured (however unconsciously) in terms of living labour expended? How can the capitalist profit system persist when its relations of production mandate the introduction of labour-displacing technology even while demanding the subordination of economic activity to private profit — that is, the class appropriation of surplus labour?

In an era in which manual living labour has become a less and less necessary material input to production and when even the most skilled intellectual labour is being displaced by computer software, robotics and even artificial intelligence, these questions are surely more acute than ever. The fact that the working-class majority has yet to become fully aware of them, much less willing to act on them, attests not to the failure of Marx's theories but to the tremendous power of the capitalist class and its ideological agents to systematically obscure social reality — to obstruct the spread of Marx's scientific discoveries and thereby impede the development of a socialist working-class consciousness.

Marx was certainly aware of the power of the dominant ideology to deform and even poison the consciousness of working people. But he also believed that, in the end, "social being determines consciousness." For this reason, he was hopeful that, over time, the contradictions highlighted in the above questions would become ever more obvious and that the working-class movement would discover the rational means to resolving them: the socialist program of transforming the social relations of production in such a way as to serve human need rather than capitalist profit. Historical experience has shown resoundingly that this discovery — this fundamental change in consciousness — will not occur through some sort of automatic or spontaneous process. Rather, it will require an arduous and determined political struggle — at the level of ideas and at the level of action. It is to this difficult question that we turn our attention in chapters 4 and 5.

Notes

1. Of course, the formal egalitarianism of the free market is decisively overshadowed by the massive substantive inequalities engendered by capitalist production and exchange; and the other relations that characterize capitalism — class

68

exploitation and competition — tend to undercut even the principle of "formal equality" by encouraging such anti-egalitarian ideologies and sentiments as racism, xenophobia and male dominance, all vital to perpetuating the domination of the capitalist ruling class.

2. "Financial wealth" does not include the wealth represented in home equity.

3. Mandel uses the expression "parametric determinism" to indicate "several possibilities within a given set of parameters" (1989: 121). To understand value as a "parametric determinant" is to affirm that the law of value establishes a field of possibilities within which human action is constrained but within which a range of important choices can also be made — choices that, among other things, may affect the degree to which market prices deviate from individual commodity values.

4. Marx's original plan for a work on "economics" included specific volumes on: 1) Capital, 2) Landed Property, 3) Wage Labour, 4) The State, 5) International Trade, 6) World Markets. He was only able to complete the first part of his work on Capital before his death in 1883.

5. I noted in *Invisible Leviathan*:

   It is necessary, in my view, to define variable capital as the *after-tax* wage bill of productive workers. The productive worker's *real* income is the income used to reproduce her capacity to work and to support her family, not the "income" that she allegedly "contributes" to the state. Certain transfer payments form components of "variable capital" — but such additional income is small in comparison with the taxes deducted from "gross wages." (Smith 1994a: 247, N. 14)

6. In *Invisible Leviathan* I wrote:

   The capitalist state is not a "private accumulator." Most of its revenues are obtained through taxation rather through participation in surplus-value redistribution on the basis of the general rate of profit. Rather than compete with capitals for a share of social surplus-value, the capitalist state is principally concerned with obtaining adequate value (revenue) to allow it to continuously acquit its historically developed tasks. This is not to say that the state *never* captures a portion of currently produced surplus-value in order to *expand* its activities; on the contrary, the state has exhibited a strong historical tendency to do precisely this. Yet, while the state regularly appropriates a certain share of newly created surplus-value as a means of further entrenching its role in social reproduction, it would be wrong to regard *all* of its tax revenues as a "deduction from surplus-value," just as it would be wrong to treat the tax on labour income as a deduction from variable capital. From the standpoint of the social capital, the state is a machine of social reproduction. Like any other machine, it requires maintenance, amortization, new parts, and a continuous supply of fuel and energy. Accordingly, the social capital — in whose historical interests the capitalist state functions — must set aside a considerable portion of the value it realizes (with the assistance of the state) in order to continuously finance state activity (just as it must set aside some of the same "realized value" to replenish raw material stocks, depreciated fixed capital, and expended fuel supplies in the mines, mills and factories that are the principal sites of surplus-value production). (Smith 1994a: 175)

7. Marx usually refers to the rate of profit as the ratio S/C+V, where C and V are both implicitly flow variables. But he also insists that the denominator of the rate of profit refers to the "capital advanced" — that is a stock measurement that would include fixed constant capital but exclude the flows of constant and variable capital. See Smith 1994a and Mage 1963 for further discussion.

8. Several arguments have been associated with the attempt to refute Marx's theory of a rising OCC/falling rate of profit. These include the "neutral technological progress" argument, the "rising technical composition/stable organic composition" argument, and the "choice of technique" argument. These are analyzed and evaluated at some length in *Invisible Leviathan* (Smith 1994a: Ch. 7). None, I conclude, provides a convincing case against Marx's theory.

Chapter Three

The Necessity of Value Theory

Robert Brenner's book-length essay "Uneven Development and the Long Downturn: The Advanced Capitalist Economies from Boom to Stagnation, 1950–1998"[1] has provoked more discussion and controversy on the socialist left than any other political-economic analysis in recent memory. Predictably, it has also elicited a number of highly critical responses from proponents of Marx's theories of labour value and economic crisis. Amongst other things, Brenner has been charged with a one-sided preoccupation with capital-to-capital (competitive) relations at the expense of the capital-wage labour (class struggle) relation, with misinterpreting and dismissing Marx's law of the falling tendency of the rate of profit and with ignoring Marx's value categories entirely.

As a value theorist and a proponent of Marx's theory of the falling rate of profit, I concur strongly with these criticisms of Brenner's work. Even so, they do not negate my admiration for his accomplishment, for Brenner's analysis stands as one of the few attempts by a contemporary socialist to provide a detailed analysis of the evolution of the leading advanced capitalist economies (Germany, Japan and the United States) over the course of the last half century. Moreover, much of what Brenner argues, on the basis of an impressive compilation and synthesis of "official" data sets, can, I think, be reconciled with a more fully Marxist understanding of the dynamics and laws of motion of the capitalist mode of production than Brenner himself provides. Indeed, in spite of his many anti-Marxist theoretical presuppositions, some aspects of Brenner's work may be seen as reinforcing the evidential case for an analysis of the "long downturn" — the malaise afflicting the world capitalist economy since the 1970s — that recognizes with Marx that "the true barrier to capitalist production is capital itself" (Marx 1981b: 358). None of this gainsays the fact that Brenner's study remains both analytically one-sided and theoretically inadequate — its very limitations suggesting the necessity of that Marxist value theory which the author seeks so diligently to ignore.

In what follows I interrogate Brenner's text in light of Marx's theories of value and crisis. I begin with a synopsis and critical appraisal of Brenner's study and proceed to some observations on how his analysis can be read in light of my own empirical and theoretical work in Marxist crisis theory.

Brenner's Argument:
A Synopsis and Characterization

At the core of Brenner's account of world capitalism's trajectory over the past fifty years is the centrality of profitability — and the rate of profit on manufacturing capital in particular — to the operations of the capitalist mode of production. The relatively high level of the average rate of profit in most of the advanced capitalist world in the years immediately following the Second World War is seen as the key to what is known, somewhat misleadingly, as the "post-war boom," just as its descent into a much lower range is seen as responsible for the long downturn that began in the early 1970s.

The rapid rate of growth of the capitalist world economy in the 1950s and 1960s was largely predicated on the strength of the U.S. economy (both its productive capacity and the size of its domestic market) as well as the willingness of U.S. capitalism to cultivate Germany and Japan as major trading partners and competitors in the global arena. The dynamic growth of the German and Japanese economies drove the extraordinary wave of global economic expansion that marked the 1950s and 1960s. But it is important to stress that, for Brenner,

> the ability of the German and Japanese manufacturers to wrest ever greater shares of the world market from U.S. (and U.K.) producers... made possible their postwar "miracles," [and that] this capacity to seize market share could only come into play because of the willingness of the U.S. government to tolerate not only the broad opening of the U.S. economy to overseas penetration, but even a certain decline in U.S. manufacturing competitiveness in the interests of U.S. military and political hegemony, international economic stability, and the rapid expansion of U.S. multinational corporations and banks. (1998a: 47)

Brenner does not elaborate on this point, but it clearly suggests that the post-war boom of the 1950s and 1960s was based to a considerable extent on a deliberate attenuation of the competitive relations between the leading capitalist power (the U.S.) and its German and Japanese rivals. A geo-political strategic calculation — the need to promote the stability of the world capitalist economy and to maintain the unity of the imperialist powers in the face of the "Communist threat" — overrode the normal tendency of a capitalist nation-state to press its competitive advantages to the fullest. Crucially, however, this partial suppression of the competitive dynamic of inter-imperialist relations was conditioned by — and likely conditional upon — the dramatic recovery of profitability in the U.S. made possible by the Second World War. Thus, the "long upturn" of the immediate post-war period depended upon both high profitability levels and the conscious efforts of U.S. policy-makers to subordinate the short-term competitive position of U.S. manufacturing capital to the longer-term goal of preserving world capitalism. In general terms, such an account of the long upturn seems quite plausible.

The long upturn was succeeded by a transitional period that spanned the years 1965–1973, a period Brenner refers to as the "onset of crisis." It was during this conjuncture that U.S. capitalism began to suffer a serious erosion of its hegemonic place within the world capitalist order. Profitability fell to unacceptably low levels as Germany and especially Japan sought to further enlarge their shares of the world market. The costs of prosecuting its dirty, losing war in Vietnam also weighed heavily on U.S. imperialism, both economically and politically. At the same time, in many advanced capitalist countries, the costs associated with maintaining low unemployment and popular social-welfare programs began to have a negative impact on economic growth and profitability. Nixon's competitive devaluation of the U.S. dollar in 1971 signalled the onset of renewed inter-imperialist rivalry. By 1974, the stage was set for the most serious international recession since the 1930s — a slump triggered by sky-rocketing oil prices, but whose backdrop was a decline in rates of profit throughout much of the advanced capitalist world.

The global recession of 1974–75 was to provoke a major offensive by capital against labour in a number of key capitalist countries, including the U.S., and it was to be followed by even more serious slumps in the early 1980s and 1990s. The turn to monetarism and neoliberalism and the deflationary tendencies these produced were cushioned, however, by the fiscal stimulus associated with "military Keynesianism" and the expansion of both public and private debt in the U.S.

The inauguration of the Clinton administration, coinciding with the end of the Cold War, marked a significant turning point in U.S. policy in relation to the global economy. Clinton's commitment to the elimination of deficit spending, which had previously tended to reflate the U.S. and global economies, broke a pattern that had persisted for some three decades. The result was that "by the midpoint of the 1990s, a certain recovery of the U.S. economy had... been purchased at the cost of exacerbating international stagnation" (Brenner 1998a: 157).

The most important part of Brenner's study is his account of the factors that produced and sustained the long downturn in the world capitalist economy, which began in the mid-1970s and has persisted to the present day. The seriousness of this downturn is well documented. In the U.S., during the period 1973–96, the growth of GDP per hour worked averaged 0.9 percent, well under half the historical average for the previous century, while the average for the 1990s (up to 1996) fell to 0.7 percent (1998a: 3).

Comparison of the periods 1950–70 and 1970–93 shows serious declines in such key economic indicators as the net profit rate, growth of output, capital stock formation, labour productivity and real wage growth throughout the G-7 core of the world capitalist economy. Meanwhile, unemployment soared, particularly in the eleven countries of the European Union, where, in 1996, it averaged 11.3 percent — higher than the average annual rate of unemployment for the sixteen leading capitalist economies during the Great Depression.

At one level, Brenner's explanation for the long downturn is quite straight-forward. Proceeding from Duménil and Lévy's (1993) defence of the central role of the rate of profit in regulating the performance of capitalist economies (a thesis central to classical and Marxist economics alike), he argues that falling profitability throughout the advanced capitalist world produced a serious decline in the rate of growth of investment and output, especially in manufacturing. This in turn led to a fall in the rate of growth of productivity, falling real wage growth and increases in unemployment. Accordingly, Brenner's key analytical task becomes one of explaining the underlying causes of the profitability crisis.

Rejecting both the "fundamentalist" Marxist account of a rising organic composition of capital as well as the dominant "supply side" accounts of profits squeezed by rising real wages, declining productivity or welfare-state expenditures, Brenner suggests that the source of the profitability crisis of the past twenty-five to thirty years has been "overcapacity and overproduction which resulted from intensified, horizontal inter-capitalist competition." This intensified competition is "itself the manifestation of the introduction of lower-cost, lower-price goods into the world market... at the expense of already existing higher cost, higher price producers, and their profitability and their productive capacity." Brenner offers not only an empirical and historical analysis of the fall in profitability, but a general theoretical framework for explaining it. Its point of departure is the "unplanned, uncoordinated, and competitive nature of capitalist production," while its upshot is the conclusion that downturns produced by crises of profitability are likely to persist so long as the afflicted economies prove unable to reduce and profitably reallocate productive resources in such a way as to overcome overcapacity and overproduction in manufacturing.

This general theoretical framework is fully consistent with the emphasis that Brenner accords to the conscious attenuation of inter-capitalist competition in explaining the long upturn after the Second World War, and places him within the broad tradition of Marxist crisis theory associated with the concept of "disproportionality." A possible consequence is that Brenner's analysis could be seen as lending itself, as one critic has suggested, to the idea that the U.S., the European Union and Japan might "jointly agree to co-ordinate their production and share out markets more equitably" as a solution to the downturn (Kilmister 1998). Such a prescription would be reminiscent of social-democratic nostrums of the 1920s, according to which "the anarchy of capitalist markets" could, in principle, be replaced with an "organized capitalism" (Hilferding) or some form of "ultra-imperialism" (Kautsky). However, Brenner seems to recognize that the general crisis of profitability of the advanced capitalist economies over the past three decades has not only resulted from heightened inter-capitalist competition but has also created conditions that encourage less, not more, cooperation between the leading imperialist states as they seek to enlarge their market shares at each other's expense. Surveying the global economic scene at the end of the 1990s, Brenner observes: "We may be on the verge of still another, perhaps even more brutal, round of that heavily zero-sum battle for world markets in manufacturing, under conditions of slow growing demand, that has for so long stood in the way of renewed economic dynamism" (1998a: 256).

How, then, does Brenner explain why profit rates displayed a secular decline? His answer is that, as a result of unbridled inter-capitalist competition, producers are "unable to markup prices over costs sufficiently to maintain their established rates of return" (96). In other words, profits are squeezed by the inability of producers to "realize" prices that are adequate in relation to rising costs. Building upon Marx's own insights into the profitability problems posed by fixed capital investments, Brenner focuses on the dilemmas facing established manufacturers when, having sunk their capital in technologically or economically obsolescent fixed capital assets, they are confronted by competition from newcomers using cheaper, more advanced means of production. So long as the established manufacturers can continue to realize an adequate rate of return on their circulating capital (raw materials, wage costs and so on) they may resist "exiting" the production line or retiring their outmoded fixed capital assets. Moreover, since the established producers also have significant advantages over new entrants in terms of market contacts and knowledge-based assets of various kinds, they have a fighting chance to meet the competitive challenge of lower-cost producers. Due to inadequate exit of obsolescent fixed capital assets and even whole firms, the competition between established high-cost producers and their lower-cost upstart competitors leads to a growing problem of overcapacity and overproduction, and with this comes the "realization" problems that cause industry-wide profit rates to fall.

In a more recent article, Brenner summarizes the place of this analysis in his overall account of the origins and persistence of the long downturn:

Why, in line with standard expectations, didn't firms suffering from falling profitability in their lines shift into other lines of production to a sufficient extent to alleviate overcapacity? To this question, it seems to me there are three general answers. First, the great corporations of the United States, Germany and Japan that dominated world manufacturing appeared to have much better prospects for maintaining and improving profitability by seeking to improve competitiveness in their own lines than in reallocating into others. They had great supplies of sunk capital that they had already paid for in their own lines; they had long-established relations with suppliers and customers that could not be easily duplicated in other lines; and they had developed, over a long period, hard-won specialized technological knowledge that was useful only in their own line. Thus during the 1970s and after, U.S., German and Japanese corporations did not generally relinquish their positions unless they were forced to, with the result that there was insufficient exit and little alleviation of manufacturing overcapacity. Second, even despite the reduced profitability in world manufacturing lines, low-cost producers based especially in East Asia found it profitable to enter many of those lines, just as had their predecessors from Japan. There was therefore too much entry, further exacerbating overcapacity. Finally, Keynesian policies, which became universal in the 1970s and persisted in the United States into the early 1990s, actually contributed to the perpetuation of overcapacity and overproduction and thus helped to keep down rates of profit in aggregate. By increasing demand, deficit spending and easy credit thus allowed many high-cost, low-profit firms that would otherwise have gone bankrupt to continue in business and maintain positions that might otherwise have been occupied by low-cost, high-profit producers. Keynesianism thus unquestionably rendered the long economic downturn milder, but also made it longer, staving off a 1930s-type depression but at the cost of reducing the system's dynamism by keeping in business firms that made low profits and did little investing. (1998b: 5)

The affinity of Brenner's account with "disproportionality" theories of capitalist crisis has already been noted. It should now also be clear that his general approach has something in common with "underconsumption" theory in its stress on realization problems and the problem of deficient effective demand. Unlike classical underconsumption theory, however, Brenner's analysis gives pride of place to falling profit rates in explaining the long downturn, a position normally associated with the "fundamentalist" falling-rate-of-profit accounts, which he rejects on theoretical grounds. It is the specific way in which Brenner combines these elements of Marx's own theory of crisis that gives his analysis its distinctive character, just as it is his refusal to integrate them with other key elements of Marx's theory that accounts for its inadequacy.

"Problems of Realization" and the Falling Rate of Profit: A Value-Theoretical Approach

In what might be seen as the central theoretical statement underpinning his analysis, Brenner writes:

> I start from the premise that, under capitalist social-production relations, the generalization of the individual norms of profitability maximization combined with the pressure of competition on a system-wide scale tends to bring about the growth of the productive forces and overall productivity, with the result that, on the assumption that the real wage remains constant, both the rate and the mass of profit rise, assuming there are no problems of realization. But given capitalism's unplanned, competitive nature, realization problems cannot be assumed away. The same cost-cutting by firms which creates the potential for aggregate profitability to rise creates the potential for aggregate profitability to fall, leading to macroeconomic difficulties. (1998a: 24)

This passage provides considerable insight into the key problems with Brenner's theoretical framework. In the first place, Brenner suggests that realization problems associated with overproduction are primarily the result of the unplanned and competitive nature of capitalism. In Marx's theory, to the contrary, the inability of capitalists to realize prices adequate to sustain profitability stems from a crisis in valorization — that is, from inadequate production of new value and of surplus value in particular. This crisis of valorization manifests itself within the sphere of circulation as a lack of effective demand, but its roots lie in the replacement of living labour in production by increasingly sophisticated labour-saving technology. The displacement of living labour from production has the effect of reducing both the income of the workforce (resulting in declining demand for consumer goods) and the magnitude of profit in relation to the capital invested (resulting in declining demand for so-called "capital goods"). Under such conditions, capitalists are unable to realize prices that are in line with the anticipated rate of return on their invested capital.

The phenomenon of "falling prices" stems in large part from efficiencies imposed under the whip of market competition, but such price adjustments are not the cause of problems of realization. A "realization crisis" arises only when the realized prices of commodities are inadequate to sustain the average rate of profit on an economy-wide scale. Thus, to blame a fall in the rate of profit on "problems of realization" is something of a tautology. What must be explained is why prices relative to costs (capital investment) cannot be sustained at levels that permit a stable (or better yet, a rising) rate of profit.

As suggestive as his account of inter-capitalist competition is in explaining the staying power of high-cost fixed capital assets and the debilitating effect of the resulting overcapacity and overproduction on prices, Brenner fails to provide an answer to this question. For he is unable to explain why the sale of manufactured commodities at unprofitable prices fails to liberate demand for other commodities enjoying higher than average profit margins, and why productive capital would not move massively enough into such profitable new lines to ensure a stable average rate of profit on an economy-wide scale. To put the matter slightly differently, Brenner is unable to account for the aggregate fall in purchasing power (in relation to the total capital invested) that prevents aggregate prices from remaining at levels compatible with a stable average rate of profit.

In contrast to Brenner's analysis, Marx's theories of value and of the falling rate of profit provide the conceptual resources needed to address this problem, and, *inter alia*, to salvage the most viable aspects of Brenner's own account. It should be stressed that an adequate solution to this problem would seem to be mandatory for any account of the long downturn that, like Brenner's, traces its source and intractability to a generalized crisis of profitability across the advanced capitalist world, and not simply to a particular distribution of profits amongst competing capitals and capitalist economies.

Marx's theory of labour value involves the defence of two fundamental propositions. The first is that living labour is the sole source of the new value that is the social substance of wages and profits. The second is that total value (previously existing as well as new) exists as a definite quantitative magnitude at the level of the capitalist macro-economy — a magnitude that sets definite limits on profits, wages and the realizability of prices set by capitalists seeking "reasonable" profit margins. Marx's theory of the falling rate of profit is crucially predicated on the truth of these propositions. Indeed, they can be regarded as necessary, if not entirely sufficient, presuppositions of his argument that capital's displacement of living labour from production will produce a crisis of valorization and a downward pressure on the average rate of profit, whether or not this displacement involves an elevated level of labour productivity.

If the two propositions central to Marx's theory of value can be sustained (and I believe they can), then the contradiction between capital's continuous success in increasing productivity at the micro-level of the individual firm and the tendency of the capitalist macro-economy to descend into periodic crises of profitability and deficient effective demand can at last be adequately explained. Contrary to conventional economic theories that assume a monotonic relationship between rising labour productivity and economic prosperity, Marx's value-theoretic analysis of capitalism recognizes that the "life blood" of the capitalist economy is not material output (the use values that satisfy people's needs and fancies), but surplus value, that is, the value of the material output newly created by living labour above and beyond the value embodied in wages. The social content of this surplus value is precisely the exploitation of living labour by capital — the specifically capitalist form in which surplus labour is extracted from the direct producers by the capitalist owners of the means of production.

The non-obvious, and even counterintuitive, relationship between productivity and the average rate of profit is the starting point of the following formulation by Marx of his "law of the falling tendency of the rate of profit" in *Capital* III:

> The progressive tendency for the general rate of profit to fall is... simply the expression peculiar to the capitalist mode of production of the progressive development of the social productivity of labour.... Since the mass of living labour applied continuously declines in relation to the mass of the objectified labour that it sets in motion, i.e., the productively consumed means of production, the part of this living labour that is unpaid and objectified in surplus-value must also stand in an ever-decreasing ratio to the value of the total capital applied. But this ratio between the mass of surplus-value and the total capital applied in fact constitutes the rate of profit, which must therefore steadily fall. (Marx 1981b: 319)

In a later passage, Marx states:

> The barriers to the capitalist mode of production show themselves as follows: 1) in the way that the development of *labour productivity* involves a law, in the form of the falling rate of profit, that at a certain point confronts this development itself in a most hostile way and has constantly to be overcome *by way of crises*; 2) in the way that it is the appropriation of unpaid labour in general... that determines the expansion and contraction of production, instead of the proportion between production and social needs, the needs of socially developed human beings. (Marx 1981b: 367, emphasis added)

Productivity growth is, of course, a matter of central concern to capitalists, for it is precisely by enhancing productivity that individual capitalist firms seek to reduce their costs per unit of output and thereby enlarge their market share and mass of profits. But it is only because individual firms can realize (or capture) the surplus value produced by workers employed elsewhere in the economy (as a result of competitive processes of surplus-value redistribution in circulation) that labour-displacing productivity enhancements are a viable micro tactic of individual capitals in trying to sustain or enhance their profitability. What is rational from the point of view of the individual firm in the short term, however, is inimical to the interests of capital in general in the medium to long term. The very means used by firms to enhance labour productivity diminish the role played by living labour in production and thereby force down the general or average rate of profit. In other words, the unintended and unanticipated consequence of efforts by individual capitals to reduce their reliance on living labour in production in order to increase their share of social surplus value is a proportionally reduced role in production for the living labour, which is the sole input capable of producing this social surplus value. Capitalists compete to increase their share (profit of enterprise) of a pie (social surplus value) that is expanding at a rate slower than the expansion of their combined investments — and this is the necessary consequence of a shift away from the employment of variable capital (the productive living labour that directly produces surplus value) toward ever-greater investments in constant capital (the elements of the process of capitalist production and reproduction that play only an indirect role in the production of surplus value).

Marx's account of the contradiction between the rationality of individual capitalist firms in promoting labour-displacing technological innovation and the macro-level requirements of the social capital to maintain the general rate of profit is an instance of a macro-micro contradiction under capitalism that Brenner himself claims to take as "his point of departure": the individual investors' unconcern for or inability to take account of the effects of their own profit-seeking on the profitability of other producers and of the economy as a whole." Yet, as we have seen, Brenner rejects Marx's understanding of the relationship between micro-level productivity enhancements and a declining average rate of profit, arguing that "the growth of the productive forces and overall productivity" produces a *rising* rate and mass of profit, provided there are no problems of realization and assuming a constant real wage.

In taking this stand, Brenner echoes the neo-Ricardian critique of Marx, the hallmark of which is a failure to appreciate the importance of the contradiction between "the natural" and "the social" in explaining the laws of motion of capitalism. Indeed, the conflation of the natural and the social is central to Brenner's misinterpretation of the "fundamentalist" Marxist theory of the falling rate of profit:

> According to the fundamentalist Marxist thesis, in order to compete, capitalists must cut costs by increasing mechanization, manifested

in a rising organic composition of capital (capital-labour ratio). But, in so doing, they cannot avoid bringing about a fall in the aggregate rate of profit because the rising organic composition of capital issues in an increase in the output-labour ratio that is insufficient to counteract the parallel fall in the output-capital [ratio?] that it also brings about. The rate of profit falls… because, with the real wage assumed constant, investment in mechanization cannot but result in an increase in labour productivity (output-labour ratio) that is more than cancelled out by a decrease in capital productivity (real output-capital ratio). Were this theory correct, what would logically be entailed is the impeccably Malthusian proposition that the rate of profit can be expected to fall because, as a direct result of capital accumulation, overall productivity — productivity taking into account both labour and capital inputs — can be expected to fall. (1998a: 11)

Thus, Brenner accuses Marx of attributing falling profit rates to declining "overall productivity" despite Marx's explicit statements to the contrary!

Brenner's gloss of "the fundamentalist Marxist thesis" involves a refusal to recognize the critical distinction that Marx makes between the production of material output and the production of value and surplus value. Marx's view is that overall productivity — material output in relation to physical inputs of all kinds — can be expected to rise as a result of capital accumulation and associated technological innovation. But this tells us nothing about what is happening in the realm of values. A completely automated economy, in which production is carried out entirely by robots, could continue to register rapid growth in overall productivity (as defined above), but it could not produce any new "value" in Marx's sense.

What, then, is "value"? In Marx's theory, value is neither a psychological relation of people to things (as in neoclassical, marginalist theory) nor a relation between things and other things (as in neo-Ricardian surplus theory), but rather a social relation of people to people in the context of a society-wide division of labour. For Marx, a commodity is a product of labour that is produced with a view to its sale in the market. Every commodity has a utility (a use value) as well as an exchange value (the power to command some sort of remuneration in exchange: a price). But the exchange value of a commodity is merely a form of appearance of the commodity's value, with which it rarely coincides directly. The value of a commodity is an expression of its relationship to all other commodities as a product of the social division of living labour. Accordingly, the value of a commodity is determined by the amount of socially necessary labour time required for its production; but its exchange value will deviate from this value as a result of other factors bearing upon price formation (including, crucially, surplus-value redistributions in circulation). However much individual prices and values diverge (owing to transfers and redistributions of value effected through market processes), total prices must equal total values — for without the social relations of capitalist production expressed by "value" (whose substance is nothing other than abstract social labour), the economic category of price could have neither theoretical pertinence nor concrete existence. The upshot of this argument is that "material wealth," under capitalist social production relations, is necessarily measured in terms of abstract socially necessary labour, the phenomenal form of which is money.

The logic of capitalist development, defined by the exploitative and antagonistic relation between capital and labour, as well as the competitive relations between capitals, is to continuously reduce the socially necessary labour time required to produce a given quantity of material output. This means that as the magnitude of physical or material output expands, the quantity of value it represents may well decrease. In view of this, it is entirely possible for material productivity to grow as the production of surplus value declines. Indeed, the ever-sharpening contradiction between humanity's command over nature in production (expressed in the growth of productive forces embodying labour-saving technology) and the social-structural imperatives of capitalism to exploit wage labour and therefore to measure "wealth" and economic performance in terms of abstract labour time (money) is central to Marx's understanding of the historical limits of the capitalist mode of production.

All of this is overlooked by Brenner, who, in the last analysis, seems unable to acknowledge that there can be a contradiction between progress in overcoming the technical-natural obstacles to increased material productivity and the class-appropriative requirements of valorization — that is, between the "natural" and the "social" dimensions of capitalist production. The consequence is that Brenner cannot see that the labour-saving technological innovation that enhances productivity must also, at the macro level, reduce the magnitude of aggregate values that are the basis of aggregate prices. Yet this phenomenon is at the root of the problem that Brenner emphasizes but fails to theorize: the problem of "realization." Once this phenomenon is acknowledged it becomes clear that aggregate prices must fall as the values sustaining them recede, and it is precisely this that accounts for the inability of capitalists to command prices for their commodities, in the aggregate, that can sustain the average rate of profit.

Eschewing the value-theoretic aspects of Marx's theory of crisis, Brenner is obliged to base his alternative account of capitalist crisis on what is clearly a much more "manageable" contradiction: the contradiction between unbridled inter-capitalist competition and the social capital's need to plan the economy in such a way as to avoid problems of realization. Abstracted and isolated from the class-relational contradictions that Marx highlights (and which are themselves an expression of the growing incompatibility between the social form and the technical-natural content of capitalist production), this latter contradiction emerges as one that, in principle, can be significantly mitigated within the framework of a reformed capitalism. Thus, Brenner's analysis tends to lend itself to a liberal-reformist program of imposing "capital controls" and "supra-national economic planning" as a means of addressing the self-destructive dynamics of inter-capitalist competition — precisely the sorts of ideas that are now gaining ground in bourgeois circles as the nostrums of neoliberalism begin to lose their lustre (Soros 1997).

This is the greatest danger of Brenner's analysis: that at a time when the long downturn may well be issuing into a global depression, it diverts attention away from Marxist analyses that point unmistakably to the conclusion that the problem is not merely with the unplanned and unduly competitive nature of the capitalist system, but with the impossibility of further human progress (defined as a qualitative extension of human productive capacities) on the basis of the class-exploitative and antagonistic social relations of capitalist production.

Productivity, Valorization and
the Problem of Unproductive Labour

Brenner's empirical analysis, I suggested earlier, can be interpreted as reinforcing the evidential case for a more fully Marxist account of the long downturn. It does so at two levels. First, it undermines the empirical grounds for more traditional neo-Ricardian, supply-side accounts of "the profit squeeze" — which suggest that rising real wages and/or declining productivity growth were primarily responsible for falling profit rates. Second, it presents data that, when interpreted through the lens of Marx's value theory, tell a story that is consistent with Marx's expectation that the average rate of profit will fall as a result of a rising organic composition of capital, that is, a rising ratio of dead to living labour in production.

Despite many shared theoretical assumptions, Brenner departs from supply-side neo-Ricardian accounts of the long downturn in his insistence that the profitability crisis has not been the result of rising labour strength but the result of manufacturing overcapacity and overproduction leading to falling prices. In general terms, such an analysis is not inconsistent with the fundamentalist Marxist view that the value of the constant capital stock (money-capital invested in means of production) has grown faster than the value embodied in variable capital (the wage bill) and surplus value (the income of the capitalist class), with the result that the organic composition of capital ($C/s+v$) has risen and the average rate of profit (s/C) has fallen.[2] Indeed, when specified in terms of Marx's value categories, Brenner's findings with respect to the fall in the output-capital ratio seem to be in accord with theoretical expectations of a rising organic composition of capital.

It is noteworthy that Brenner largely ignores the extensive empirical literature by Marxist political economists that has sought to test Marx's hypothesis that a falling average rate of profit is caused by, or at least correlated with, a rising organic composition of capital (Mage 1963; Moseley 1991; Shaikh and Tonak 1994; Smith 1994a). Much of this literature lends support to the fundamentalist view, especially those empirical studies that, on the basis of Marx's own theory, insist on the critical importance of distinguishing between productive and unproductive labour in the measurement of Marx's value categories. Indeed, the productive-unproductive labour distinction has been central to most Marxist attempts to refute the "rising labour strength" account of the profitability crisis. Brenner's analysis is the first serious study, within an ecumenically defined Marxist tradition, to simultaneously reject this account and to dispense with the productive-unproductive labour distinction.

That Brenner does not refer to the problem of unproductive labour is hardly surprising, for virtually all proponents of Marx's view of the question accept the value-theoretic assumptions upon which it is based. To be sure, an increasing number of non-Marxist economists entertain the idea that certain categories of labour are intrinsically less productive than others, without embracing any notion of labour value. But the fact remains that, amongst Marxist political economists, Marx's theory of labour value and the productive-unproductive labour distinction are seen as closely intertwined. The reason is simple. For Marx, productive labour is precisely labour that is directly and immediately involved in the production of surplus value; it is wage labour that participates in the valorization process via its direct involvement in the production of commodities. It follows that the Marxist concept of unproductive labour is not at all a normative concept. Indeed, Marx allows that many types of labour (including non-capitalist forms of production labour) can be considered socially useful, and even socially necessary in many different senses, without being "productive." In contemporary capitalism, many wage and salary earners engage in activities that are socially necessary to the social capital (from retail sales to working for the capitalist state), but they are by no means productive of surplus value on that account. Many of these workers perform labour that is indispensable to the transfer of surplus value from productive capital to unproductive capital, and in this sense they make possible the profits that are realized by commercial and financial capitals; but in so doing they do not enlarge the total magnitude of social surplus value available for distribution within the capitalist class (see appendix 2 of this volume).

The importance of this theoretical issue is obvious when one considers the expansion of "socially necessary unproductive labour" (SNUL) in twentieth-century advanced capitalist economies. Official government statistics fail to distinguish between labour income accruing to productive and SNUL wage labourers. At the same time, aggregate productivity measures tend to examine output in relation to hours worked by both productive and SNUL wage and salary earners. To be sure, productivity figures for the manufacturing sector alone provide a fairly good indication of the real trend in labour productivity amongst productive workers in that sector of the economy (since the majority of the manufacturing labour force is productive of surplus value), but even here trends can be skewed by the changing ratio of productive to unproductive labour in manufacturing. The point is that, as the SNUL workforce has grown as a percentage of the total workforce, conventional measures of productivity growth have tended to understate the real growth of productivity amongst productive workers, because it is only the productive sector of the workforce that is responsible for the creation of the value by which gross output is measured. This is not to suggest that the SNUL segment of the labour force does not produce a material output that can be measured (in physical terms); but it is to insist that the portion of material output that takes the commodity form (and is measured in dollar figures in national income accounts) is solely produced by productive labour.

All of this has important implications for assessing Brenner's empirical observations in light of Marxist theory. For one thing, Brenner notes that, historically, productivity growth throughout the G-7 has been lower in non-manufacturing sectors than in manufacturing and that the rate of growth of productivity in non-manufacturing in the U.S. fell to shockingly low levels between 1979 and 1995 compared to manufacturing. Consider also Brenner's observation that between 1965 and 1973 (the period of the onset of crisis) "aggregate profitability in the G-7 economies outside of manufacturing fell by only about 19 percent — compared to 25.5 percent in G-7 manufacturing — despite the fact that unit costs of production seem to have risen considerably faster outside manufacturing than within it" (1998a: 136–37). To assess the significance of these trends in value-theoretic terms, we would have to examine the ratio of productive to unproductive labour in these different sectors of the economy and the transfers of value occurring between them. Assuming that a proportionally larger portion of social surplus value is produced in manufacturing than in non-manufacturing sectors, we might hypothesize that one of the reasons for the larger fall in manufacturing profitability relative to non-manufacturing sectors might be changes in the distribution of surplus value that favour unproductive (commercial and financial) capital (and perhaps the capitalist state) at the expense of productive (industrial) capital. Because Brenner does not consider the possibility of inter-sectoral transfers of value, as between productive and unproductive spheres, such an explanation for the severe decline in manufacturing profitability during the critical period of 1965–73 is not available to him. The result, as we have seen, is that the decline in manufacturing profitability is entirely explained in terms of falling prices resulting from intensified inter-capitalist competition.

For reasons I have already sketched, Brenner's explanation of the origin and persistence of the profitability crisis strikes me as both one-sided and under-theorized. At the same time, my own empirical work on the Canadian economy and the empirical work of other Marxist political economists on the U.S. economy support an explanation that is consistent with what Brenner calls "fundamentalist" Marxist theory. This explanation highlights two major phenomena: a secular increase in the organic composition of capital and a rising ratio of unproductive to productive labour in the wage-earning workforce. Together these two phenomena have contributed to what might be called a rising "value composition of output" — in which the total costs of capitalist production and social reproduction have grown faster than the new value created by productive living labour.

As already noted, an important point of departure for the renaissance of empirical work in "fundamentalist" Marxist crisis theory was the reassertion of the salience of Marx's distinction between productive and unproductive labour. In particular, Shaikh and Moseley have demonstrated in their respective studies that attempts to analyze post-war developments and to test Marx's theory of the falling rate of profit by including the wage bill of unproductive labour in the Marxian category of "variable capital" can only lead to skewed and inconclusive results. On the other hand, once variable capital (v) is restricted to the wage bill of productive workers it can be shown that, in the American economy at least, the rate of surplus value (s/v) rose even as the rate of profit (s/C) and the ratio of total profits to total wages fell (Moseley 1991; Shaikh and Tonak 1994).

My work on the Canadian economy also establishes a rising rate of surplus value throughout the long upturn of the 1950s and 1960s, but it differs from the approach of Shaikh and Moseley in a number of ways. Most importantly, it rejects the inclusion of the SNUL wage bill, as well as taxes, as "non-profit components" of social surplus value, and associated attempts to distinguish between "gross" and "net," or "Marxist" and "conventional," rates of profit. Moreover, by excluding SNUL and tax revenues from the category of surplus value, my work establishes an even stronger tendency for the organic composition of capital (C/s+v) to rise alongside a falling rate of profit than does the work of Shaikh or Moseley. Table 3.1 shows the results of my empirical study of the Canadian economy as informed by this specification of Marx's fundamental value categories.

Following the pioneering work of Shane Mage, I have argued elsewhere (see appendix 2 of this volume) that the increasingly important SNUL wage bill is most appropriately treated as a component of the constant capital *flow*

Table 3.1: The Marxian Ratios, Canada 1947–1991

Year	S/C (Rate of profit)	S/V (Rate of surplus value)	C/(S+V) (Organic composition of capital)
1947	0.1366	0.4764	2.362
1948	0.1418	0.4839	2.299
1949	0.1564	0.5436	2.251
1950	0.1788	0.6488	2.201
1951	0.1716	0.6615	2.319
1952	0.1739	0.6617	2.289
1953	0.1521	0.5952	2.449
1954	0.1355	0.5687	2.675
1955	0.1569	0.6586	2.529
1956	0.1542	0.6676	2.596
1957	0.1281	0.5906	2.898
1958	0.1221	0.6027	3.079
1959	0.1319	0.6644	3.024
1960	0.1171	0.6098	3.235
1961	0.1162	0.6302	3.325
1962	0.1249	0.6786	3.237
1963	0,1232	0.6709	3.258
1964	0.1421	0.7758	3.076
1965	0.1305	0.7552	3.296
1966	0.1287	0.7020	3.206
1967	0.1202	0.6789	3.364
1968	0.1214	0.6978	3.386
1969	0.1171	0.6967	3.508
1970	0.1006	0.6297	3.841
1971	0,0994	0.6382	3.921
1972	0.1067	0.6825	3.801
1973	0.1079	0.6856	3.769
1974	0.1325	0.9403	3.657
1975	0.0901	0.6073	4.192
1976	0.1248	0.8192	3.607
1977	0.1089	0.7316	3.876
1978	0.1184	0.8147	3.791

continued on next page...

Year	S/C (Rate of profit)	S/V (Rate of surplus value)	C/(S+V) (Organic composition of capital)
1979	0.1302	0.9205	3.682
1980	0.1222	0.8822	3.834
1981	0.1282	0.9463	3.794
1982	0.0939	0.7714	4.637
1983	0.1156	0.9029	4.106
1984	0.1391	1.0541	3.691
1985	0.1326	0.9755	3.725
1986	0.1226	0.9038	3.874
1987	0.1342	1.0047	3.735
1988	0.1388	1.0141	3.627
1989	0.1243	0.9308	3.879
1990	0.1068	0.8632	4.336
1991	0.0884	0.7366	4.801

— as a special type of overhead cost borne by the social capital as a whole. It should be noted that in the measurement of the rate of profit (s/C) and the organic composition of capital (C/s+v), such a procedure does not inflate the magnitude of C because this latter magnitude refers only to the value of the constant capital *stock* (of which the SNUL wage bill is not a component).

My treatment of the SNUL wage bill and most tax revenues as elements of the constant capital flow is controversial. Marxists who reject the productive-unproductive labour distinction generally treat the SNUL wage bill in the private sector as a component of variable capital and taxes as part of social surplus value. Those who defend the distinction generally follow the convention established by Sweezy and Gillman of treating all unproductive costs (in both the private and state sectors) as non-profit elements of social surplus value. It seems to me that the approach of treating SNUL and unproductive costs in general as part of constant capital allows us to preserve the most important insights proffered by each of these contending theoretical camps.

Unfortunately, textual exegesis of Marx does not provide a solution to the problem of how unproductive labour costs should be treated in relation to the value categories. In discussing labour employed by commercial capital, for example, Marx suggests in one passage that this unproductive labour is exchanged with "variable capital," in another that is "a deduction from surplus value" and in still another that it adds "previously existing value" and "constant capital" to the commodity product. Despite Marx's failure to provide a clear resolution of the issue, however, a strong case can be made that the constant-capital specification of SNUL and of other unproductive overhead costs of the social capital is entirely warranted, not least because it avoids the fetishistic reduction of the value category of constant capital to "physical means of production" and allows instead for a conception of constant capital as the value expression of all those elements of production and reproduction that "frame" the valorization process. Just as variable capital contributes directly to the production of surplus value through its exchange with productive living labour, constant capital contributes indirectly to the valorization process through its exchange with the tools, machinery and raw materials with which productive labourers work, as well as the "social machinery" that makes possible the realization of value and the institutional conditions of capital accumulation (including the capitalist state).

By contrast, the treatment of SNUL as a non-profit component of social surplus value has a highly problematic consequence. It suggests that the investment that the social capital makes in SNUL — in order to decrease the turnover time of capital or to maintain the functions of the capitalist state, for example — is a form of discretionary spending that, in one period, can be increased to prime effective demand, and, in another, decreased in order to expand the profit component of social surplus value. Such a view of the matter understates the necessary functions of SNUL (a point that is forcefully, and quite correctly, driven home by many opponents of the productive-unproductive labour distinction) while also overestimating the ease with which value can be reallocated from SNUL activity to the "profit component" of surplus value.

The constant-capital specification permits us to recognize the fact that SNUL constitutes a critically important component of the investment that the social capital makes in the overall process of capitalist production and reproduction. By the same token, however, it highlights why the expansion of SNUL is likely to have a negative long-term impact on profitability and capital accumulation. For while SNUL's socially necessary functions can un-doubtedly assist in maintaining the rate of profit (by, amongst other things, counteracting unfavourable conditions of "realization" that can negate values), its expansion involves an increase in the overall investment in the circulating constant capital, which finds expression in the total value of gross output. Other things being equal, an increase in SNUL must produce an increase in what I have called the "value composition of output" — the ratio of constant capital (previously existing value) to new value in the gross product — and this is likely to be associated with a declining average rate of profit. Indeed, in examining the Canadian economy between 1947 and 1980, I found that different components of the constant capital flow grew at different rates over a stretch of history that was marked by a long-term decline in the average rate of profit. Circulating constant capital consumed in manufacturing grew by a factor of 18 between 1947 and 1980, while the tax flow increased by a factor of 26 and the SNUL wage bill by a factor of 36. Overall, the value composition of gross output increased by more than 50 percent over this thirty-four-year period (Smith 1984). These figures suggest that the growth of SNUL has been an important supplementary factor in depressing the rate of profit, even though the primary factor was the rising organic composition of capital.

Conclusion

In my book *Invisible Leviathan*, I suggest that the growth of socially necessary unproductive labour alongside a rising organic composition of capital attests to a certain "adulteration" of Marx's law of the tendency of the rate of profit to fall and invites a new way of appreciating the declining dynamism of the capitalist mode of production:

> [If] the growth of constant capital in relation to newly created value once signified a growth in the productivity of labour, it now *also* signifies a relative diminution of productive labour in relation to socially-necessary unproductive labour. If Marx argued that the rate of profit would fall cyclically (and perhaps secularly) due to progressive increases in the technical and organic compositions of capital, profitability now seems to be subject to a downward pressure stemming both from technical changes enforced by capitalist competition *and* from the circumstance that a diminishing percentage of the working class is involved in surplus value production, as distinct from realization. If capitalism's tendency to promote the "objective socialization" of labour and of production once reflected its historically progressive role in developing the forces of production, it now *also* reflects a hypertrophy of the capitalist state and the sphere of circulation — a hypertrophy which impedes the advance of the productive forces by diverting enormous economic resources *away from* production. (Smith 1994a: 180–81)

This way of assessing the capitalist mode of production at the end of the twentieth century is very remote from the picture painted by Brenner, notwithstanding his gloomy prognostication of a looming global recession. There is nothing in his account that allows us to assert that the capitalist mode of production has long since entered a stage of decline — of "historical structural crisis." Instead, Brenner invites us to fix our attention on the "unplanned, uncoordinated and competitive" character of capitalist production even as he insists that "the capitalist mode of production distinguishes itself from all previous forms by its tendency to *relentless and systematic development of the productive forces*" (10, emphasis added). In a world in which over a third of the global labour force is either unemployed or underemployed; in which the diffusion of advanced technology to those who desperately need it is blocked; and in which the continued measurement of wealth in terms of abstract social labour (that is, the law of value) has become an obstacle to the qualitative expansion of material output and to the extension of global human capacities, one wonders how Brenner can fail to see that capitalism has long since forfeited any claim to so progressive a mission. As troubling as this question might be to Brenner's socialist conscience, I am convinced that it is not likely to arouse his or anyone else's intellect outside of a serious engagement with Marx's theory of value. A fully adequate critique of capitalism's historical limits continues to suggest the latter's necessity.

Notes

1. Brenner's article (1998a) is better known as "The Economics of Global Turbulence: A Special Report on the World Economy, 1950–98," the title that appeared on the cover of *New Left Review*. An expanded and updated version was published by Verso under the title *Economics of Global Turbulence* in 2006.

2. The organic composition of capital is here represented as the ratio of the constant capital stock to the sum of two flows of new value: variable capital and surplus value. The rate of profit is represented as the ratio of surplus value to the value of the constant capital stock. The upper case C is meant to distinguish the *stock* of constant capital from the *flow* of circulating constant capital (usually represented by a lower case c).

Chapter Four

Class Struggle and Socialist Transformation: Beyond the Law of Value

The Working Class, Value and Anti-Capitalist Struggle

Marxist socialism has always been committed to the idea that the working class not only has an abstract historical interest in abolishing capitalism but is also strategically positioned to end the rule of capital and undertake the socialist/communist reorganization of society. Given the recent, decades-long passivity of the Western working class (even in the face of a persistent capitalist offensive) and the declining influence of socialist ideas in the organized labour movement since the collapse of Soviet Bloc "socialism," Marx's original vision of workers' revolution may seem fantastically quixotic to many of us today — particularly if the working class is defined, as it so often is, to exclude the more skilled and better educated salary earners. But once it is understood that the working class, as Marx defined it, constitutes a decisive majority of the population of the developed capitalist countries, and once it is stipulated that this majority should be able to rally the support of at least some segments of the professional-managerial and intellectual "middle classes" in its more serious confrontations with a capitalist order that is not merely in decline but in a state of decay, the idea of workers' revolution begins to lose its aura of unrealism — while the antithetical notion of capital's "eternal rule" acquires the unmistakable aspect of a fantastic dystopia.

Marx's Proletarianization Thesis

In the *Communist Manifesto* and other early writings, Marx refers to the inevitability of a process of polarization between the two fundamental social classes of capitalist society, the bourgeoisie and the proletariat, and a concomitant decline of all other classes. Furthermore, in the famous, climactic chapter of *Capital* I, entitled "The General Law of Capitalist Accumulation," Marx predicted the historical ruination of the middle class and its proletarianization consequent to the concentration and centralization of capital. This may be referred to as Marx's "proletarianization thesis." Has this thesis turned out to be correct?

Before we can answer this question, two preliminary observations are in order. The first is that Marx, unlike many Marxists, never disqualified all "unproductive" labourers from the ranks of the working class understood as the "collective labourer" (Carchedi 1977, 1991). The second is that Marx seemed to think that unproductive labour was a phenomenon subject to historical decline with the further development of capitalism. In this latter regard, he turned out to be both correct and incorrect. Marx was certainly right to expect that the traditional ranks of the unproductive labour force — domestic servants and other hangers-on of the privileged classes — would decline over time. But his expectation was wrong insofar as it failed to anticipate the emergence and significant expansion of new types of unproductive labour — the socially necessary yet unproductive workers employed by the state and by commercial, financial and industrial capital (clerks, bookkeepers, accountants, civil servants and so forth). Arguably, Marx's failure in this regard may have stemmed from an overly optimistic view that capitalism would not overstay its historical welcome. The expansion of a socially necessary yet unproductive workforce may be seen, after all, as a by-product of a rather long and drawn-out historical-structural crisis of the capitalist mode of production. Even so, the proliferation of such labour can only be properly understood in light of the operations of the capitalist law of value, in particular the effects of the law of the falling tendency of the rate of profit.

While Marx never disqualified all unproductive labourers from the ranks of the proletariat, the same cannot be said for a great many twentieth-century class theorists, non-Marxist and Marxist alike. For example, it has been all too common for neo-Weberian and functionalist theorists to distinguish between "white collar" and "blue collar" workers and to rather impressionistically draw a class line between them. In a similar vein, Nicos Poulantzas (1978) has argued, from an ostensibly Marxist standpoint, that those wage labourers who are not directly productive of "material commodities," as well as those engaged in "mental labour" and/or supervisory functions, are most appropriately classified as constituents of a "new petty-bourgeoisie."[1]

Other Marxist theorists have maintained that membership in the working class should be reserved for those wage labourers who directly create surplus value, whether in the course of producing goods or services. J.K. Lindsey (1980), for example, argues that the "production working class" should be distinguished from the "circulation working class" on the grounds that the former is *exploited* while the latter is merely oppressed. He makes the unobjectionable point that the relation between production and circulation workers is not an antagonistic one; yet this sits uneasily with his view that circulation workers, along with the members of what he calls an "ideological class," live off the surplus value appropriated by capitalists. Like many Marxists, Lindsey fails to distinguish between the different forms of unproductive labour and then mistakenly asserts that all unproductive labour is "exchanged with revenue." In this way, socially necessary unproductive labourers are treated, in value-theoretical terms, as a kind of "luxury good" of the social capital, employed at the sufferance of the bourgeoisie and supported out of the revenue component of social surplus value. Even though socially necessary to the reproduction process of capitalist society, these workers are regarded no more as victims of capitalist exploitation than are the domestic servants with whom they are theoretically conflated.

I have elsewhere given an extended argument for rejecting such an understanding of socially necessary unproductive labour (see appendix 2 of this volume). One thread of this argument deserves some special consideration here, however, since it is directly relevant to Lindsey's mistaken notion that circulation workers are not exploited.

In his discussion of the costs of circulation in *Capital* II, Marx notes the case of a "buying and selling agent" who sells labour power to a capitalist:

> Whatever his payment, as a wage-labourer he works for part of the day for nothing. He may receive every day the value product of eight hours' labour, and function for ten. The two hours' surplus-labour that he performs no more produce value than do his eight hours of necessary labour, although it is by means of the latter that a part of the social product is transferred to him. (1981a: 210)

Two critical points are made in this passage. The first is that the working day of this unproductive wage labourer is, like that of a productive labourer, divided into two components: one during which "necessary labour" is performed, and another during which "surplus labour" is performed. The second point is that none of this labour is productive of value. Rather, all of the labour performed is simply a means of transferring a portion of the social product from the sphere of production to the sphere of circulation. The significance of the unpaid portion of the unproductive labourer's work day is that it permits the labourer's (commercial capitalist) employer to appropriate a part of the product that has been transferred through the efforts of the buying and selling agent.

These considerations enable us to understand Marx's otherwise mystifying reference in *Capital* III to the "variable capital" that the commercial capitalist exchanges for the unproductive labour of commercial workers. Recall that the specific contributions of commercial and financial capitals to reducing the costs of circulation within the overall division of labour between industrial, commercial and financial capital are the basis for their participation in the formation of a general rate of profit and the distribution of aggregate surplus value among the various capitals according to "capital advanced." Productive capital shares a portion of the social surplus value it produces with commercial and financial capital. In the case of commercial capital, Marx defines this sharing mechanism as follows:

[Commercial] capital makes a profit by not paying productive capital in full for the unpaid labour contained in the commodity... and, as against this, itself receiving the additional portion which it has not paid for once the commodity has been sold. Commercial capital's relationship to surplus-value is different from that of industrial capital. The latter produces surplus-value by directly appropriating the unpaid labour of others. The former appropriates a portion of this surplus-value by getting it transferred from industrial capital to itself. (Marx 1981b: 407)

However, a condition for the transfer of surplus value to commercial capital is the performance of unpaid labour (surplus labour) by commercial capital's (unproductive) employees:

The very function by virtue of which the commercial capitalist's money is capital is performed in large measure by his employees, on his instructions. Their unpaid labour, even though it does not create surplus-value, does create his ability to appropriate surplus-value, which, as far as this capital is concerned, gives exactly the same result: i.e. it is its source of profit. (407)

It follows that the capital the commercial capitalist exchanges for the labour power of commercial workers is "variable" only from the standpoint of commercial capital. From the standpoint of the social capital as a whole, however, it must be considered an overhead cost of capitalist reproduction — a component of constant capital. None of this suggests that circulation workers are not exploited by capital, but it does suggest that they are subject to a somewhat different mode of exploitation.

The different locations of production and circulation workers within the overall process of capitalist reproduction should nevertheless be noted. Circulation workers, along with workers employed or maintained by the capitalist state, are centrally involved (whether consciously or unconsciously) in the reproduction of capitalist social relations, whereas production workers are directly and centrally involved in the production and reproduction of the "material" elements of society. It is conceivable that this circumstance could make circulation and "public sector" workers less likely to develop an anti-capitalist consciousness than workers involved in production. Even so, such a hypothetical difference in consciousness is no reason to say that these unproductive workers are not exploited or that they belong to a different social class than production workers. What's more, it is doubtful that such a difference in consciousness can be convincingly established, much less linked to different structural locations in reproduction. Indeed, over the past few decades, unproductive public-sector workers (teachers, civil servants, health-care workers, etc.) have often assumed a pre-eminent role in working-class struggles against neoliberalism and capitalist austerity.

Although a clarification of Marx's ideas regarding socially necessary unproductive labour is of great moment to a value-theoretical mapping of the contemporary class structure, it can hardly resolve all of the important questions under debate. For example, Erik Olin Wright (1978), following a cogent critique of Poulantzas' catch-all category of the "new petty bourgeoisie," fruitfully suggests that "positions within the social division of labour can be objectively contradictory" and, on the basis of this insight, identifies several contradictory class locations positioned in between the bourgeoisie, the proletariat and the (traditional, self-employed) petty bourgeoisie. For Wright, contradictory class locations can exist between any two of these classes, suggesting that the individuals occupying such locations share structural characteristics in common with more than one class (for instance, a factory supervisor who "commands" the labour of others but who is also directly involved in production and subject to exploitation).[2] Robert Weil (1995) takes Wright's argument one step further, arguing that petty-bourgeois commodity producers within capitalist society also constitute a contradictory class location — insofar as they act out the roles of both capital and wage labour.

Whether ambiguously positioned wage labourers like engineers and managers should be conceptualized as members of a contradictory class location, a "service class" (Abercrombie and Urry 1983) or a "new middle class" (Carchedi 1987), the analysis of their proliferation under advanced capitalism can only benefit from a Marxist value-theoretical perspective that recognizes that the problems of value production and realization call forth an ever-more elaborate technical and social division of labour — that is, an increasingly differentiated occupational structure that tends to obscure the real contours of the class structure.

How do these observations pertain to Marx's thesis concerning the progressive polarization of the capitalist class structure and the historical tendency toward the proletarianization of ever-larger segments of the population under contemporary capitalism? In my view, they substantially support it. The complexity of the contemporary class structure is most readily apparent within the working class itself, which has become increasingly differentiated with respect to its roles in social reproduction. At the same time, the growing weight of the working class is also indirectly reflected in the fact that the "contradictory class location" or "new middle class stratum" that has experienced the greatest expansion in advanced capitalist societies over the course of the past century is precisely that which straddles the bourgeoisie and the proletariat.

Value, Class Struggle and Bureaucracy

The problem of how the productivity-increasing imperative of the capitalist law of value has been "adulterated" over the long course of capitalist development cannot be adequately specified without reference to the central role played by class conflict. Purely structuralist accounts of Marx's economic laws of motion tend to view the class struggle as a mere epiphenomenon of the "objective" contradictions of capitalist production/reproduction. The implication of such a view is that class practices, or strategies, can have little impact on the overall direction of capitalist development. Yet precisely because subjectively oriented practices do not belong to a realm autonomous from "objective laws," but, to the contrary, belong to the same order of social being (Smith 2009), a value-theoretical account of capitalist development must specify the ways in which the class struggle impacts on the expression — that is to say, the concrete historical forms — of these laws.

Precisely because capitalism encompasses an antagonistic relation between capitalists and workers, as well as a competitive relation between private commodity producers, a strong tendency exists for capitalists to reduce their costs of production through labour-saving and/or labour-displacing innovation. In this connection, capitalists derive two main functional benefits from the resulting increase in the technical composition of capital: it promotes the "real subsumption" of labour under capital; and it reproduces the reserve army of unemployed workers required to maintain a downward pressure on wages. Both of these benefits to capital are substantial and even indispensable for subjective as well as objective reasons. The reproduction of unemployment, for example, is not only useful in keeping the labour movement "off balance" and in mitigating wage-push/profit-squeeze phenomena, it is also vital to instilling a sense of insecurity in workers, rendering them less likely to undertake militant anti-capitalist action. Similarly, while the real subsumption of labour by capital involves an increased production of relative surplus value, it also entails a continuous deskilling of qualified labour, a process that fosters the capital-fetishistic notion that labour is a mere adjunct to the independent power of capital.

But this doesn't tell the whole story. Not only do workers resist technological redundancies and deskilling technical change, they also react to the crisis tendencies bred by a rising organic composition of capital. Moreover, it is precisely because workers have an anti-capitalist option open to them (namely, the struggle for a socialist transformation of society) that the capitalist class must tread carefully in its efforts to follow the objective dictates of the capitalist law of value. While workers (consciously or unconsciously) can and do challenge the limits of the law of value, capitalists can seek only to modify the effects of the law of value in accordance with their class interests, including their interest in maintaining some reasonable level of class peace.

What this suggests is that the laws of motion of capital create a framework within which a multitude of choices are made pertaining to class practices. Capitalists have no option but to limit their class practices to this framework, and they bend every effort to get the working class to do the same (very often, it should be said, with the indispensable assistance of trade union officials and reformist "socialists"). Yet the working class remains within this framework only to the degree that the consciousness of workers remains limited to it. Bourgeois class interest dictates that capitalists respect and obey the law of value, just as proletarian class interest dictates that workers repudiate and seek to supersede it.

The historical tendency of the class struggle within capitalism has been to push toward an ever greater "objective socialization" of the reproduction process. On the one hand, a key aspect of the progressive historical mission of capitalism has been to promote "the growth of technical coordination, interdependence and integration *in production*, by which capitalism increasingly generates the negation of the private labour and private production from which it was born — first inside single factories, then within a number of production units and branches of industry, and finally between countries" (Mandel 1975: 595, emphasis added). On the other hand, the pressure of the class struggle and of capitalism's mounting contradictions has forced the capitalist class to submit to a process of "unproductive socialization," through which the overhead costs of capitalist reproduction (the state, the administration of industry, the sales effort, finance and credit) have grown enormously. Given the antagonistic and exploitative character of capitalist social relations of production, the predominant organizational mode emerging from these socialization tendencies has been the "bureaucratic mode."

The essence of all bureaucracy, and especially industrial bureaucracy, is a thorough-going division between mental and manual labour (Braverman 1974; Deutscher 1973; Sohn-Rethel 1978; Clawson 1980; Mandel 1992). Such a division is implicit in the real subsumption of labour by capital as this was conceived by Marx, and is rendered explicit in the principles of scientific management elaborated by Frederick W. Taylor among others. Short of a complete elimination of living labour from production, what the capitalists seek to achieve is effective control over the labour process and a qualitative attenuation of the class struggle within the workplace on terms favourable to surplus-value production. In general, this project is furthered by efforts to continuously "transfer" the skills formerly wielded by living labourers to machinery, thereby eliminating all vestiges of "craft production" — a state of affairs in which the more skilled workers perform both brain work (planning) and manual functions. The separation of conception and execution, together with the relegation of living manual labour to mechanically repetitive tasks, is integral to a capitalist class strategy to enforce the domination of capital over the working class within production (what Marx referred to as the "despotism of the factory regime"). The essential content of this strategy is a "cognitive appropriation" of the skills and technical knowledge of skilled craftspeople, their incorporation into machinery through scientific and technological innovation and the development of a managerial-bureaucratic layer whose task is both to ensure the technical efficiency of the production process and, under the guise of "maintaining labour discipline," undercut any tendencies toward worker control of the labour process.

It should be emphasized that the above features of the bureaucratization of industry are promoted by value relations in general, and not only by class struggle at the point of production. Moreover, the tendency toward the deskilling and dequalification of labour is partially offset by a counter-tendency toward the creation of new types of skilled labour, a process that is itself a consequence of the drive of capitalist firms to reduce production costs per unit of output in order to more effectively meet the challenges of competition.

The real subsumption of labour by capital attests to the ongoing role of capital in enhancing the productivity of labour at the level of the individual productive enterprise. For Marx, this role is historically progressive and its results form the material presuppositions of socialism:

[To] the degree that large industry develops, the creation of real wealth comes to depend less on labour-time and on the amount of labour employed than on the power of the agencies set in motion during labour-time, whose powerful effectiveness is… out of all proportion to the direct labour-time spent on their production, but depends rather on the general state of science and on the progress of technology, or the application of science to production. (1973: 705)

This passage clearly shows that Marx didn't condemn capitalism for its tendency to free material production from the need for living labour of all types; rather, he indicted it because it could not realize the full potential of the technological revolutions that it sponsored under the whip of the law of value. The tragedy, for Marx, was not that craft skill, a relic of the "artisanal mode of production," was giving way to automation; the tragedy was rather that capitalist relations of production, involving the measurement of social wealth in terms of labour time, reserved all the benefits of automation for the capitalists, while condemning the working class to increasing alienation, economic insecurity and cognitive degradation.

Technological revolutions are one thing, however, and bureaucratization something else again. The claim of most sociological apologists of industrial bureaucracy is that bureaucratic organization — the centralization of knowledge about production in the hands of a "hired-gun" managerial stratum enjoying the confidence of the capitalist owners — is an essential ingredient to optimal productivity and efficiency in industrial enterprises. But this is a claim that can be easily dismissed. For while the separation of conception and execution might be a necessary feature of labour-saving technological innovation, the "division of head and hand" does not immediately follow from this, especially as the role of the "hand" continues to decline in importance with the automization/robotization of large-scale industrial production processes. There is really no reason why "conception" cannot become a responsibility of all of the associated producers, regardless of their specialized roles in the technical division of labour — no reason except for the class imperative of capital to hoard an esoteric body of knowledge useful to fortifying its domination over the labour process.

In sum, it is vitally important from a value-theoretical standpoint to distinguish those aspects of the real subsumption of labour by capital that promote the productivity of labour and real progress in liberating human labour from drudgery, from those aspects that involve a bureaucratic expropriation and centralization of knowledge and decision-making in the hands of capitalist management. The latter aspects pertain to the exploitative capitalist form of the law of value, while the former pertain to a perennial tendency of the law of value to promote technical rationality — a tendency that capital supports only up to a point. To state this proposition a little differently, the bureaucratic organization of the production process is not a necessary by-product of labour-saving technological innovation. To the contrary, the displacement of living labour from production and the spread of automation, robotics and computers should undermine any purely "technicist" rationale for bureaucratic relations of authority, while liberating the social time required to educate and involve the associated producers as a whole in the management of industry — and of society as a whole.

The Value of Labour Power:
Labour Market Segmentation and Working Class Fragmentation

As already pointed out, the tendency toward the deskilling and homogenization of the working class is offset to some extent by a counter-tendency toward the creation of new skills and qualifications. This counter-tendency is partly dictated by the exigencies of technological innovation in the ongoing quest of capitals to reduce unit costs of production. However, differentials in wages are not solely the result of differences in levels of skill, and processes of deskilling/reskilling may be somewhat incidental or tangential to other factors that contribute significantly to labour market segmentation and class fragmentation.

The value of individual labour powers is by no means simply determined by an "objective" calculus in which the cost of reproducing the ability to work is defined as the sum of physiological subsistence expenditures plus the educational and other costs incurred by workers in acquiring, exercising and maintaining a particular set of skills. In *Capital* I, Marx argues that the value of labour power has a historical and moral component as well (1977: 274–75). Marx is ambiguous on the point, but it seems appropriate to apply this consideration to the definition of the value of both "simple" and "qualified" labour power. From this perspective, the incorporation of a social-constructionist view into a theory of labour power valuation becomes a rather straight-forward matter (Thompson 1989).

Qualified labour is not entirely synonymous with skilled labour. Nor are skills entirely objective attributes of individual workers who have incurred determinate costs in acquiring them. To put the matter bluntly, a qualification for a relatively privileged and well-paid position within the division of labour may simply be maleness, white skin or the right social connections (whether with capitalist management or the director of a union hiring hall). Similarly, the criteria for distinguishing between skilled, semi-skilled and unskilled work tasks may have less to do with formal education and training than with how these tasks are distributed to workers in terms of their gender, race and other status backgrounds. For example, a highly talented seamstress may be defined as semi-skilled and a male truck driver as skilled simply because the very notion of skill has been traditionally associated with male craft organization.

More generally, the value of labour power is determined to a considerable extent by prevailing social norms, lifestyle expectations, racial, ethnic and gender inequalities, and other strictly non-economic considerations. In the world of commodities, the social equality of commodity-producing labour is the rule and the level playing field the accepted norm. But commodities share the real world with human beings whose social relations and consciousness reflect the influence not only of commodity production and exchange but also long-standing cultural traditions and cross-cultural antagonisms. Not surprisingly, it is precisely in the determination of the value of individual labour powers that these relatively autonomous cultural influences can be most profoundly felt — trampling underfoot all attempts to "objectively" compare the value of different work tasks. (It is precisely this consideration that makes the demand for "equal pay for work of equal value" so very problematic.)

In a provocative contribution, Michael Lebowitz argues:

> [The] value of labor-power has a tendency to adjust to its price — rather than the reverse! Accordingly, Marx was wrong to state that "as with all other commodities, so with labour, its market price will, in the long run, adapt itself to its value" (Marx, [*Value, Price and Profit*]). Rather than a fixed magnitude, the set of necessities entering

into the value of labor-power is inherently variable: "This historical or social element, entering into the value of labour, may be expanded or contracted, or altogether extinguished, so that nothing remains but the physical limit." (1991: 144–45)

In my view the burden of Lebowitz's critique of Marx's contradictory formulations in *Value, Price and Profit* (1865) is unobjectionable, and I share his regret that neither Marx nor his immediate successors elaborated the sort of "political economy of the working class" that Marx had apparently envisaged for his planned volume on wage labour. The struggles of the working class, both its victories and its defeats, have a major bearing on how the price and therefore the historically and morally determined value of labour power are established in any given period.[3]

The same point applies to qualified as well as to unqualified labour powers. Even so, it should be remembered that the variability of the value of labour power pertains principally to the historical, social or moral elements in its determination, while physical limits provide an enduring objective floor below which the quality of even the simplest, most unskilled labour power is seriously compromised. The value of the necessities entering into this physical floor may be said to determine the subsistence component of the price of labour power, just as the total price of specific labour powers, mediated by cultural and class-struggle factors, will determine the historically constituted value of labour power.[4] Yet the necessities comprising the subsistence component of the wage is itself subject to changing historical conditions. For example, in the early days of the industrial revolution, workers usually lived within walking distance of their workplace, and for this reason, transportation costs didn't enter into the value of labour power. But today such costs are largely unavoidable, and the worker's wage must be adequate to cover them. What is still subject to historical, moral or class-struggle adjudication, however, is whether the wage should be sufficient to provide the worker with bus fare, a bicycle, a modest automobile or a sport utility vehicle!

The substantially arbitrary or contingent ways in which the value of labour power may be determined beyond the physiological minimum necessary to the social reproduction of its simplest forms suggests the possibility that a redistribution of value may occur among workers just as it occurs among capitals (even though, of course, for different reasons and through different mechanisms). Diverse levels of class organization (unionization, in particular), gender, ethnic and racial discrimination, and culturally constructed definitions of skills and qualifications may enter into the distribution of the value "available" to wage and salary earners and may thereby contribute to invidious political divisions within the working class. Whether furthered by the capitalist ruling class or by workers themselves, such fragmentation can only contribute to the emergence of disparate, and quite contradictory, forms of working-class consciousness.

Class Consciousness: Regional and International Dimensions

International capital mobility and the dismantling of barriers to "free trade" within the capitalist world market promote the equalization of profit rates on a world scale. This, in turn, allows for the possibility of significant transfers of surplus value across national lines. The more prominent the tendency toward the equalization of profit rates on a world scale, the more scope there is for technologically superior capitalist countries to offset crises of profitability at the expense of weaker trading partners. The pool of social surplus value available for distribution amongst individual capitals becomes internationalized, and the distribution of this surplus value determines the relative fortunes of countries, regions and even whole continents.

On a world scale, the distribution of internationalized social surplus value comes close to resembling a zero-sum game, particularly under conditions of economic contraction and crisis within the capitalist world economy as a whole. The condition for prosperity, growth and rising average living standards in one zone of capitalist economic activity becomes the failure of other zones to adequately compete and prevent a transfer of value to the more competitive zones.

Workers living in the more "advanced" or "developed" zones of the world capitalist economy enjoy the benefits of an economic environment that is not only wealthier but also less prone to the most severe manifestations of capitalist economic crisis. Indeed, through the various mechanisms of international value transfer, the developed capitalist zones use the less developed zones as shock absorbers for the crisis tendencies originating in their own economies. The third-world "debt crisis" of the 1980s is a prime example of this phenomenon (George 1988; Magdoff 1992). It goes without saying that individual developed countries or trading blocs will seek to export their crisis tendencies to other developed regions as well. The possibility of resolving the domestic manifestations of capitalist crisis at the expense of other regions, other countries and other nations encourages a tendency on the part of working people to seek a solution to their economic problems in regional, national or continental (trade-bloc) terms. Such strategies almost invariably involve a perspective of collaboration with one's "own" capitalist class in "winning the war for markets" and frequently contain significant elements of racism and xenophobia. As such, they are profoundly at odds with the internationalist working-class perspective, which alone can counter the logic of a law of value that refuses to recognize either national boundaries or regional peculiarities, and that operates in such a way as to seduce the unwary into a class-collaborationist perspective of "beggar my neighbour" competition.

The Uneven and Discontinuous Growth of Class Consciousness

Our discussion up to this point has identified a plethora of factors that may affect the consciousness of working-class people as they wrestle with the persistent social and economic problems bred by capitalism. These factors range from the uneven impact of capitalist crisis tendencies on different segments of the international working class, to racial and gender inequalities countenanced by cultural traditions, to skill differentials, to the dull compulsion of fending for one's self and one's family in an insecure economic environment. To these factors must be added, of course, the conscious efforts of the capitalist class to diffuse its values and worldview to the wider working population through the mass media, the churches, the educational system and the family.

Despite the large number of factors that serve to obstruct the emergence of an anti-capitalist, socialist consciousness on the part of the working class, such a consciousness has repeatedly and stubbornly asserted itself. Often it is confined to relatively small segments of the working class (as it clearly is today in the United States and Canada). But at other times, it has embraced the majority of the working class and seriously posed the question of working-class power and the socialist transformation of society (as it did, for example, in Russia in 1917, in Germany in 1918–19 and 1923–24, in Spain in 1936–37, in Italy in 1920, 1945–47 and 1969, in France in 1936 and 1968, in Chile in 1970–73, in Portugal in 1974–75, in South Africa in the 1990s and in Venezuela today). The fact that such a consciousness could emerge at all, given the strength of the factors arrayed against it, calls for some explanation. The explanation that Marx himself adduced remains the most compelling: the working class, despite its divisions and its relative dearth of resources, is united by powerful common interests that periodically assert themselves in the most unexpected of ways and that demand the formulation of a common working-class program based on socialist principles and goals.

The development of socialist consciousness within the working class is a powerful tendency apparent in the real history of the capitalist mode of production — a tendency rooted in the social being and common historical interests of working people. But like every tendency it is confronted by powerful counter-tendencies that determine a definite unevenness in its articulation and spread, counter-tendencies that always threaten its reversal. This uneven and discontinuous quality of the development of socialist class consciousness poses serious programmatic and strategic problems for those who have achieved something more than a visceral dislike of capitalism and a vague attraction to the socialist idea. For those who have internalized Marx's critique of capitalist political economy and come to understand the necessity of socialism, the task becomes one of decisively informing the strategic and programmatic perspectives of the workers movement with the results of Marx's scientific analysis with a view to heightening the political consciousness of the working class as a whole.

The Role of Value Theory in the Anti-Capitalist Struggle

Marx's theory of value, and his critique of capitalist political economy as a whole, is a theory of the historical limits of the capitalist mode of production and of the social forms that serve to conceal them. His scientific analysis is at once an explication of the laws of motion of the capitalist economy and an account of how false, or one-sided, ideas about that economy come to arise and flourish. No other theory, however critical of capitalism, has ever come close to elucidating both of these problems, much less establishing their common foundation in value relations.

The programmatic upshot of Marx's analysis of capitalism is that the latter is not at all susceptible to socialist transformation through a process of gradual, incremental reform and that neither is it capable of a progressive, crisis-free evolution that would render the socialist project, in some sense, dispensable. Capitalism must be destroyed root and branch before there can be any hope of social reconstruction on fundamentally different foundations, and such a radical reconstruction is vitally necessary to ensuring further human progress.

Despite the urgency of socialist transformation, none of the objective laws of motion of capitalism can bring about a final and irrevocable breakdown of the capitalist system. Capitalism may be digging its own grave, but it will never carry out its own execution. Its burial awaits the concerted action of a class-conscious working class. The central practical problem facing Marxian socialism is that under conditions of advanced capitalism (which alone can furnish the material presuppositions for a dynamic socialist transformation) the working class has so far failed to carry through its anti-capitalist struggle to the end.

In part, this failure may be attributed to insufficient class consciousness, in part to strategic or even tactical errors on the part of revolutionary workers movements (for instance, Germany 1919–24) and in part to the outright betrayal of revolutions by the ostensible leaders of the working class (for example, Spain 1936–37). By themselves these factors go quite far in explaining why, despite the experience of depressions and wars, and social decay amidst material plenty, the working class in advanced capitalism has not yet risen to its historic task of overthrowing the regime of capital. The question is thus posed: what program can assist the proletariat in bridging the gap between its existing consciousness and practices and the consciousness and action needed for successful anti-capitalist struggle?[5]

In the history of Marxist socialism, programs embodying a strategic orientation to bridge that gap have often been called "transitional." *The Communist Manifesto* is in this tradition, as are the *Theses on Tactics* and other declarations of the first four congresses of the Third (Communist)

International. Its most comprehensive and eloquent expression was elabo-rated in *The Death Agony of Capitalism and the Tasks of the Fourth International*, the famous "Transitional Program" adopted at the founding conference of Leon Trotsky's Fourth International in 1938 (Trotsky 1973a, 1997).

The hallmark of the transitional programmatic conception is its attempt to overcome the dichotomization of a "minimum program" of struggle for reforms within capitalism and an abstract "maximum program" which promises the eventual substitution of socialism for capitalism (a dichotomiza-tion formalized in the German Social Democracy's *Erfurt Program* of 1891). A transitional program seeks to transcend this dichotomy by articulating a system of demands that anticipate the social and political content of a workers state and the early stages of socialist construction. These demands (a sliding scale of wages and hours, workers' control of production, the expropriation of industry without compensation, workers' defence guards and so on) are meant to intersect the immediate, largely defensive struggles of the working class as these unfold within capitalism, while at the same time projecting "solutions" that, taken together, serve to disintegrate the social, political and military power of the capitalist class. In the words of the Third International: "In place of the minimum programme of the centrists and reformists, the Communist International offers a struggle for the concrete demands of the proletariat which, in their totality, challenge the power of the bourgeoisie, organize the proletariat and mark out the different stages of the struggle for its dictatorship" (Communist International 1980 [1921]: 286).

Fundamentally, the transitional program is predicated on the inevitability of capitalist crises and class struggles stemming from the inherent contra-dictions of capitalism. The program permits the vanguard of the working class to build a bridge, at first through militant action, and then in political consciousness, between the immediate struggles of the working class and the programmatic goal of a workers socialist government.

A basic theoretical presupposition of the transitional program is that socialists must take into account the following two factors affecting the de-velopment of workers' class consciousness: on the one hand, it is profoundly conditioned by the "fetishisms" inherent in the capitalist relations of produc-tion as well as by ideologies rooted in the "appearance of things" under capi-talism; on the other hand, it is shaped by the experience of struggle against the material depredations of the capitalist system and, under conditions of systemic crisis, the floodgates of consciousness can be opened to possibilities that are not normally entertained by the great mass of working people.

Although sometimes conceived as akin to Andre Gorz's (1973) "anti-capi-talist structural reforms," transitional demands form part of an articulated program of open-ended anti-capitalist struggle. Only when they are dissoci-ated from the overall system of demands and thereby "fetishized" (which invariably involves a qualitative attenuation of their thrust) can they devolve into simple reform measures serving a closure of struggle. As a "system" of demands, in resolute opposition to all bourgeois-reformist programs, a transitional program leads "unalterably to one final conclusion: the conquest of power by the proletariat" (Trotsky 1973a: 75).

The logic of the transitional programmatic conception is illustrated by even so modest a transitional demand as the "sliding scale of wages and hours." The sliding scale of hours is not only the "socialist solution" to the problem of unemployment under capitalism, it is a veritable prefiguration of the system of work in socialist society — "the total number of workers divided into the total number of hours" (Trotsky 1973a: 128). Entirely counterposed to the bourgeois-reformist conception of "work-sharing," it proposes that any shortening of the workweek to address the problem of unemployment must entail no diminution in the living standards of the working class. A concrete application of the demand is the call for "30 hours' work for 40 hours' pay" when workers are being laid off due to labour-saving technological innovation or economic contraction. The social logic of this demand is quite clear: technological innovation should accrue to the benefit of workers rather than capitalists, and the right of workers to employment should not be threatened by episodic market conditions. Similarly, the demand for a full sliding scale of wages (also known as "indexation for inflation") seeks to guarantee the workers' share of national income by removing wage levels from the adjustments of the capitalist price structure. All in all, the thrust of the sliding scale of wages and hours is to strike a blow against the reification of labour power in the capitalist economy by systematically challenging its status as a commodity. Challenges of this sort to the social logic of the capitalist law of value are absolutely necessary if the workers movement is ever to advance its struggle to the level of expropriating capitalist industry and establishing a workers government.

An adequate class-struggle socialist program must obviously address the many factors that may contribute to the fragmentation of working-class struggles. Transitional and democratic demands pertaining to the specific problems confronting women, minority and immigrant workers must be integrated into the program if it is to build a bridge wide enough and strong enough to accommodate the working class as a whole. (Indeed, it is only in this way that a socialist workers movement can politically defeat the reformist sectoralism associated with postmodern "lifestyle" and "identity" politics.) Furthermore, the perspective of struggle around a transitional program must be linked to an internationalist strategy of organizing workers across national lines. Only through a conscious internationalization of the struggle can workers avoid tying their material interests to the competitive performance of their "own" capitalists on the world market.

The transitional program and the strategic orientation it embodies for mobilizing the working class against capital is consistent with Marx's critique of capitalism in the sense that it challenges the social logic of value relations. But certain limitations of this programmatic-strategic conception should be noted. First, its efficacy is largely predicated on the existence of widespread sympathy for socialism as the pre-eminent goal of the labour movement, as well as on the existence of a layer of working-class militants who consciously seek the ousting of reformist labour leaders and the construction of a class-struggle leadership. While present to some degree in Latin America, South Africa and certain parts of Asia, neither of these conditions obtains today in North America, and they are clearly less present in Europe today than at most other times in the past century. These circumstances underscore the need for those who have achieved a revolutionary socialist consciousness to wage a determined fight to preserve and disseminate the programmatic legacy of Marxism, both through propaganda and cadre development and through exemplary forms of trade union activity and other mass work based on a transitional program. Only by waging such a fight (and not just on their own national terrains but on an international scale) can socialists prepare the way for linking the program of Marxist socialism to the mass anti-capitalist struggles that are likely to emerge and multiply as the crisis of capitalism deepens.

Value Theory and Socialist Construction

Up to the 1970s, the Soviet model of "socialist construction" remained an immensely powerful pole of attraction for major segments of the Western working class as well as for the impoverished masses of the colonial and semi-colonial world. The Soviets' successes in "extensive economic growth" in the 1930s and again in the immediate post-war period (up to about 1965) commanded the admiration of the majority of those who longed to throw off the yoke of capitalism and imperialism and to embark on the building of a socialist society free of want and extreme social inequality. Not surprisingly, many admirers of the Soviet achievement were inclined to regard the draconian, corrupt, repressive and anti-democratic features of the Soviet system as "necessary evils" — departures from socialist principle that were, in any case, hypocritically exaggerated by anti-socialist forces. What seemed unarguable to those who "wanted to believe" was that Soviet "actually existing socialism" had eliminated unemployment, modernized a vast and backward economy at breakneck speed and provided by the 1950s a level of basic material security for its people that was, in some respects, superior to conditions prevailing in even the richest capitalist countries. By the early 1960s Soviet Premier Nikita Khrushchev's boast that the Soviet Union would soon reach the stage of full-fledged "communism" appeared quite plausible to many who had already been awed by the rapid recovery of the Soviet economy in the aftermath of the terrible devastation of the Second World War. As early as 1937, in *The Revolution Betrayed*, Leon Trotsky provided an incisive account of the impressive accomplishments of the Soviet planned economy while also pointing to the contradictions and limits of the Stalinist bureaucratic-command structure that administered it:

> The progressive role of the Soviet bureaucracy coincides with the period devoted to introducing into the Soviet Union the most important elements of capitalist technique. The rough work of borrowing, imitating, transplanting and grafting was accomplished on the bases lain down by the revolution. There was, thus far, no question of any new word in the sphere of technique, science or art. It is possible to build gigantic factories according to a ready-made Western pattern by bureaucratic command — although, to be sure, at triple the normal cost. But the further you go, the more the economy runs into the problem of quality, which slips out of the hands of the bureaucracy like a shadow. The Soviet products are as though branded with the gray label of indifference. Under a nationalized economy, quality demands a democracy of producers and consumers, freedom of criticism and initiative — conditions incompatible with a totalitarian regime of fear, lies and flattery. (1970a: 275–76)

A faint echo of Trotsky's indictment of bureaucratic commandism in the Soviet "degenerated workers state" was sounded some fifty years later by Mikhail Gorbachev as part of his call for restructuring following the Brezhnev "era of stagnation": "In the last fifteen years the national income growth rates had declined by more than a half and by the beginning of the eighties had fallen to a level close to economic stagnation. A country that was once quickly closing on the world's advanced nations began to lose one position after another" (1987: 19).

Superficially, Gorbachev's reform policies of glasnost and perestroika appeared to have affinities with Trotsky's programmatic admonition of 1932: "Only the interaction of three elements, of state planning, of the market and of Soviet democracy can provide the country with correct leadership in the transitional epoch [to socialism]" (1973b: 275). But it was soon apparent that Gorbachev's policies were inspired, not by Trotsky, the leader of the left opposition to Stalin, but much more by Nikolai Bukharin, co-author with Stalin of the doctrine of "building socialism in one country" and the leader of the right wing of the Communist Party of the Soviet Union in the 1920s.

Bukharin was the prophet, within ostensibly Marxist thought, if not within the socialist tradition as a whole, of what is today referred to as "market socialism." The attraction of this notion to reform-minded bureaucrats like Gorbachev is easy to understand. It is an approach that seeks to resolve the problems associated with transitional socialist economies without introducing the political forms of an authentic workers democracy and without seeking a socialist division of labour on an international scale. As the experiences of Yugoslavia, Hungary and the Soviet Union amply confirm, it is also an approach that has been manifestly incapable of addressing the immense accumulated problems and contradictions of decades of Stalinist bureaucratic mismanagement, waste and authoritarian rule.

The tendency of Stalinist bureaucracies, Gorbachev's included, to seek a solution to the crisis of the "command-administrative" system through increasing reliance on market mechanisms reflected neither the practicality nor the feasibility of the so-called "market-socialist" alternative. Rather, it reflected the belief of these bureaucratic oligarchies that market-oriented reform was the only alternative to the status quo compatible with the perpetuation of their material privileges and monopoly of political power. In hindsight, we know that the Gorbachevite turn to market socialism in the U.S.S.R. was simply the penultimate chapter in a process of counter-revolution that began with Stalin's political expropriation of the working class in the 1920s and culminated with the installation of Boris Yeltsin's openly pro-capitalist regime in 1991.[6]

I will not enter here into a full-scale analysis of the lessons of "socialist construction" in the erstwhile countries of "actually existing socialism," or the factors leading to the terminal crisis of this system (on this topic, see Smith 1996–97). But the still-strong influence of the market socialism idea on socialist-minded workers and intellectuals, in East and West alike, suggests that the lesson most widely drawn in this regard has been that the crisis of the Communist regimes was pre-eminently a crisis of "planned economy" and that the indicated antidote was a reassertion of the role of market relations in coordinating economic activity and enforcing efficiency. True, most Western advocates of market socialism have also invoked the necessity for democracy and human rights in a healthy socialist society. But the prevailing tendency is to view democracy as an end in itself rather than as a key ingredient in socialist economic development. Indeed, on this view, democracy for the producers and consumers is often considered to be one of those institutional externalities that may actually impede economic efficiency and growth.

The optimal articulation of the three elements that Trotsky pointed to as indispensable to socialist economic development — central planning, the market and workers democracy — is undoubtedly problematic. But this articulation problem will remain resistant to a satisfactory resolution so long as debate on the political economy of socialism is confined within the parameters of the false dilemma: either bureaucratically centralized state planning or workers' self-management of enterprises within a socialist market economy. Other models are possible and deserve to be explored, and it is gratifying that the issue has been seriously engaged by a growing number of Marxists over the past quarter century (Mandel 1986, 1992; Spartacist 1988; Elson 1988; Bottomore 1990; Samary 1991; Laibman 1992; Flaherty 1992; URPE 1992; McNally 1993; Cockshott and Cottrell 1993; Ollman 1998). A touchstone for this discussion should remain Trotsky's own proposal for a democratically centralized planning system that would rely on (socialized) market mechanisms for as long as these may be required:

> The problem of the proportionality of the elements of produc-tion and the branches of the economy constitutes the very heart of socialist economy.... The innumerable living participants in the economy, collective and individual, must serve notice of their needs and of their relative strength not only through the statistical determinations of plan commissions but by the direct pressure of supply and demand. The plan is checked and, to a considerable degree, realized through the market. The regulation of the market itself must depend upon the tendencies that are brought out through its mechanism. The blueprints produced by the departments must demonstrate their efficacy through commercial calculation.... The art of socialist planning does not drop from heaven nor is it pre-sented full-blown into one's hands with the conquest of power. This art may be mastered only by struggle, step by step, not by a few but by millions, as a component part of the new economy and culture. (1973b: 265, 274, 260)

Trotsky emphasized that planning is by no means a self-sufficient method of regulating the economic affairs of human beings but is critically dependent on other principles of social and economic organization:

> [A] successful socialist construction is unthinkable without including in the planned system the direct personal interests of the producer and consumer, their egoism, which in its turn may reveal itself fruit-fully only if it has in its service the customary reliable and flexible instrument, money. The raising of the productivity of labour and bettering of the quality of its products is quite unattainable without an accurate measure freely penetrating into all the cells of industry — that is, without a stable unit of currency.... For the regulation and application of plans two levers are needed: the political lever, in the form of a real participation in leadership of the interested masses themselves, a thing which is unthinkable without Soviet [council]

democracy; and a financial lever, in the form of a real testing out of a priori calculations with the help of a universal equivalent, a thing which is unthinkable without a stable money system. (1970b [1937]: 67–68)

This vision of socialist construction may seem to be something of a retreat from Marx's program of transcending market and monetary relations in the creation of a society in which human beings consciously direct their affairs. But bear in mind that Trotsky is speaking here of the transition to socialism, and that he regards socialist planning as an "art" that must be mastered by millions "as a component part of the new economy and culture." What vistas will open up with the democratic involvement of millions of people in social and economic planning cannot be predicted with precision from our present historical vantage point. All that can be said with certainty is that for an indefinite period following the conquest of power by the working class and its allies, socialist planning will continue to coexist with and rely heavily on market mechanisms and monetary instruments.

But the question remains: would the survival of money and the market signify the survival of the law of value? The answer is, yes, up to a point. The survival of market and money categories could only mean that society is continuing to allocate resources and distribute income in accordance with the measurement of labour time. But in a centrally planned economy, under the democratic management of the associated producers and consumers, the measurement of wealth in terms of socially necessary labour time would cease to be the dominant principle of economic regulation and resource allocation. Moreover, the abolition of private ownership in the means of production and of enterprise competition oriented toward profit maximization would destroy the two pillars of the capitalist law of value, rendering obsolete the quest for surplus value as the motor force of economic activity. The survival of "exchange value" in such a post-capitalist society would not, in other words, entail the survival of surplus value. Human activity could henceforth be geared toward the satisfaction of human needs and the all-round development of the human personality rather than toward the appropriation of wealth in the socially antagonistic form of private profit. But for this to happen, socialist exchange value would have to be the "form of appearance" of a new set of social relations based pre-eminently upon cooperation, solidarity and democracy, and not upon the invidious enterprise competition that currently fashionable models of market socialism openly posit and even celebrate (see, for example, Nove 1983, 1987; Le Grand and Estrin 1989).

This much is clear: the models of market socialism that have issued from the crisis of Stalinism could not fail to perpetuate and entrench all the characteristic evils associated with the value relation (from unemployment to the division of mental and manual labour) that Marxist socialism has always set its sights on eliminating. Marx's theory of value stands as a constant reminder of the limits to the historically progressive role of commodity exchange and as a challenge to reconstruct society on fundamentally different foundations. As such, it directs us to look beyond "that which exists" to that which ought to and could exist once the constraints of the value form are socio-historically transcended and human beings determine, in defiance of the supposedly eternal law of value, to assume mastery of their own collective destiny.

Notes

1. Ellen Meiksins Wood, in her important book *The Retreat from Class*, identifies Poulantzas (1978) as the "forerunner" of a (non-class struggle) "new 'true' social-ism" that has been embraced by many erstwhile Marxists, among them Gorz (1982) and Laclau and Mouffe (1985). As Wood demonstrates well, Poulantzas's erroneous theoretical conceptualizations of class were very much in the service of a Maoist and then a Eurocommunist politics oriented toward subordinating the independent workers' movement to a class-collaborationist "popular front" alliance. The influence of such Stalinist conceptions continues to inform the theory and politics of many who now identify themselves with "post-Marxist socialism."

2. Wright's later neo-Marxist works on social class (which reflect, among other things, a movement in the direction of Weberian and neo-Weberian conceptions) are decisively influenced by the neo-Ricardian critique of Marx. While often hailed by non-Marxist sociologists as more rigorous than his earlier work, they actually evince weaknesses that can be traced back to Wright's abandonment of Marxian value theory, which he once embraced.

3. My agreement with Lebowitz on this point does not extend to all aspects of his argument concerning the "political economy of the working class." See Lebowitz 2003 for a complete statement of his views. For one of several important cri-tiques, see Fine 2008.

4. Not the least of these "cultural" circumstances concerns the issue of whether the value of labour power is normatively equated with an individual or family wage. Marx suggests that the value of labour power must take into account the wage labourer's obligation to support non-wage-earning family members (a spouse, dependent children, etc.). But this is not always the case, especially under conditions of increased labour force participation by women (which may or may not be the result of a decline in the real wages of male workers and which may or may not promote such a decline). Related to this issue is the still-unresolved debate surrounding the contribution of unpaid domestic labour to the reproduction of the commodity labour power and therewith (indirectly) to the production of surplus value in the public economy.

5. In providing some elements of an answer to this question I will focus here on programmatic issues (narrowly defined) and leave the strategic and tactical issues of working-class political organization to the side.

6. In saying this, I am, of course, following Trotsky's thesis that the Soviet Union was a "degenerated workers' state" from 1924 on. Central to Trotsky's view is the idea that the Stalinist bureaucracy was by no means a finished "ruling class" but rather a "parasitic oligarchy" that would either be removed by a working-class political revolution or pave the way for a return to capitalism. On this view, the Soviet transitional society was by no means indicative of the "general laws of modern society from capitalism to socialism" but rather "a special, exceptional and temporary refraction of those laws under the conditions of a backward revolutionary country in a capitalist environment" (Trotsky 1970a: 7). Accordingly, the lessons of the Soviet experience pertain mainly to "the application of socialist methods to the solution of pre-socialist problems" (1970b: 57) under conditions of extreme bureaucratic deformation of those methods.

Chapter Five

The Global Crisis, Marxism and the Malaise of the Anti-Capitalist Left

Throughout the 1990s, in the wake of the Soviet Bloc collapse and the re-surgence of a globalizing capitalism, antagonists of Marxism argued, with predictable alacrity, that the only sensible thing for its one-time proponents to do would be to admit that the socialist project had ended as an unrealizable utopia and consign the theories supporting it to the trash heap of history. Marxism, we were repeatedly told, was effectively dead — except in the minds of a few hopeless dogmatists. To varying degrees, Francis Fukuyama's thesis, according to which liberal-democratic capitalism had triumphed as the non-transcendable final chapter of human history, was accepted widely — and not only by aggressively pro-capitalist ideologues but also by many progressive-minded activists and a good number of disillusioned erstwhile Marxists.

Partly in reaction to the bleak and often disastrous results of capitalist restoration in Eastern Europe and the former Soviet Union and partly due to the emergence of a militant anti-corporate-globalization movement, the political and intellectual climate had undergone a sea-change by century's end. Far from producing an improvement in human well-being and security, capitalism's triumph had resulted in the premature deaths of millions in the former Soviet Bloc and reinforced a virulent neoliberalism that was devas-tating much of the semi-colonial world while also corroding the Western "welfare state" (Petras and Veltmeyer 2001). The opening years of the new century witnessed the descent of global geo-politics into a squalid clash of fundamentalisms and the recrudescence of a particularly adventurist and bellicose form of neo-colonialism (the U.S.-led occupations of Afghanistan and Iraq), as well as stagnation and austerity across broad swaths of the world economy (Ali 2002; Achcar 2002; Blackwell, Smith and Sorenson 2003; Harvey 2005). These developments encouraged a revival of interest in Marxism both as a tool of analysis and as a guide to changing the world. Today, at the close of the first decade of the new millennium, there are sub-stantial reasons to think that this revival will gain momentum as the current global economic crisis lays waste to the lives of tens and perhaps hundreds of millions of people (McNally 2009b).

That said, Marxism continues to face a severe crisis of credibility. The popular identification of Marxist socialism with the failed Soviet system remains a formidable problem, and, owing in good part to the stubbornness of this identification, new, non-Marxist forms of radical thought have won the allegiance of many activists who regard themselves as anti-capitalist.[1] Most of these radical activists identify with an amorphous "global social-justice movement," which addresses a range of issues from ecological sustainability, fair trade and global poverty to racism, gender inequality and economic democracy, with a minority self-identifying as "independent socialists." Amongst the most militant of these activists, a new generation of anarchists has emerged whose prejudices against Marxism seem particularly strong.[2]

In light of all this, the question is posed: Why do the Marxists persist? What sustains us in our commitment to a body of ideas and a vision of social change whose global appeal has undergone such a drastic decline over the course of a single generation? The answer, I think, should be apparent to anyone with even a limited knowledge of the complex history of Marxist socialism. For a great many reasons, Marxism has never been a seamless or monolithic body of ideas, and so activists and intellectuals have always had a variety of different and competing ostensible Marxisms with which to identify. The simple and perhaps paradoxical fact is that many of us saw in the events of the late 1980s and early 1990s (that is, in the disappearance of what had passed for "actually existing socialism" or "Communism") a vindication of the fundamental ideas of "our Marxism." None of these events had forced upon us the conclusion that our ideas had been proven wrong, even if other ostensible Marxisms had not withstood the test of time and experience nearly as well. Accordingly, many of us felt a profound intellectual and moral responsibility to resist the zeitgeist of capitalist triumphalism and to stand firm in defence of certain fundamental Marxist truths.

What are those truths? I believe they can be summed up in two main propositions. The first is that capitalism is a historically specific mode of production and societal form that had, by the early twentieth-century, exhausted its potential to promote continued human progress. By human progress I mean not just improvements in technical gadgetry or collective scientific understanding, but real advances in realizing the productive and creative capacities of each and every human individual. The second is that the attempt to construct a systemic alternative to capitalism in the twentieth century — in the first place in the Soviet Union — foundered decisively on the Stalinist project of building "socialism in one country" under the leadership of a nationalistic-bureaucratic oligarchy hostile to the Marxist principle of the democratic self-emancipation of the working class.

In what follows, I summarize the evidence supporting each of these propositions and consider what each suggests about the responsibilities and challenges confronting the socialist left — and would-be progressives in general — in the twenty-first century.

The Decadence and Decay of Capitalism

The first proposition, regarding the historical limits of capitalism, should be understood as a much stronger statement than another that has been frequently defended by leftist intellectuals in recent years. It has been common enough for Marxist, "neo-Marxist" and even many non-Marxist intellectuals to argue that fundamental aspects of Marx's analysis of the capitalist mode of production remain fully relevant to our present situation: that the phenomena of alienation, commodity fetishism, exploitation, capital accumulation, overproduction, internationalization of capital and so on are all still very much with us, and that so long as these facts of capitalist life persist there will continue to be a place for a Marxist analysis of them. This line of argumentation, coupled with well-founded outrage over the moral decadence of contemporary capitalism, is certainly both correct and compelling as far as it goes. By itself, however, it is insufficient to support the idea — which is crucial to a transformative socialist project — that capitalism has long since entered into world-historical crisis and decline.

What gives Marx's theory its great force and originality is the fact that it furnishes a powerful scientific basis for the proposition that the capitalist system not only ought to be superseded by socialism but that it must be if human civilization is to avoid a catastrophe and chart a progressive and sustainable path forward. Marx's critical analysis of capitalism discloses the dynamic — the laws of motion — through which capitalist development undermines itself and fosters increasingly serious crisis tendencies, while also creating the material conditions for the transition to a new, socialized mode of production and a classless society. Having established a world market and an intricate international division of labour, capitalism reaches a point of maturity where the forces of production must be liberated from the perverse logic imposed by capitalist social relations — or these relations will eventually destroy the productive forces, and much else besides. In such an era, we are confronted, in the words of Rosa Luxemburg, with the alternatives of "socialism or barbarism."

Historical experience fully confirms this prognosis. Two world wars in the last century testify to how capitalist accumulation and competition can lead to the massive physical destruction of both capital and human lives. The deaths of over a hundred million people from starvation in each and every decade since the last world war; the horrors of innumerable regional conflicts and the massive, wasteful expenditures on armed forces by large and small nations alike; the bondage of at least 26 million chattel slaves in India, Africa and the Western hemisphere — all this and much more attest to how a world dominated by capital has been unable to secure peace, security or a decent standard of living for the great majority of humanity. Beyond this overwhelming evidence of actually existing capitalist barbarism, the dire

119

threats posed by the rampant degradation of the biosphere and the spectre of thermonuclear warfare suggest that we are now very probably confronting the alternatives of socialism or human annihilation.

To be sure, much controversy surrounds Marx's analysis of capitalism's laws of motion. Yet a hundred and fifty years on, it retains a remarkable power. Once widely presumed to be dead and buried, Marx's theories of labour value, capitalist crisis and a falling average rate of profit have returned with a vengeance in recent decades — revived not so much by Marxist scholarship as by the real trends and vicissitudes of capital accumulation itself.

What other economic theory can match Marx's in explaining why, despite ongoing productivity gains and enormously improved productive technology, the living standards of much of the world's population, including the working-class majorities of many advanced capitalist nations, have declined in recent decades? What explanation for this phenomenon is more compelling than Marx's own — one that highlights the continuing (unconscious, market-mediated) measurement of wealth in terms of "abstract social labour" in an era in which living labour is a less and less significant material input to production? Furthermore, what rival economic theory has been more prophetic than Marx's in insisting upon the globalizing and concentrating imperatives of the capitalist accumulation process? At the turn of the twentieth century, most social scientists, and not a few "revisionist Marxists" like Eduard Bernstein, disputed Marx's law of the concentration and centralization of capital. Yet who today would contest the accuracy of Marx's forecast that capitalism promotes a process of "objective socialization" in which more and more of the economic activity of humanity is brought under the control of a smaller and smaller number of giant capitalist concerns? With transnational corporations comprising over fifty of the world's hundred largest "economies" and with annual sales of the top two hundred transnational corporations accounting for close to a third of global GDP (Anderson and Cavanagh 2000), Marxists are surely on firm ground in pointing to the extraordinary predictive power of Marx's analysis and, more importantly, insisting with him that so great a concentration of economic power in private, self-interested hands constitutes a formidable obstacle to the well-being and progress of the great majority of humankind.[3]

On a whole series of issues pertaining to the basic dynamics and logic of capitalist development, the past few decades have given Marxists an abundance of reasons to affirm that many of Marx's most important predictions have proved remarkably accurate. Numerous studies have now established that Marx was right to think that the average rate of profit would fall over the long term and that this would be associated with the displacement of living labour from production through technological innovation (that is, a rising organic composition of capital). As Marx anticipated, profitability crises have indeed been answered by capital with attempts to lower real wage levels, intensify the labour process, undermine workers' rights and cut or eliminate popular social programs that have negative implications for private profitability. At the same time, the world economy has created a huge "surplus population" of over 1.3 billion unemployed and underemployed people, a mass of human beings whose capacity for productive activity is being squandered by global capitalism, and which is now expanding rapidly due to the current global slump (ILO 2001, 2009). The near-universal monopoly exercised by the capitalist class over the world's most powerful means of production can only mean that the advanced technologies that capitalism has brought into being will not be used to raise the productivity of the economically marginalized with a view to meeting human needs, but will be used instead as pawns in a competitive, class-antagonistic game whose overriding object remains the amassing of private profit.

None of this is registered by Marxism's obituary writers. Instead, what is usually stressed (all too often in smug, self-satisfied fashion) is the purported failure of Marx's predictions that the working class would (a) eventually become a revolutionary class "for itself" and (b) proceed to build an egalitarian socialist society in which political power would be democratically exercised by the "associated producers." The failure of the first prediction is said to demonstrate that Marx assigned too great a significance to class struggle in human affairs and harboured illusions in the revolutionary capacity of the working class; the failure of the second is said to show that democracy and "economic collectivism" are incompatible and that any attempt to move beyond capitalism can only lead to the rise of a totalitarian social order dominated by a new class of state bureaucrats. Such, at any rate, is the "politically correct" balance sheet on Marxism that is assiduously promoted by an army of mainstream academics and pundits — and accepted to varying degrees by many contemporary radical intellectuals and activists.

A compelling Marxist response to this familiar critical assessment of Marxist theory and practice exists, but it is rarely addressed by Marx's critics or even by many of his would-be defenders. In what does it consist? In the first place, it involves an insistence upon an accurate historical accounting of the record of working-class struggle against capitalism. While it is true that history has seen only one successful working-class, socialist revolution — the Bolshevik-led revolution of 1917 in Russia — it is utterly wrong to suggest that the working class has not shown a revolutionary capacity in a great many other times and places since Marx's time. That this history is not only ignored but deliberately buried by the enemies of Marxist socialism should surprise no one. That it is often unknown or at least understudied by many of today's leftist intellectuals and activists is a rather striking confirmation of Marx's thesis that the educators must themselves be educated.[4]

Marx's confidence in the ability of the revolutionary working class to build an egalitarian socialist order on the road to a classless society also appears to have been misplaced in view of the record of "socialist construction" in the past century; but once again, a careful historical appreciation of these experiences suggests that the assumptions upon which that expectation was based have been scarcely refuted. Indeed, if anything, the historical record confirms, albeit in the negative, Marx's warning that a fully socialist/communist transcendence of capitalism would require highly developed forces of production brought into being by capitalism itself — among them: a worldwide division of labour, a technologically sophisticated productive apparatus and a well-educated working class capable of assuming the tasks of democratic self-administration. It is only too obvious that the conditions under which countries like the Soviet Union and China attempted socialist construction in the twentieth century were marked instead by a comparatively low level of development of the productive forces so defined.

The End of Soviet-Bloc Stalinism

This brings us to the second truth that I referred to earlier: that Stalinism — the social phenomenon of bureaucratic rule on the basis of collectivized property that characterized all of the nominally socialist countries — was a nationalist and fundamentally anti-working-class departure from Marxism in the realms of both theory and practice. From this standpoint, the demise of Stalinism in the Soviet Bloc countries in no way signifies the death of authentic Marxism (Smith 1996–97).

Three further observations need to be made in this connection. The first is that the end of the Stalinist projects in the former Soviet Bloc confirms Marx's proposition that the practical premise for the development of fully socialist institutions, relations and practices is the abolition of capitalism on a world scale and the incorporation of the productive forces created under capitalism into a worldwide socialist division of labour (a socialist globalization). Without this, Marx and Engels observed:

> *want* is merely made general, and with destitution the struggle for necessities and all the old filthy business would necessarily be reproduced…. Empirically, communism is only possible as the act of the dominant peoples "all at once" and simultaneously, which presupposes the universal development of productive forces and the world intercourse bound up with communism. (1969: 37, emphasis in original)

Proceeding from these observations, Leon Trotsky (1970a) elaborated a powerful Marxist analysis of the Stalinist "bureaucratic degeneration" of the

Soviet workers state as early as the 1930s — one that withstood the test of time remarkably well. Indeed, his analysis was unique in predicting the ultimate fragmentation of the Soviet bureaucratic oligarchy, which occurred in the late 1980s and early 1990s, as well as the growing attraction of a program of capitalist restoration to significant segments of the Soviet *nomenklatura*. According to Trotsky, only the international extension of the revolution to the citadels of world capitalism, through a process of permanent revolution, could open a road to a healthier socialist transition in the Soviet Union and to the triumph of world socialism.

In his memoirs, Leopold Trepper, the head of the Soviet "Red Orchestra" spy network in Nazi-occupied Western Europe, paid tribute to the Trotskyist opposition to Stalin's regime—a regime that Trepper had served throughout the Second World War despite his growing misgivings that it had betrayed the principles of the October socialist revolution:

> The Trotskyites can lay claim to this honor. Following the example of their leader, who was rewarded for his obstinacy with the end of an ice-axe, they fought Stalinism to the death, and they were the only ones who did. By the time of the great purges, they could only shout their rebellion in the freezing wastelands where they had been dragged in order to be exterminated. In the camps, their conduct was admirable. But their voices were lost in the tundra.

> Today, the Trotskyites have a right to accuse those who once howled along with the wolves. Let them not forget, however, that they had the enormous advantage over us of having a *coherent political system* capable of replacing Stalinism. They had something to cling to in the midst of their profound distress at seeing the revolution betrayed. (Trepper 1977, emphasis added)

The Trotskyist political system to which Trepper referred encompasses many elements, but a key element — implacable opposition to Stalinism combined with unconditional defence of the Soviet Union against any and all attempts at capitalist restoration (either from within or without) — was always the touchstone of orthodox Trotskyism. In a pithy, yet definitive, programmatic statement of 1939, Trotsky wrote:

> [The] question of the overthrowing of the Soviet bureaucracy is for us subordinate to the question of preserving state property in the means of production in the U.S.S.R.; [the] question of preserving state property in the means of production in the U.S.S.R. is subordinate for us to the question of the world proletarian revolution. (1970b: 21)

Trotsky's insistence on defending the bureaucratized Soviet workers state from the forces of capitalist counter-revolution was rooted in the conviction that the socialist elements of its transitional economy — collectivized property, central planning and the state monopoly of foreign trade — represented precious gains for the workers of the Soviet Union. While progress toward full socialism required the triumph of the socialist revolution on a world scale, the preservation of such a transitional economy was no less important to the international working class than the preservation of their trade unions, which are likewise often dominated by conservative bureaucratic apparatuses.

The idea that the transitional, putatively socialist economies of the twentieth century constituted important historic gains for the working class finds powerful support in a study published in 1991, the year in which capitalist counter-revolution triumphed in the Soviet Union. Working with Human Development Index (HDI) data compiled by the United Nations Development Programme, Francois Moreau generated a set of comparisons between two broad groups of countries for the year 1987. The first group comprised capitalist economies at two levels of development: the capitalist core and the capitalist periphery. The second group comprised transitional economies, also at two levels of development: the relatively advanced Eastern European economies (including the U.S.S.R.), and the "third world" transitional economies (including China, North Korea, Vietnam and Cuba). The results of this analysis are contained in table 5.1.

While core capitalist countries like the U.S., Canada and Britain ranked highest on the Human Development Index, peripheral capitalist countries like India, Nigeria and Brazil ranked lowest. At the same time, the average HDI of the transitional countries — as of 1987, when they were still nominally

Table 5.1 Indicators of Development, 1987

Type of economy and level of development	Per capita product ($)	Life expectancy (years)	Literacy rate	Human development index (Maximum = 1000)
Capitalist Core	14,164	76	97	970
Cap. Periphery	1,928	59	58	529
Cap. World	4,684	63	67	629
Trans. E. Europe	5,540	71	98	916
Trans. 3rd World	2,051	69	70	710
All Transitional	3,001	70	78	764

Note: Means for each group of countries, weighted by population. Source: Moreau 1991.

124

socialist — ranked well above the average HDI for the capitalist world as a whole. In terms of its HDI index, Mexico emerged as an average capitalist country. Summing up, Moreau commented: "What the UNDP analysis shows, no doubt without consciously intending to do so, is that transitional societies have actually achieved a higher level of 'human development' for a given level of economic development than capitalist countries" (1991: 141).

Shortly after the publication of this UNDP data, most of the transitional economies were dismantled and reabsorbed into the capitalist world system. The relative political stability and the absolute wealth and power of the capitalist core proved to be a decisive obstacle not only to the spread of transitional-socialist economic forms but even to their preservation in most of the countries in which they had taken root. As Trotsky predicted, the subordination of the world revolution to the nationalist objective of building socialism in one country — the political policy pursued by the Stalinist regimes presiding over all of the transitional economies — had contributed to a decisive strengthening of world capitalism (notwithstanding the economic turbulence it was experiencing) and had thereby prepared the way for a historic roll-back of the "socialist beginnings."

This leads us directly to a third observation. If, in the historic contest between Stalin's program of "socialism in one country" and Trotsky's "permanent revolution," the latter now appears fully vindicated, it is nevertheless clear that the revolutionary Marxism that Trotsky represented continues to be accorded surprisingly little consideration by non-Trotskyist leftists and Marxist intellectuals.[5] The reasons for this are worth exploring, I think, for they reveal a great deal about the current disorientation of the radical left and highlight some important obstacles to the re-emergence of a serious global movement toward socialism.

The Revival of Gradualism

The immediate political beneficiary of the collapse of Stalinism within the international labour movement was unquestionably social democracy. By the 1990s, however, it was abundantly clear that the great majority of social-democratic parties had long since abandoned any project of fundamental social transformation. When and if it was still used at all, the phrase "democratic socialism" (as originally formulated in opposition to "totalitarian communism") had ceased to refer to a programmatic goal — a socialist society involving democratic planning — and had come to refer exclusively to a strategy of gradual, piecemeal reform of capitalism "through the ballot box." The social-democratic project had become entirely one of administering capitalism "humanely" — and pre-eminently within the bounds of "one's own" country. The fact that, by the 1990s, most governing social-democratic parties had also embraced the neoliberal agenda of austerity and deep cuts to the social welfare functions of the capitalist state only confirmed that social democracy's first loyalty was not so much to "capitalism with a human face" as to "capitalism as such."

The collapse of Stalinism and the sharp rightward turn of social democracy created a renewed opportunity for many academic Marxist intellectuals and self-styled independent socialists to carve out a specific political niche for themselves, one simultaneously critical of contemporary social democracy and hostile to an undifferentiated Leninism. Whether acknowledged or not, the socialism they have sought to promote is remarkably similar, in programmatic and strategic terms, to the Marxism of the Second International (1889–1914). This is a socialism committed to a gradualist strategy and to what are often called "inclusive" (that is, non-vanguardist) organizational forms. It is also a socialism whose implicit point of departure is the notion that, for the foreseeable future at least, the global spread of capitalism is likely to remain inexorable.

Such a prognosis carries with it profound programmatic and strategic implications, the main one being that a socialist transformation cannot be on the immediate agenda and that there may yet be considerable scope for significant "progressive reform" within the framework of capitalism. Implicitly rejecting Trotsky's (1998 [1938]) call for a transitional program of working-class struggle — a necessarily revolutionary struggle for a system of demands that prefigure the social, political and economic content of a future workers state — many of today's independent socialist intellectuals openly or tacitly embrace the "minimum-maximum" programmatic approach of pre-First-World-War social democracy, as classically codified in the Erfurt Program of 1891.[6] "Socialism" is talked about as a distant goal, as the "maximum program" they hope somehow, someday to realize. But the real program of struggle in the here and now is a "minimum program" of reforms to be realized within capitalism, a program of ameliorating the conditions of the working masses, extending and expanding "democracy" and incrementally weakening the prerogatives of capital.[7] Accordingly, many contemporary Marxist intellectuals have associated themselves with liberal-reformist initiatives like "alternative budgets" that entirely accept the framework of the capitalist economic order, as well as promoting anti-corporate-globalization measures (such as the "Tobin tax") that seek to discourage and regulate capital flows across national borders, but fail to pose the question of the expropriation of capital. In response to the financial crisis of 2008, many have raised the call for the nationalization of the banks, echoing conservatives like Willem Buiter who have argued that such a measure is desperately needed to stabilize capitalism.

The favoured vehicles for such initiatives are often not even political parties in the classical social-democratic mould (a broad "party of the whole class") but rather "grassroots social movements," "structured movements against capitalism," world or regional social forums and "inclusive" cross-class coalitions (such as the misbegotten "Respect" project in Britain) that are reminiscent of the Stalinist-led popular fronts that derailed working-class revolts in Spain, France and Italy in the 1930s and immediately following the Second World War.

The odd thing is that this neo-reformist perspective is championed by many social-justice activists, independent socialists and Marxist intellectuals without any attempt to link it to a theoretical analysis of contemporary capitalism that clearly supports it. Yet the absence of such analysis is hardly surprising, for trends in the world economy over the past thirty years have provided little reason to think that capitalism has resumed a historically progressive trajectory. What is called "corporate globalization" is the form that the internationalization of capital has taken in a new world situation defined in large part by the disappearance of most of the erstwhile socialist (that is, bureaucratized workers) states. What is called "neoliberalism" is the class-struggle program that capital has implemented over the past thirty years to jack up the rate of exploitation and arrest the decline in the rate of profit at the expense of the working class. And what is called "financialization" is really just an admission by the capitalist class that its decaying profit system can only survive through the proliferation of fictitious capital and the accumulation of unsustainable debt. The most compelling proof that we have not been living through an era of renewed capitalist ascendancy (or even an "expansionary long wave" of the Kondratieff type) is that neither the restoration of capitalism in the former Soviet Bloc nor the partial reopening of the People's Republic of China to capitalist exploitation has been accompanied by dramatically higher rates of growth in global output or in improved prospects for progressive social reform anywhere in the world (oil-rich Venezuela representing one of the very few exceptions). Stagnation and austerity have remained pervasive on a global scale, and the neoliberal era has now culminated in the worst economic slump since the Great Depression. All of this suggests, forcefully and unmistakably, that a worldwide socialist transformation cannot be delayed for long without putting at risk the very survival of the human species.

Facing up to this reality and developing a political practice adequate to the challenges it poses is unquestionably the central responsibility confronting the radical left. What then accounts for the implicit denial of this reality by leftists who continue to embrace what the American Trotskyist leader James P. Cannon once called "inch-at-a-time reformism"? In part it can be explained by the pre-eminence within the contemporary radical left of academics. Owing to their relatively privileged social location and the liberal, class-collaborationist pressures of their milieu, even avowedly

Marxist academics have never been particularly good at envisioning or promoting a class-struggle politics. Occupying a contradictory class location, leftist academics are influenced, if not entirely seduced, by many of the characteristic prejudices of the traditional petty bourgeoisie: illusions in the bourgeois-democratic electoral process, a distaste for the sharper forms that the struggle between labour and capital can assume and a belief in the possibility of reconciling antagonistic classes through reason, compromise and gradual social reform. What's more, they have a proclivity to jealously guard their "independence" and display an unwillingness to subordinate their individual interests, whether material or intellectual, to the needs of a determined movement to achieve world socialism.

In my view, these considerations go far to explain the widespread disdain within the academic "independent socialist" milieu for "vanguardism" (that is, serious attempts to unite revolutionary socialist activists into disciplined, programmatically based organizations) and so-called "insurrectionary socialism," as well as a corresponding attachment to gradualism and left-reformism.[8] Social reality may thunder that the struggle to rid the world of capitalism is an urgent necessity, but the "social being" of the academic leftist urges a political practice that falls well short of a full-blown attack on the capitalist system.

Similar considerations apply in explaining the persistent unwillingness of so many leftist intellectuals to question the Leninism-Stalinism amalgam that is routinely used to dismiss Trotsky's Marxism — arguably the only programmatically coherent alternative to the failed national-reformist projects of "parliamentary socialism" (social democracy) and "building socialism in one country" (Stalinism). The conventional wisdom amongst a great many of these intellectuals seems to be that the traditional social-democratic critique of Leninist communism has been substantially vindicated. Accepting the premise that Stalinism was the logical and necessary outgrowth of Leninism (an idea that was tirelessly disputed and, in my view, completely demolished by Trotsky), they exhibit an unseemly haste — even eagerness — to conclude that the Stalinist debacle confirms the folly of Lenin's attempt to forge a revolutionary Marxist alternative to the social-democratic Second International. At the level of theory, this conclusion sanctions the notion that the gradualist democratic socialism once advocated by the mass social-democratic parties is the only feasible Marxist alternative to the imaginary amalgam known as Leninism-Stalinism-Communism, and that fidelity to Leninist principles by Trotskyists shows that they are perilously close to "totalitarianism." A tendentious reading of the history of Leninism is thus adduced to support the rehabilitation of classical social-democratic politics and "strategy" (or, less frequently, a neo-anarchist perspective of "changing the world without seizing state power"). It is adduced, in other words, to support a politics that has no real prospect of success.

The essential problem with this left-social-democratic approach is that it fails to confront the altogether obvious fact that the struggle to abolish capitalism (however that abolition might be conceived) is no easy task — that any serious struggle will encounter the determined resistance of the capitalist class and its agencies at every level. One does not need to defend each and every action taken by Lenin's Bolsheviks following Russia's socialist revolution in order to see that the fundamental tenets of Lenin's strategy — the need for a disciplined and programmatically cohesive "democratic-centralist" party, a resolute commitment to the political independence of the working class on the basis of an internationalist socialist program and a perspective of "smashing" the existing capitalist state machine and replacing it with organs of working-class power (a system of "council democracy") — are entirely indispensable to any determined effort to uproot the capitalist order and achieve socialism.

No doubt this claim will be denounced by many as an example of "dinosaur Marxism" and "ultra-left sectarianism." But the stubborn fact remains that the avowedly anti-Leninist radical left has yet to articulate any serious, much less convincing, alternative to the body of program and strategy developed by Lenin's Bolsheviks in the early years of the Third (Communist) International and subsequently augmented by Trotsky and his followers after the Stalinist degeneration of the international communist movement.

Unfortunately, instead of paying heed to the "lessons of October" or the hard-won lessons of other important working-class revolts, contemporary radicals are much more likely to agree with Susan George's dismissive suggestion that a "twenty-first century 'revolution' might, perhaps, occur in several ways, but the storming of the Winter Palace isn't one of them" (2004: 93). Of course, George doesn't comment on what those several ways might be. Nor does she acknowledge that the conquest of the seat of state power by insurrectionary forces (whether that seat is the Winter Palace, Westminster or the Washington capitol) is a *necessary*, if not entirely sufficient, condition for the victory of any revolution worthy of the name. But then, the real purpose of George's argument against an "all-consuming one-off revolutionary transformation" (whatever that might mean) is not to urge the formulation of a better, more "up to date" revolutionary strategy, but rather to reject the very idea of preparing for a decisive confrontation between an insurgent mass anti-capitalist movement and the repressive agencies of the capitalist order. She writes:

> I can barely visualize what such a gigantic one-off event might look or feel like, but history suggests it could only come about after a series of wrenching crises in which millions would suffer and thousands die.... Frankly, I hope such traumatic events can be avoided. (93)

In this single passage, George succeeds in distilling much of the confused thinking that prevails not only in the "global justice movement" (of which she is a prominent spokesperson) but also amongst many "independent socialist" Marxists. To be a revolutionary socialist — a Leninist or a Trotskyist — is not to hope for "traumatic events"; it is to expect them and also to prepare for them. Indeed, it is to recognize that humanity lives with them now and must continue to live with them as long as the rule of capital continues. Furthermore, to be a revolutionary socialist is to recognize that, periodically, mass struggles of workers and other popular forces must come face to face with the question of state power, and that decisive (and often bloody) show-downs will occur irrespective of whether a revolutionary vanguard party is present and poised to lead an insurgent mass movement to victory.

Replying to a critique of "insurrectionary socialism" by the independent socialist Ralph Miliband some years ago, I wrote:

> Ultimately, the question [of the relevance of the lessons of the October Revolution] concerns whether — in the context of episodes like the Russian Revolution of 1917, the Spanish Revolution of 1936, or the Portuguese Revolution of 1975 — one will take one's stand with those seeking to limit the mass movement to constitutionalist avenues or with those seeking to lead the working class forward to the conquest of state power. To be a Trotskyist means to affirm well in advance of such revolutionary situations which side one will take in the midst of a decisive confrontation (a situation of "dual power), and it is to proclaim the need to construct a party that will know how to resolve the confrontation decisively in favor of workers' power. Such a Trotskyist party will certainly distinguish itself from other organizations on the Left in non-revolutionary conjunctures as well, but it will do so precisely as an organization of militants participating in broader movements of struggle against exploitation, oppression, and social injustice — articulating these struggles with a program of socialist transformation... and, through it all, cultivating a spirit of revolution that has at its core a fundamental disrespect for the constitutional limitations, legal framework, and repressive agencies of the capitalist state. (Smith 1996–97: 58–59)

To make such an argument is not to indulge in sectarianism or to build castles in the sky. It is to emphasize what Susan George herself tells us "his-tory suggests" — that wrenching crises can indeed give birth to revolutionary (and counter-revolutionary) events. What distinguishes George and other left-reformists from revolutionary Marxists is not realism or their pious hopes that traumatic events can somehow be avoided. Rather it is their determination to turn a blind eye to the elementary responsibility incumbent on all those who would lead the charge for "global social justice" — to learn the lessons of history and to build the political instruments needed to win real victories in the struggle to change the world. In what way is it realistic to reject the need for a programmatically coherent revolutionary socialist party with a clear strategic orientation and tested tactical capacities, while urging on a rising movement of workers, peasants and social-justice activists to confront a well-organized and violent counter-revolution? Hasn't this scenario played out far too many times over the past century (in Spain, in Indonesia, in Chile, etc.), and haven't these defeats led precisely to the demoralization and defeatism that now make it so very difficult for Susan George, and even many socialists to her left, to "visualize" another October revolution? No, such a perspective is not realism. It is not even simple naiveté. A better name for it would be political irresponsibility.

The Pivot of Consciousness

As the ideological pathologies associated with the collapse of Stalinism begin to abate and new possibilities open up for political and theoretical clarification, one can only hope that an increasing number of social-justice activists and self-styled independent socialists will put aside their residual prejudices and begin a serious engagement with the revolutionary Marxist tradition represented by Lenin and Trotsky. In my opinion, this is a *sine qua non* for the rebirth of a genuine socialist project.

To be sure, sympathetic engagement with Trotskyism is hardly a talisman — or a guarantee of anything. Just as there are many ostensible Marxisms on offer, so too are there many ostensible Trotskyisms. Some are programmatically indistinguishable from the left reformism they claim to combat, while others are characterized by extreme sectarianism. Regardless of what might be said about specific Trotskyist currents, however, it is imperative that the foundational theses and principles of the Trotskyist movement receive the sober consideration they deserve from all socialist intellectuals and activists seeking a more just and egalitarian world.

Rather than expending precious time and energy debating postmodernist fashions, catering to a lifestyle, counter-culture politics or formulating policy recommendations for capitalist governments, the radical socialist left (within the academy and without) must begin to explore issues that speak to the problems of a revolutionary political practice and a transformative socialist project. In this connection, a number of crucial questions posed by the theory and the practical experiences of Trotskyism need to be addressed. These questions include:

1) Are there reasonable grounds for claiming that the twentieth century witnessed several opportunities for working-class revolutions, opportunities thwarted by the weakness, ineptitude or betrayal of working-class

leadership? If so, what are the principal lessons of those revolutionary (or near-revolutionary) situations?

2) Is the present crisis of humanity reducible to the crisis of working-class leadership, as Trotsky argued in 1938? Does the regression in class consciousness and socialist commitment throughout the world, especially since the early 1990s, require modifications to this thesis? And does the demise of Stalinism in the international labour movement and the current global economic crisis open up new possibilities for the construction of revolutionary oppositions to the bureaucratic misleaders?

3) What are the conditions for the construction of a revolutionary Marxist organization that can avoid the opportunism, sectarianism, bureaucratism and cultism that have afflicted so many avowedly Leninist and Trotskyist organizations?

4) What does it mean to have a strategy centred on the working class today, and how should this be understood in a global context? What orientation is needed to the existing mass working-class organizations and in particular the trade unions?

5) What is the significance of the so-called "new social movements" for a working-class centred socialist strategy? How can socialists relate constructively to and win the allegiance of those participating in struggles on behalf of racial minorities, women, immigrants and other victims of "special" oppression?

6) How can Marxist-socialist ideas be most effectively popularized in a world dominated by capitalist mass media? What kinds of socialist education, agitation and propaganda should be prioritized, and what forms should these take?

7) What lessons can be drawn from the twentieth-century experience in "socialist construction," and how can these lessons be applied to "erecting in thought" an attractive alternative to the capitalist global order?

8) What is the contemporary meaning of Marxist internationalism? If nationalism has been the bane of the dominant politico-ideological expressions of the labour movement over the past century, how can it be combated? What should an internationalist program and perspective for contemporary socialists look like, and how might it be implemented?

9) What are the real meanings of "sectarianism" and "dogmatism" in the contemporary context? Is it not sectarian for erstwhile Trotskyists to cling dogmatically and nostalgically to the icon "Trotsky" even after they have effectively abandoned the revolutionary core of Trotsky's thought? And is it not sectarian for "independent socialists" to refuse to engage in debate and sometimes in joint actions with those more authentic Trotskyists who have not abandoned their revolutionary commitment?

This latter question brings to mind an instructive example of the malaise and disorientation that currently exists on the socialist left. On May 1, 2008, the International Longshore and Warehouse Union (ILWU) shut down every port on the U.S. West Coast in an illegal eight-hour strike against the Iraq War — the only successful labour strike against U.S. military intervention ever organized in the United States and an inspiring example of the kind of action that must multiply if the capitalist order is ever to be brought to its knees. It should surprise no one that this event was met with silence by the capitalist mass media (except in cities that were directly affected). What perhaps is surprising (not to say disheartening) is that the great majority of the "socialist and anti-imperialist left" ignored — indeed, effectively boycotted — a public forum in Toronto a few months later where one of the key organizers of that strike, the ILWU militant and socialist Jack Heyman, was the featured speaker. No doubt this boycott was largely attributable to the fact that the forum had been organized by a Trotskyist group that many consider sectarian! The meeting attracted about fifty people — but none, it seemed, from the International Socialists, the Communist Party, the New Socialists, Socialist Project or most of the other organized socialist groups on the Toronto left. Conspicuous by their absence too were most of Toronto's more prominent academic Marxists.

This de facto boycott poses another important question: what can be said about "anti-sectarian" leftists who place their disdain toward a particular left group ahead of the opportunity to learn about and discuss such a historically significant labour-based political action? What does this sort of "anti-sectarian" sectarianism reveal about the real priorities and principles of much of the ostensibly socialist left?

10) What is the proper relationship between revolutionary strategy and tactics? Why is it that, in the name of the latter, so many Trotskyist groups have allowed themselves to be propelled to the right and to effectively abandon the former? Consider just one example: can the insistence of so many Trotskyist groups to almost always give "critical" electoral support to one or another "labour based" party be justified any longer? The "critical support" tactic was originally conceived by revolutionary leader V.I. Lenin as a means to expose the ostensibly socialist but actually pro-capitalist leadership of a "bourgeois workers party" before its working-class base — to "support" these opportunists in the same way that "a rope supports a hanged man." Arguably, however, a tactic that made sense in relation to the British Labour Party in the 1920s has been transformed by many of today's ostensible Leninists and Trotskyists into a means of training would-be revolutionaries in opportunist maneuvering and political support for the lesser evil. Isn't the call for a vote to a political

party that doesn't even pretend to champion a socialist program — that fails to draw a class line in even a crude way — just a way of signalling one's intention to abandon Marx's class-struggle socialism and to enter the arena of capitalist politics?

These are some of the more important questions that socialist activists and intellectuals need to explore in the coming period if the consciousness of progressive activists is to be directed away from reformist gradualism (or, alternatively, from romantic, anarchist-style resistance to capitalist injustice) and toward a serious fight to achieve world socialism. If only one tenth of the human energy that is now expended on reforming capitalism, protesting its depredations and cobbling together electoral alliances within the arena of bourgeois politics could be channelled instead into an effective revolution-ary/transformative political practice, one suspects that the era of socialist globalization would be close at hand.

Conclusion

The objective, historical conditions for a socialist transformation are not only ripe; they have become altogether rotten. The global capitalist order is pres-ently in an advanced state of decay. The vital task today is to bring human consciousness and activity — the "subjective factor" — into correspondence with the urgent need to confront and transform that object reality. Given the worldwide regression in class consciousness that has occurred among working people over the past generation, those who maintain an attachment to the socialist idea, in the first place leftist intellectuals, bear a heavy responsibility to play a positive role in fulfilling this task. But to do so they must shed their contempt for programmatically based vanguard organizations; recognize, with Lenin, that "socialist consciousness" will not develop spontaneously within the working class or its potential allies; and rediscover the vocation of earlier generations of radical intellectuals: to champion ideas and pro-grams that pose a fundamental challenge to the bureaucratic, pro-capitalist misleaderships of organized labour (Butovsky and Smith 2007; Goldfield and Palmer 2007).

In the mid-1990s, I published a piece that was devoted to assessing Trotsky's theoretical and political legacy, the damage done by Stalinism to the socialist project and the disorientation pervading much of the indepen-dent socialist milieu. The conclusion to that article, I believe, retains all of its relevance for socialist intellectuals and activists today:

> Those of us who remain seriously committed to *socialism* — not to "advanced democracy," not to "a family of the Left," and not to "capitalism with a human face in one country" — must learn to

work and argue with each other in the context of genuine "united fronts." We must learn, as Lenin and Trotsky's early Communist International urged, to "march separately but strike together." We must learn to accept with good grace the criticism of groups either larger or smaller than our own as a condition not only for joint action but for the clarification of political differences and the eventual regroupment and unification of socialist forces on principled, and hopefully more adequate, foundations. Only in this way can a healthy socialist praxis begin to mature in this post-Stalinist era. Beyond this, we must all seek a political practice that is appropriate to our political understanding, without gratuitously vilifying those whose understanding has led them in different directions. We must seek, in other words, to avoid both opportunism and sectarianism — the opportunism which tempts us to keep our ideas under wraps until the dawning of a better day, and the sectarianism which deludes us into thinking that the organizational interests or political shibboleths of a single group can or ought to supersede the needs of the broader movement. In this spirit, the socialist Left as a whole could do worse than to reflect upon and take to heart the "rules" that Trotsky elaborated for his "world party of socialist revolution" at its founding conference in 1938: "To face reality squarely; not to seek the line of least resistance; to call things by their right names; to speak the truth to the masses, no matter how bitter it may be; not to fear obstacles; to be true in little things as in big ones; to base one's program on the logic of the class struggle; to be bold when the hour of action arrives — these are the rules of the Fourth International" (1998: 68). (Smith 1996–97: 64–65)

Notes

1. For an interesting exchange of views, see the debate between Michael Albert and Alex Callinicos 2003.

2. It is significant that the best known and most influential radical academic in the world today is probably Noam Chomsky, whose impressive critiques of the U.S. Empire display an intellectual rigour that is conspicuously lacking from his tendentious passing shots at the revolutionary Marxism of Lenin and Trotsky (see, for example, Chomsky 2004: 69–70). Chomsky's anti-Bolshevism is informed by a peculiar mix of liberalism and anarchism but also resembles that of many contemporary Marxist academics in its appeals to crude anti-communist prejudices. For substantial Marxist critiques of the anarchist tradition, see Spartacist 2001 and IBT 2002.

3. For further elaborations on this theme, see chapters 13, 15, 17, 34 and 37 of Blackwell, Smith and Sorenson 2003.

4. An outstanding educational resource on this question is the British-based journal, *Revolutionary History*.

5. A notable exception is the work of historian Bryan D. Palmer. See in particular his impressive biography of James P. Cannon (Palmer 2007). See also Workman 2009, whose critique of the contemporary left in Canada complements my own in several respects.

6. See Trotsky 1998. This edition of Trotsky's manifesto, published by the International Bolshevik Tendency, is particularly recommended for its excellent introductory and supporting materials.

7. See, for example, most of the more directly political articles that have appeared in such academic Marxist journals as *New Left Review* and *The Socialist Register* in recent years.

8. For a response to the "independent socialist" critique of Trotskyism as "insurrectionary socialism," see Smith 1996-97: 56–62. The case for a class-struggle strategy in the labour movement, involving the coalescing of an anti-bureaucratic, socialist vanguard, is made in Butovsky and Smith 2007.

The Controversy Surrounding
Marx's Theory of Value

In chapter 2, it was noted that the most common, and seemingly cogent, criticism of Marx's theory of value — one endlessly repeated by mainstream economists — rests on a basic misunderstanding of the theoretical purpose served by Marx's premise in *Capital* I that "commodities are sold at their (labour) values." Marx advanced this premise neither as a statement of empirical fact nor as an explanation of the formation of market prices but primarily as a simplifying device to demonstrate that the creation of surplus value depends on the exploitation of wage labour in production. It is one element in a procedure of "theoretical abstraction" that provisionally suspends certain aspects of concrete reality in order to bring into clearer focus other aspects (a procedure not entirely unknown to mainstream economists, who routinely entertain far more unrealistic assumptions — such as "perfect competition" — in the construction of their own theoretical models). Once this is understood, the standard, common-sense criticism of Marx's theory of labour value loses all its force.

Nevertheless, some other, more serious, objections to Marx's theory have been put forward by a range of critics, including many who are otherwise sympathetic to his theoretical and political projects. These criticisms have ignited disputes that have led to the formation of several schools of thought regarding the theoretical content and methodological underpinnings of Marx's *Capital*. A comprehensive discussion of those disputes cannot be undertaken here, but a brief survey of a few of the major currents within "the value controversy" may be of interest to some readers.

Our starting point is the controversy surrounding Marx's presentation of the transformation of commodity values into prices of production. No attempt will be made here to explore all aspects of this controversy or to defend a definite position within it. Instead, the following discussion is intended merely as a springboard to a consideration of a number of more fundamental issues in Marx's value theory: those pertaining to the relationship between the form of value and the magnitude of value.

The first major critique of Marx's transformation procedure was elaborated by the Ricardian economist Ladislaus von Bortkiewicz (1975 [1907]) and later popularized by Paul Sweezy (1968 [1942]). According to von

Bortkiewicz and Sweezy, Marx failed to consider how his theoretical formula for the transformation of commodity values into prices of production can be reconciled with the model of simple reproduction outlined in the second volume of *Capital*. But even more crucially, his transformation procedure is faulted because "it excludes the constant and variable capitals from the transformation process, whereas the principle of the equal profit rate… must involve these elements" (von Bortkiewicz 1975: 201). To correctly transform commodity values into prices of production, von Bortkiewicz claimed, the values of the input commodities c and v (which together constitute the "cost price" of the commodity) need to be transformed in accordance with the general rate of profit along with the newly produced surplus value.

This latter premise of the von Bortkiewicz/Sweezy critique has been cogently challenged from somewhat different angles by Mage (1963), Mandel (1981) and, more recently, the proponents of the Temporal Single System Interpretation (TSSI) of value theory (Freeman and Carchedi 1996; Kliman 2007). What these replies to Bortkiewicz/Sweezy have in common is an insistence that the cost price of a given commodity input to production should be seen as a form of value that has already been transformed in a previous production cycle. As Mage puts it: "the difference between the value created by [an input commodity's] production and its price of production has *already* been transferred to other capitalists through the average rate of profit" (1963: 243, emphasis in original). The price paid by a capitalist for an input commodity finds a renewed value expression as the value of the money-capital invested in its purchase (Smith 1994a : 104–105). Therefore, the Bortkiewicz/Sweezy "solutions" are wrong to insist that "prices of production of inputs should be calculated within the same time-span as prices of production of outputs" (Mandel 1981: 22–23). This is important, it is claimed, because these stratagems render it difficult if not impossible to simultaneously maintain the aggregate equalities "total prices = total value" and "total profits = total surplus value," thereby calling into question the core postulates of Marx's theory of value.

Notwithstanding these arguments, other Marxists have continued to insist that Marx's own transformation procedure is indeed flawed and that what they see as his "dual system" of values and prices of production needs to be refined in order to meet the challenges of Bortkiewicz and such "neo-Ricardian" critics as Steedman (1977). (For surveys of two phases of the debate, see Mandel and Freeman 1984; Freeman, Kliman and Wells 2004.)

At issue in the debate between proponents of dual-system, temporal single-system and other notable interpretations of Marx's value theory and transformation procedure (including those of Foley 1986 and Moseley 1993) are two questions: 1) the relationship between the value form and the value-magnitude in Marx's theory; and 2) the place within it of such concepts as "economic equilibrium" and a "general rate of profit." The discussion that follows is primarily concerned with the first question.

The Ricardian-Marxist Orthodoxy and the Rise of Neo-Ricardianism

Faced with the Bortkiewicz critique, an earlier generation of Marxist economists (Sweezy 1968; Dobb 1973; Meek 1956) succumbed to an approach that seemed close to Marx on substantive issues while more rigorous on technical ones. Unfortunately, the failure of these "orthodox" Marxist economists to pay heed to Marx's value-form theory and to fully appreciate the profound methodological differences between Marx and that classical exponent of "profit rate uniformity" David Ricardo led to their defence of a "Ricardian Marxism." This decisively compromised their ability to meet the neo-Ricardian challenge posed by Piero Sraffa and other proponents of what might be called "Ricardianism minus a labour theory of value" — a challenge that began in the 1960s.

The hallmarks of what came to be known as "neo-Ricardian Marxism" were the claims that a theory of labour value is inessential to a theory of exploitation and surplus generation; that models of economic reproduction that entertain the notion of a surplus must assume the actual existence of a "uniform rate of profit" (rather than a mere tendency towards the equalization of profit rates); and that wages ought to be considered the crucial "independent variable" of capitalist development — and wage inflation the root cause of a falling rate of profit.

The Rediscovery of Value-Form Theory

In reaction to the exhaustion of orthodox Marxist value theory and to the Sraffian/neo-Ricardian challenge, new interpretations of Marx emerged in the 1970s. These interpretations emphasized the critical character of Marx's project and pointed to Marx's analysis of the value form as an area of his theory that had been given insufficient attention by the orthodox (Ricardian-Marxist) value theorists. One of the currents developing out of this rediscovery of the value form (what today is often called "value-form theory") went so far as to see Marx's analysis of the value form as not only the core of his theory of value but also as a basis for abandoning his value-magnitude analysis.

In the first chapter of *Capital* I, Marx identifies the "substance" of value as "abstract labour," defined as labour abstracted from its concrete utility-shaping characteristics and conceived as an aspect of the homogeneous mass of social labour entering into the production of commodities. The measure of this value-creating substance is socially necessary labour time, defined as "the labour-time required to produce any use value under the conditions of production normal for a given society and with the average degree of skill and intensity of labour prevalent in that society" (1977: 129). It follows from this that: "The value of a commodity is related to the value of any other commodity as the labour-time necessary for the production of the one is related to the labour-time necessary for the production of the other" (1977: 130).

Marx's subsequent analysis of exchange value (or the form of value) identifies two "poles" of the value relation, the relative form of value and the equivalent form:

> Whether a commodity is in the relative form or in its opposite, the equivalent form, entirely depends on its actual position in the expression of value. That is, it depends on whether it is the commodity whose value is being expressed, or the commodity in which value is being expressed. (1977: 140)

Further analysis of this relation discloses three peculiarities of the equivalent form. First, "use-value becomes the form of appearance of its opposite, value" (1977: 148) due to the fact that the physical body of the commodity standing in the equivalent form expresses the value of commodities standing in the relative form. It follows from this that the concrete labour going into the production of this commodity stands in a relation of equivalence to the abstract labour "embodied" in the commodities standing in the relative form. Hence, "concrete labour becomes the form of manifestation of its opposite, abstract human labour" (150). This leads directly to a third peculiarity: the equivalent form reveals that "private labour takes the form of its opposite, namely labour in its directly social form" (151).

The reversals suggested in this analysis of the value form are of central importance to Marx's whole value theory. Within value relations, Marx asserts, use value appears as value, concrete labour as abstract labour, and private labour as social labour. The commodity is a unity of use value and value, but this dual character of the commodity is only expressed when its value has a form of appearance distinct from its natural (use-value) form. This form of appearance is its money exchange value.

Marx's derivation of the expanded form of value from the simple form, of the general form from the expanded form, and of the universal money form from the general form constitutes a brilliant logico-historical unfolding of a result that is clearly central to his theory: "Money as the measure of value is the *necessary* form of appearance of the measure of value which is immanent in commodities, namely labour-time" (Marx 1977: 188, emphasis added). The peculiarities of the equivalent form, to which we have already referred, find final expression in the money commodity.

This analysis points directly to the problem of distinguishing between the commodity's natural/use-value aspect and its socio-economic or value aspect. It is hardly surprising then that Marx follows up his value-form analysis with his famous discussion of the "fetishism" of commodities, a concept that is central not only to his critique of political economy but to his critique of capitalism as well. According to Marx, the forms of appearance of value lead us away from the recognition that commodities both reflect and give expression to definite social relations existing between commodity producers. Indeed, value relations systematically encourage a confusion of the natural and the social, and this fetishistic confusion creates the illusion that, as producers, people can relate to one another only through the mediation afforded by "things."

Following his initial discussion of value as "socially necessary abstract labour," Marx's analyses of the value form and of commodity fetishism serve to explain his unwillingness to follow David Ricardo in directly proceeding from the "magnitude of value as labour time" to the money-price of commodities. Indeed, it is in just this way that Marx establishes his theory of value, not as a theory of market-price formation (after the fashion of Ricardo's labour theory of value), but as a basis for disclosing the macro-economic processes issuing from the contradictions of the commodity form of the product of labour. Still, the relevance of such an investigation, as he makes clear, can only be grasped by those prepared to recognize that the product of labour can assume different (that is, non-commodified) forms and that the social form of the division of labour need not be that of private exchange.

At one level, Marx's analysis of the value form appears to relieve the value theorist of any obligation to address the problem of the magnitude of value as this was traditionally conceived in Ricardian political economy. Indeed, many value-form theorists have conceded that the neo-Ricardian criticisms of Marx's value-magnitude analysis are correct and that Sraffa's physical-magnitude model of economic reproduction (which dispenses with labour values) is a superior tool of macro-economic analysis (Himmelweit and Mohun 1981; Elson 1979). Where the orthodox school of value theory subordinated the value form to the value-magnitude analysis, these value-form theorists have done precisely the reverse. The only real "continuity" between them lies in their mutual dissociation of the "quantitative" and "qualitative" aspects of Marx's theory.

An important consequence of the preoccupation with the "form of value" over the "magnitude of value" is a tendency to go beyond the correct perception that interaction occurs between production and the other moments of reproduction (circulation, exchange, consumption) to the conclusion that, under capitalism, exchange emerges as the predominant moment. Such an approach is not at all the same as saying that exchange is the social form of a commodity-producing economy — as argued by the famous Russian value-form theorist of the 1920s, I.I. Rubin (1973). Indeed, by implicitly rejecting the primacy of production, it involves a complete abandonment of Marx's social ontology and a major concession to neoclassical marginalism as well as neo-Ricardianism. In fact, through an excessively qualitative focus on micro-economic exchange relations, these value-form theorists draw dangerously close to a simple identification of value and price. Such a drift is particularly evident in the following statement: "The transformation from Volume I [of *Capital*] to Volume III is not a transformation from value to price, but from value and price considered purely from the point of view of production to value and price as modified by circulation and capitalist competition" (Gerstein 1986: 68). And further: "I locate the creation of value not in production but at the articulation of production and circulation" (De Vroey 1981: 173). The logic of such identification is also evident in Himmelweit and Mohun's discussion and in that of Elson, despite occasional references to "value produced in production" and the like. In this connection, Lipietz noted that the failure of the French value-form school "to deal with the problem of magnitude had an unexpected result: they abandoned the pole of substance and slipped irresistibly towards a purely formal and subjectivist theory of value" (Lipietz 1985: 158).

Fundamentalist Value Theory

Lipietz's reference to the "pole of substance" is a convenient point of departure for an attempt to assess the value controversy as a whole on what I have called a "fundamentalist" basis, that is, a basis that recognizes the importance of both aspects of Marx's fundamental theoretical program: the analysis of the form and the magnitude of value.

The emphasis on the value form is associated with an attempt to radically differentiate Marx's notion of "abstract labour" from a (Ricardian) notion of "embodied labour." Indeed, many value-form theorists regard the distinction between an "embodied-labour theory of value" and an "abstract-labour theory of value" as both the starting point and the terminus of any Marxist attempt to respond to neo-Ricardian criticisms. The fundamentalist position is that while such a distinction is of vital importance, it remains necessary to tackle the neo-Ricardian challenge head on. It's not enough to say that the neo-Ricardians have misunderstood Marx's theory of value; it is also necessary to demonstrate the macro-economic superiority of Marx's value-magnitude analysis over the Sraffian physical-magnitudes model of the neo-Ricardians.

Marx's concept of "abstract labour" is the vital conceptual nexus between his value-form and value-magnitude analyses. Since abstract labour for Marx is the substance of value, it needs to be referred to whether one is discussing the qualitative (form-analytic) or the quantitative (magnitude) aspects of his theory of value. My contention is that in avoiding the controversy surrounding the value-magnitude analysis many proponents of value-form theory have redefined abstract labour in a fashion that misrepresents Marx's theoretical project. In their hands the concept has become a theoretical rationale for denying that value exists as an "objective, quantitatively determined magnitude" and for obfuscating the processes through which value is created.

In contrast to this equivocation, the fundamentalist value theorists refuse to relinquish the historical-materialist principle that what transpires in exchange must be regulated and dominated by the way in which social labour time has been allocated in the sphere of production. This notion permits a conception of abstract labour as the reflection in thought of the real social processes through which commodities are produced for the purpose of sale and the realization of profit. Abstract labour and value now appear as the results of commodity production; both are created through the real activity of producing commodities before the latter enter the realm of exchange.

Such an approach leads to a reinstatement of the notion of "socially necessary labour time," which is central to Ricardian and neo-Ricardian interpretations of Marx. At the same time, however, it is linked to a concept of how commodities "represent" value rather than "embody" labour time. This concept is well-specified by Anwar Shaikh:

> It is clear in Marx… that it is not the historical cost of a commodity in labor time, but rather its current cost of reproduction, which determines the magnitude of a commodity's Value. As such, it is not a question of the labor time "embodied" in a commodity but of the social cost which the current production of the commodity entails. (1977: 113)

This understanding of labour value informs Shaikh's "iterative" approach to the transformation issue, as informed by the value-form analysis.

For the fundamentalists, abstract labour (as the substance of value) serves to link the value-form and value-magnitude analyses and consequently is measurable in two senses: at the level of exchange or circulation, money appears as its sole measure; but at the level of production, the concept is conceptually apprehended and measured in terms of labour time.

By denying that abstract labour can be measured at the level of production in terms of socially necessary labour time, value-form theorists render consistent their theoretical revision according to which value is created, if only in some final sense, in exchange. Fundamentalists overturn this revision by showing how the "form of value" and the "magnitude of value" are contradictory only in the sense that they are conceptual reflections of the real contradictions of commodity production:

Labour involved in the production of commodities produces value, while exchange merely realizes it in money-form. It is only because of this that Marx can distinguish between the amounts of value and surplus-value created in commodity production and the generally different amounts realized through exchange. (Shaikh 1981: 274, emphasis in original)

On the basis of this common core of understanding of Marx's value theory, the (otherwise heterogeneous) fundamentalist school has elaborated a formidable response to the neo-Ricardian/post-Sraffian challenges over such matters as the transformation problem, the alleged redundancy of the value-magnitude analysis to a physical-magnitude analysis and the so-called "joint production problem" (Shaikh 1977, 1981; Foley 1986; Mandel and Freeman 1984; Moseley 1993; Freeman and Carchedi 1996; Kliman 2007). Unfortunately, the attention given to answering the technical points of the neo-Ricardians has not always been matched by attention to the larger methodological and ontological issues that are key to differentiating the Marxist-fundamentalist theory from virtually every other theory of value, Marxian and non-Marxian alike.

The Ontology of Abstract Labour and Value

Marx's procedure in the first chapter of *Capital* I is implicitly to establish "value" as a general or universal concept corresponding to a real social process. This holistic commitment is rendered explicit in a passage from his appendix to the first German edition of *Capital*, where he speaks of a "reversal, whereby the sensuously concrete is considered as only the form of appearance of the abstract universal, as opposed to the case where the abstract universal is a property of the concrete." No less than the other reversals peculiar to the equivalent form of value, this reversal, for Marx, "characterizes the value expression" (1953: 271; cited in Fischer 1982: 31).

Marx's observations here would seem to support the notion that abstract labour — as a real structure — finds expression through the concrete particulars of the products of labour. Thus, to conceive of abstract labour as a "universal structure" (or, more dynamically, as a "universal process") is not to deny that it finds particular expressions or concrete forms (in which, indeed, it is apprehended as a "property of the concrete"); rather, it is to insist that it has an existence that is independent of these concrete particulars as well. The quantitative dimensionality of abstract labour is, therefore, not confined to concrete particulars (the money-form), but exerts itself also at the level of its social-structural existence (as socially necessary labour time).

In my view such a conceptualization is the implicit ontological basis of the fundamentalist approach to value theory. As we have seen, the core fundamentalist account recognizes the importance of both the "magnitude of value" and the "form of value." The magnitude-of-value problematic directs attention to the macro-level and to the measurement of value in terms of socially necessary labour time. The form-of-value problematic directs attention to the micro-level issue of the quantitative relation between particular commodities as expressed through the money form.

The dissociation of these problematics can only lead to a dualism of universal and particular, that is, to a denial of their dialectical unity. In practical terms such a dualism must eventuate in that methodological privileging of "the particular," which is characteristic of all theories of value that focus on the "individual commodity" at the expense of an understanding of "the world of commodities." Such an approach is characteristic of Ricardo's theory (despite his concern with the macro-economic issue of the distribution of income between classes), of Mill's "cost of production" theory and of neoclassical marginal-utility theory. Orthodox (Ricardian) Marxist value theory is characterized by an uneasy, and ultimately untenable, compromise between a dualistic and a dialectical (monistic) handling of the universal/particular relation, while neo-Ricardianism represents a bold reassertion of a dualistic position, but one that accords an analytical privilege to "macro-level" economic phenomena (abstracted from any theory of value). Pure value-form theory, in this context, can be interpreted as a reassertion of the micro-economic side of Marx's value theory (the function of which is to remind us that the product of labour is valorized only by virtue of the existence of determinate social relations) within a theoretical space that accepts both a dualistic framework and a macro-economic analysis that eschews any value-magnitude theory. For these reasons, pure value-form theory can be seen as a philosophizing or sociologizing current within the value controversy, one at odds with Marx's dialectical-monistic social ontology (Smith 1994a; see also Smith 2009).

What needs to be stressed by the Marxist fundamentalists in relation to pure value-form theory is that money becomes the form of value precisely in its role as the universal equivalent. To cite Marx: "Since all other commodities are merely particular equivalents for money, the latter being their universal equivalent, they relate to money as particular commodities relate to the universal commodity" (1977: 184). Money, as the universal commodity, is the expression of undifferentiated abstract labour. Significantly, Marx goes on to say that "the money-form is merely the reflection thrown upon a single commodity by the relations between all other commodities" (184). This can be expressed otherwise as follows: money is the form of appearance or "reflection" of a real structure of abstract labour that mediates the relations between commodities. Yet to understand this structure and its mediating role, one must look to the macro-level problem of the magnitude of value. Hence, abstract labour needs to be conceived as a structure (of relations) grounded in production but reflected by individual commodities in the sphere of circulation — and this is precisely the general position taken by the fundamentalist school of value theory. It is solely on this basis that the fundamental postulates of Marx's value theory can be sustained: that living labour and living labour alone is the source of all newly produced value (including surplus value) and that value exists as a definite quantitative magnitude at the level of the capitalist economy as a whole.

Socially Necessary Unproductive Labour in Contemporary Capitalism

In this appendix I survey a number of key issues pertaining to a Marxist "value-theoretical" interpretation of the distinction between productive and unproductive labour.[1] By "value-theoretical" I mean an approach predicated on Marx's labour theory of value and informed by his historical-materialist critique of commodity and capital fetishism (Marx 1977: 163–77, 983, 1003, 1046; Smith 1994a). What distinguishes my treatment from most previous treatments of these issues is my contention that the income of the great majority of unproductive workers is most appropriately conceived as an "overhead cost" of the capitalist system as a whole: in value-theoretical terms, as elements of the "constant capital" whose use values are consumed in the reproduction process of the social capital, but whose value is preserved and reappears in the gross value of output. This approach, though proposed by Shane Mage as early as 1963, has received scant attention in the Marxian literature. Its great merit, in my view, is that it helps to resolve many of the long-standing theoretical difficulties with well-established Marxian treatments of unproductive labour by scrapping the curious convention of treating the wage bill of unproductive workers as a non-profit component of social surplus value and by acknowledging that some forms of unproductive labour are vitally necessary to sustaining profitability and to reproducing the institutional framework of the valorization (value-expansion) process.

I begin with a review of the main elements of Marx's (incomplete) account of unproductive labour. This is followed by a critique of conventional Marxian conceptualizations of unproductive labour and the case for subsuming "socially necessary unproductive labour" under an expanded concept of constant capital. The implications of this approach are then explored in relation to Marx's theory of profitability crisis and in connection with the experience of the Canadian economy. I conclude with some general theoretical considerations on productivity trends under advanced capitalism.

Marx and the Problem of Unproductive Labour

All forms of unproductive labour have one obvious thing in common: none, by definition, is "productive." The simplest way to begin is therefore to establish how Marx defines "productive labour."[2] In all of his writings on the subject, Marx is unequivocally clear that his concept of productive labour is by no means coextensive with "production labour," that is, manual and/or mental labour directly involved in the production of useful things or effects. Production labour is not specific to the capitalist mode of production; it is also performed in non-capitalist modes of production (for example, feudalism) and in non-commodified spheres of capitalist society (for example, domestic labour). Productive labour, on the other hand, is labour that is productive for capital; it is labour that not only produces commodities (marketed use values) but also is employed by capital and creates surplus value. For Marx, this last is the key criterion. Labour may be in the employ of capital and yet not be productive. It may even produce a measurable "output" in physical terms and/or assist individual capitalists in realizing a profit, and yet still not be productive. Labour is "productive" in the specifically capitalist sense solely when it participates directly in a labour process that augments social surplus value — the surplus value that is generated on an economy-wide scale on behalf of "capital in general."

We are now in a position to distinguish between the main *forms* of unproductive labour. Two principal forms are already indicated: (1) labour that belongs to non-capitalist socio-economic activities and therefore cannot serve to augment social surplus value (the labour of self-employed commodity producers is a major instance of this form within capitalist societies); and (2) labour that is in the employ of unproductive capital and therefore "facilitates" the valorization process but does not contribute directly to the augmentation of social surplus value. To these should be added: (3) labour that is supported by the capitalist state and likewise contributes "indirectly" to valorization and accumulation through its role in maintaining the institutional framework of capitalist society; and (4) labour in the employ of productive capital that nevertheless contributes only indirectly to valorization and accumulation (supervisors, security guards and so on).

The last three forms of unproductive labour — what might be referred to as "circulation labour" (form 2) and "social-maintenance labour" (forms 3 and 4) — have expanded considerably under advanced capitalism, while the first form has declined precipitously. Yet it was undoubtedly only this first form that Marx had in mind when he enunciated his much-quoted but quite misleading definition of unproductive labour as "labour which is not exchanged with capital, but *directly* with revenue, that is with wages or profit" (Marx 1978a: 157, emphasis in original).

In *Capital* II and *Capital* III, Marx unequivocally affirms the existence of forms of unproductive labour that are not exchanged with revenue but rather with capital. In these later treatments, Marx is preoccupied with the specifically capitalist incarnations of unproductive labour: the socially necessary forms of unproductive labour that serve the reproduction of the capitalist socio-economic order. To be sure, in *Capital* II Marx still refers to unproductive workers "who receive for their services a part of the luxury expenditure of the capitalists" and "who are themselves to this extent a luxury item" (1981a: 486). But the main focus is no longer on "form 1" unproductive labour of the luxury type. Rather it has shifted to unproductive labour in the sphere of circulation and to unproductive labour as a cost of circulation. The activities of buying, selling and bookkeeping are singled out by Marx as types of unproductive labour with a very different import than the unproductive labour of butlers, maids and stable boys:

> Labour-power and labour-time must be spent to a certain degree in the circulation process.... But this now appears as an additional outlay of capital; a part of the variable capital must be deployed in acquiring these labour-powers that function only in circulation. This capital advance creates neither products nor value. It proportionately reduces the scale on which capital advanced functions productively. (1981a: 210–11)

Clearly, the unproductive labour to which Marx refers here is socially necessary to capital in so far as it contributes not to the "creation" of surplus value but to its "realization" in the sphere of circulation. Moreover, Marx is clear that this form of unproductive labour is exchanged with capital. Yet Marx also refers to the capital advance made to acquire these unproductive labour powers as a "part of the variable capital" — a problematic suggestion in view of his fundamental definition of variable capital as capital exchanged for labour power of the productive type (Marx 1977: 317).

This apparent contradiction in Marx's thinking on the problem of circulation labour reflects a contradiction that exists in reality: the circumstance that labour involved in the circulation of capital is "productive" from the standpoint of individual (commercial or financial) capitals, even though it is unproductive from the point of view of the social capital ("capital in general"). What we are dealing with then is a "variable capital *sui generis*" — a portion of the social capital exhibiting some but by no means all of the characteristics associated with variable capital.

In brief, circulation labour is subject to exploitation, even though it is not directly productive of surplus value. In the case of a "buying and selling agent" who works for a capitalist, Marx states that "as a wage labourer he works part of the day for nothing. He may receive every day the value product of eight hours' labour, and function for ten" (1981a: 210). Yet, "[the] two hours' surplus-labour that he performs no more produce value than do his eight hours of necessary labour, although it is by means of the latter that a part of the social product is transferred to him" (210). For the industrial capitalist who employs this type of unproductive labour, the capital exchanged with it is purely an "overhead" cost of production, a *faux frais*, which should be kept to a minimum. Such labour does not augment social surplus value, even though it "performs a necessary function, because the reproduction process itself includes unproductive functions" (209). Yet for the commercial capitalist who employs such labour, its significance is necessarily different: the surplus labour performed by such unproductive labour in the sphere of circulation is precisely the means whereby "a part of the social product" is transferred to commercial capital in the form of merchants' or financial profit. In *Capital* III, Marx states:

> Commercial capital's relationship to surplus-value is different from that of industrial capital. The latter produces surplus-value by directly appropriating the unpaid labour of others. The former appropriates a portion of this surplus-value by getting it transferred from industrial capital to itself.... The very function by virtue of which the commercial capitalist's money is capital is performed in large measure by his employees on his instructions. Their unpaid labour, even though it does not create surplus-value, does create his ability to appropriate surplus-value, which, as far as this capital is concerned, gives exactly the same result: i.e., it is its source of profit. (1981b: 407)

The fact that "buying and selling agents" in both the sphere of production and the sphere of circulation perform functions that are necessary to completing the circuit of capital (through the realization of commodity values) in no way obviates the circumstance that the paid labour of such agents will be viewed differently by industrial and commercial capitals: the former will see such labour costs as a deduction from its profits, the latter as a source of profits. Both perspectives embrace a partial truth. But the real significance of this form of labour from the standpoint of the social capital as a whole can only be grasped by taking into consideration its contributions to the overall process of capitalist production/reproduction. From this standpoint, socially necessary unproductive labour (SNUL) — whether of the "circulation" or the "social-maintenance" types — has a highly complex relationship to the valorization and accumulation processes: one that should find a subtle theoretical expression at the level of Marx's basic value categories. These categories comprise the three constituents of the value of the commodity product: constant capital, variable capital and surplus value $(c + v + s = P)$.

At different times and in different theoretical contexts, Marx subsumed the costs of SNUL under each of these categories, failing to resolve definitively the problem of how SNUL should be specified in value-theoretical terms. Unfortunately, the conventional Marxian treatment of the problem, which treats the wage bill of SNUL as a non-profit component of social surplus value (and as a straight-forward deduction therefrom), is a false solution that does justice neither to the dialectical subtlety of Marx's theory nor to the complexity of the SNUL phenomenon under capitalism.[3]

SNUL and Marx's Value Categories

The specification of SNUL costs as elements of social surplus value became a convention within Marxist discourse only with the rise of underconsumptionism in Marxian crisis theory (Sweezy 1968 [1942]). The "monopoly capitalism" school in particular has championed this specification in a fashion that has a clear affinity to its view that the key problem facing modern capitalism is one of "absorbing the surplus" (Baran and Sweezy 1966; Foster 1986). On this view, unproductive labour is functional to capitalism, not only because its on-the-job activity helps to realize surplus value, but because its consumptive behaviour generates additional effective demand for an ever-growing "economic surplus" (Tarbuck 1983). Such an analysis comes close to suggesting that unproductive labour is deliberate "make work," designed and paid for by micro-economic agents (primarily commercial capitalists) to redress a macro-economic effective-demand problem. The problem, however, is that the feedback mechanism in this particular "functional loop" would seem quite difficult to specify.[4]

Yet Marxists who do not subscribe to underconsumption theories of crisis have also accepted the dubious proposition that SNUL is paid for out of surplus value. Joseph Gillman, for example, asserts: "The whole congeries of administrative expense and selling costs, as well as rent, interest and business taxes, are all part of surplus-value" (1957: 17). This view is seconded by Anwar Shaikh, a leading proponent of Marx's law of the falling tendency of the rate of profit:

> The question Marx poses… is: out of what fund are [the] distribution activities to be supported? And the answer he gives is: out of the surplus-product, out of surplus-value. After the replacement of the costs of production, there remains the surplus product from which all further costs of capitalist reproduction must eventually be defrayed. (Shaikh 1978b: 8; see also Miller 1984; Moseley 1987; Chernomas 1987, 1990; Fine and Harris 1979)

Given the near-consensus on this point among Marxists who champion the productive-unproductive distinction, it is important to emphasize that Marx never, in fact, provided such an unequivocal answer to the question attributed to him by Shaikh. Indeed, to the best of my knowledge, the sole basis in Marx's writings for the specification of SNUL costs as paid for out of surplus value is his ambiguous reference to a "deduction from surplus-value" in the following passage from *Capital* II:

> The general law is that all circulation costs that arise simply from a change in form of the commodity cannot add any value to it. They are simply costs involved in realizing the value or transferring it from one form into another. The capital expended in these costs (including the labour it commands) belongs to the *faux frais* of capitalist production. The replacement of these costs must come from the surplus product, and from the standpoint of the capitalist class as a whole it forms a deduction of surplus-value or surplus-product, in just the same way as the time that a worker needs to buy his means of subsistence is lost for him. (Marx 1981a: 225–26)

The difficulty with this passage is that it appears to contradict Marx's treatment of commercial capital and the costs of circulation as this is elaborated in *Capital* III, as well as in some other passages of *Capital* II. Indeed, the way in which this passage has been interpreted by Sweezy, Gillman and Shaikh renders it entirely incompatible with the burden of this latter treatment, which I turn to shortly. The incompatibility disappears, however, if we amend the wording of the first sentence to read "any *new* value" instead of "any value," and if we examine the concept of a "deduction from surplus value" a little more closely.

The main preliminary point is that a "deduction from surplus value" can be understood in either a relative or an absolute sense. Proponents of the conventional specification of SNUL are clearly committed to an absolute interpretation. Yet, in a (neglected) passage where Marx actually defines this concept, such an interpretation is logically excluded:

> the actual *circulation costs* increase the *value* of the product, but decrease the surplus value.... The costs of circulation generally, in so far as their merely economic moments, circulation proper are concerned... are to be regarded as deductions from *surplus-value*, i.e., as an increase of necessary labour in relation to surplus-labour. (1973: 548, emphasis in original)

Consistent with his *Capital* III treatment, Marx is here quite clear that the costs of circulation *increase* the value of the commodity product. Yet if the circulation costs were "paid for" out of surplus value, there would be no increase in the value of the product. All that would happen is that the total surplus value would be divided between the payment of circulation (and other unproductive) costs and the revenue available for private capitalist consumption and accumulation. But since, according to Marx, these costs do increase the value of the product (without, however, adding fresh surplus value to it), any decrease in surplus value must merely be a relative one. Hence, what is involved in a "deduction from surplus value" is a relative diminution in the proportion of the commodity's value that takes the form of surplus value. If the added circulation costs did not exist (that is, were unnecessary), the absolute magnitude of "new" surplus value would not increase (indeed, it may even decrease), but this magnitude would represent a larger proportion of the total value of the commodity product. The corollary to this would be that industrial (that is, productive) capital would appropriate all of the surplus value.

It should be noted further that Marx suggests that a deduction from surplus value signifies an "increase of necessary labour in relation to surplus labour" (assuming that all circulation costs are labour costs). But if the costs of circulation are a non-profit component of surplus value, such a definition would be absurd. For if, as Marx insists, surplus value is simply a monetized form of surplus labour under capitalism, and if, as Shaikh et al. insist, a deduction from surplus value is still a "component" of surplus value, then Marx's last sentence might just as well read: "The costs of circulation… are to be regarded as surplus-labour, i.e., as an increase of necessary labour in relation to surplus-labour." Clearly, in so far as a deduction from surplus value represents an "increase in necessary labour," the wage bill of this necessary labour cannot be considered a component of aggregate social surplus value on any logically coherent grounds.

If the costs of circulation are not to be regarded as a part of the aggregate surplus value, how then should they be treated? The most adequate answer to date has been suggested by Shane Mage: "What takes place in the unproductive spheres is simply the outlay of a determined and necessary constituent part of the total social capital" (1963: 65). The inspiration for this is *Capital* III, where Marx states:

> Although [circulation capital] forms additional capital, it does not form any more surplus-value. It must be replaced out of the commodities' value, for a portion of this value must be reconverted back into these circulation costs…. (1980b: 405)

Since circulation activity can add no *new* value to the commodity product, Marx concludes that "the additional value that [the merchant] adds to commodities by his expenses is reducible to the addition of *previously existing* values, even though the question still arises here as to how he maintains and conserves the value of this *constant capital*" (1981b: 406, emphasis added). The relationship of commercial capital to the commodity product is therefore similar to that of "means of production" (machines in particular), which add "previously existing value" but can confer no new value. Such a parallel is supported by Marx's own imagery:

> *One* merchant (considered here merely as the agent of the formal transformation of commodities, as mere   buyer and seller) may, by way of his operations, shorten the buying and selling time for *many* producers. He should then be considered as a machine that reduces the expenditure of useless energy, or helps to set free production time…. The capital advance [required to meet the labour costs of circulation] creates neither products nor value. It proportionately reduces the scale on which the capital advanced functions productively. It is the same as if part of the product was transformed into a machine that bought and sold the remaining part of the product. (1981a: 209, 211, emphasis in original)

What all this implies is that the variable capital *sui generis* deployed by unproductive capital is, from the standpoint of the social capital, qualitatively similar to the constant capital deployed by productive capital. It is variable only in its ability to effect a transfer of already existing surplus value from the productive to the unproductive spheres. Moreover, whether paid for by commercial or industrial capital, the costs of circulation form a component of the capital advanced and therefore reduce the average rate of profit: "The surplus-value s remains constant, but the capital advanced C still grows from C to ^C, so that the profit rate s/C is replaced by the smaller profit rate s/C+^C. The industrial capitalist therefore attempts to keep these circulation costs to a minimum, just as he does his outlay on constant capital" (1981b: 413).

Marx's implicit treatment of unproductive labour costs as a form of constant capital finds explicit support in the way that Mage specifies the value categories:

> The difference between variable capital and constant capital is founded on their differing modes of transferring value to the commodity-product; and in the case of constant capital this characteristic mode is precisely *the addition of previously existing values*. Consequently, the appropriate treatment for the outlay on unproductive expenses in general, provided only that they are "socially necessary" under the existing form of social organization, is to regard them as part of the constant capital advanced and expended. (1963: 66, emphasis in original)

Mage applies this reasoning both to circulation labour and to the social-maintenance labour supported by the capitalist state. Nevertheless, a few qualifications are in order. Like unproductive capital in the sphere of circulation, the state carries out a range of tasks that are indispensable to maintaining the institutional framework of the valorization process. In this sense, it contributes indirectly to the production of social surplus value. Yet the capital exchanged with SNUL in the state sphere is not regarded by any segment of the social capital as contributory to profits. While the sense in which state employees perform "unpaid labour" is problematic, it is safe to say that such state-supported "social-maintenance labour" is exchanged with a form of constant capital that has even less in common with "variable capital" than that exchanged with circulation labour. "State capital" (capitalized tax revenue for the most part) is not exchanged with SNUL with a view to transferring surplus value from the sphere of production to the state, but with a view to centralizing and rationalizing some of the overhead costs of the social capital as a whole and attenuating systemic contradictions. The capitalist state obviously does not participate in surplus-value redistribution on the basis of the average rate of profit (or interest), except where it involves itself directly in commodity production (for example, nationalized industries) or circulation (for instance, nationalized banks). The great majority of its revenues are obtained through a political taxation process, which may have the appearance of "democratically" involving all citizens as "taxpayers" but which finally always amounts to a tax on the social capital.

From the standpoint of the social capital, the state is simply a massive engine of social reproduction, and, like any engine, it requires maintenance, amortization and fuel. Accordingly, the social capital must "set aside" a considerable portion of the value it realizes (and which frequently takes the form of an income tax deduction from the "gross wages" of workers) in order to finance state activity — just as it must set aside some of this same realized value to replenish raw material stocks, depreciated fixed capital and expended fuel supplies in factories and other sites of surplus-value production. State revenues differ from business revenues principally in that the former typically involve a much smaller proportion of redistributed surplus value in relation to recouped costs.

Constant Capital and Capital Fetishism

One possible objection to treating SNUL costs as a component of the constant capital flow is that constant capital is almost always thought of as "means of production" and as directly implicated in the physical process of producing commodities. But constant capital is not merely a value expression of its material forms in the immediate process of production. Rather it is one expression of the "social relation" that is capital, the other expression being variable capital. It is therefore quite reasonable to argue that the category of constant capital encompasses all those "advances" and "costs" associated with the total process of capitalist production and reproduction that are not encompassed by variable capital. If variable capital is defined as that portion of the social capital that is transformed into the living labour that is *directly* productive of surplus value, then constant capital may be defined as that portion that is transformed into all the elements of capitalist production/reproduction that are *indirectly* implicated in the total valorization process. As such, constant capital may assume the form of SNUL just as easily as it assumes the form of a drill-press, an industrial robot, a ton of steel or a cash register.

To assume that constant capital must be directly implicated in use-value production to be "indirectly" implicated in valorization is a fetishistic error. Marx's critique of fetishized political economy involves centrally a rejection of the confusion of the social and the natural aspects of production and of the product of labour. The conventional Marxian identification of constant capital with the physical means of production is no less an instance of such confusion than is the neoclassical/neo-Ricardian failure to distinguish between productive and unproductive forms of wage labour. Neoclassical economic theory cannot distinguish between the productive labour that creates the material/natural content of the commodity product and the unproductive labour that effects the sale of the commodity because sales activity (for example, the labour of the retail cashier) is conceived as the final act in the production of a use-value bearing the required commodified form. In a sense, the activity of the circulation worker is perceived as "productive" of the social form of the product of labour. The sphere of circulation, on this view, does not merely effect a change in titles of ownership and facilitate the realization of commodity values; rather, it "attaches" the commodity form to the product of labour, as a kind of social icing on the cake. By positing an external relation between the natural content and the social form of the product of labour, the neoclassical approach lays the basis for treating each as the unique "productive contribution" of, respectively, "industry" and "commerce" to the creation of "wealth" (a concept that itself conflates and confounds the material and social dimensions of production). Marx's theory of value, by contrast, is based on a dialectical conception of the form-content relation as internal and contradictory (Rubin 1973: 117). From this perspective, the conventional Marxian treatment of constant capital and SNUL concedes too much to a fetishistic view of capitalist economy, while, paradoxically, disarming the proponents of the productive-unproductive distinction of their most valuable theoretical weapon: consistency in resisting the conceptual conflation of the material/natural and the social.

The various forms of constant capital constitute elements of the total process of capitalist production and reproduction that characteristically owe their existence to the past transformation of surplus value into capital. In this sense constant capital forms part of a historically constituted social surplus product from which all systemic costs must be defrayed. But capitalized surplus value and newly created surplus value are by no means coextensive, and there is no good reason to say that the value of an industrial robot should be subsumed under the former, while the value of SNUL should be subsumed under the latter. Upon some reflection, then, it is not hard to see that what Marx said about the means of production is, in principle, applicable to the means of circulation and social maintenance as well:

> As regards the means of production, what is really consumed is their use-value, and the consumption of this use-value by labour results in the product. There is in fact no consumption of their value and it would therefore be inaccurate to say that it is reproduced. It is rather preserved.... Hence the value of the means of production reappears in the value of the product, but it is not strictly reproduced in that value. What is produced is a new use-value in which the old exchange value re-appears. (1977: 315–16)

It might be objected that when Marx speaks of the use values of means of production being "consumed by labour" and resulting in a new product he is speaking of a process that is not duplicated in the unproductive spheres. This is quite true. It may nevertheless be argued that the use values of the "means of reproduction" (including SNUL) are consumed in a process of facilitating valorization and capital accumulation, but that this consumption does not involve the consumption (that is, disappearance) of their value. Instead the value of the consumed means of reproduction "reappears" in the value of the commodity product (conceived as the gross output of the economy as a whole). In other words, two streams of constant capital value reappear in the new social product: one emanating from the immediate process of use-value production, the other from the spheres of circulation and social maintenance.

The myriad forms of constant capital share this common essence: they are means of presenting living labour as new value. Means of production, means of circulation and means of social maintenance are all indispensable to enhancing the productivity of surplus-value-producing labour, and each therefore has a claim to participating indirectly in the valorization process. It matters little that means of production are directly involved in use-value production, while the means of circulation and of social maintenance are not. What matters insofar as the valorization process is concerned is that each of these means of living productive labour represents elements of capital that can contribute to surplus-value production only as facilitators.

Living productive labour is the sole source of surplus value in Marx's theory, and it would therefore be capital fetishism to impute to constant capital in production more than an auxiliary role in the production of value, a role that is paralleled in the unproductive spheres by SNUL (Smith 1991b). This is the unmistakable burden of the following passage from Marx's *Grundrisse:*

> To the extent that the instrument of production is itself a value, objectified labour, it does not contribute as a productive force.... If capital could obtain the instrument of production at no cost, for 0, what would be the consequence? The same as if the cost of circulation = 0. (Marx 1973: 765)

Theoretical Advantages of Treating SNUL as Constant Capital

Perhaps the single greatest merit of treating SNUL as part of the constant capital flow is that it serves to underline its indispensability for capitalism. Proponents of the conventional treatment of SNUL as a non-profit component of surplus value tend either to subsume SNUL under an expanded notion of "luxury consumption" or to overstate the discretion enjoyed by capital in the disposition of the social surplus product as between productive and non-productive uses. By emphasizing the *social necessity* of SNUL for the social capital's reproduction, the constant-capital conceptualization recognizes and gives due weight to a powerful argument often advanced by critics of the distinction between productive and unproductive labour: that circulation labour (and perhaps even social-maintenance labour) contributes materially to a decrease in the turnover period of capital by increasing the velocity of commodities as they move through circulation. Such a decrease means a higher level of employment of productive labour than might otherwise be the case, and consequently an increase in the absolute magnitude of the surplus value being produced relative to the capital advanced. Marx discussed this phenomenon at length under the rubric of the "annual rate of surplus-value" (1981a: 382). Indeed, a decrease in circulation time, other things being equal, must mean an increase in the rate of profit. In light of this consideration, the Marx of *Capital* II could only have admonished the Marx of *Capital* III for assuming that an increase in the capital advanced on circulation costs could not increase the magnitude of surplus value. Due to the influence of the "annual rate of surplus-value" on the average rate of profit, the *direction* of change in the previously cited rate of profit $s/(C+{}^\wedge C)$ becomes somewhat indeterminate. (See also *Capital* III [Marx 1981b: 393].)

Nevertheless such a reduction in circulation time is by no means easily accomplished. The costs of circulation may well rise under the whip of competitive pressures without yielding significant decreases in the average turnover time of the social capital. "Circulationist" strategies may be pursued by individual capitals to shore up profit margins, but the unintended consequence of these strategies may be a downward pressure on the average rate of profit analogous to what Marx says occurs when living labour is replaced by labour-saving machinery in production. Undoubtedly, the costs of circulation have been rationalized considerably as a result of the evolving functional division of labour between industrial, commercial and financial capital. Yet it is also clear that such costs have evinced a tendency to rise as the contradictions of capitalism have intensified (Lebowitz 1972), and these rising circulation costs may, under certain conditions, contribute to a crisis of profitability.

The picture is therefore a highly contradictory one. Under conditions of increasing market accessibility, SNUL may enhance the "annual rate of surplus-value" and play a significant (if still indirect) role in augmenting social surplus value. But under conditions of market contraction and intensified competition over market shares, SNUL may only help individual capitals hold their own against competitors, permitting them to lay claim to their rightful share of a pool of surplus value that is shrinking relative to capital invested. The more autonomy commercial and financial capital (and indeed the capitalist state) have from industrial capital under such conditions, the greater the damage they may inflict upon productive capital, the valorization process and the average rate of profit. By conceptualizing SNUL as a necessary systemic overhead cost, the constant-capital approach emphasizes that capital's room for manoeuvre with respect to these problems is quite limited, giving Marx's proposition that "the true barrier to capitalist production is capital itself" (1981b: 358) a somewhat new twist.

What needs to be stressed is that none of these considerations are adequately captured in the conventional Marxian conceptualization of unproductive labour. In this conceptualization, the capitalist economy is either one in which the "economic surplus" is rising, or in which the distinction between a gross rate of profit (which abstracts from SNUL) and a net rate of profit (which does not) is a meaningful one for economic policy debates (Chernomas 1987). The constant-capital conceptualization on the other hand underlines that the fall in the rate of profit can no more be stemmed by redirecting investment from SNUL to productive labour than it can be by redirecting investment from fixed constant capital to variable capital. It is, in other words, resistant to a reformist perspective, staking its ground on Marx's own thesis that the system "moves in contradiction" and is subject to increasingly severe crisis tendencies.

The Falling Rate of Profit and Capitalist Crisis

At the centre of Marx's theory of capitalist crisis was his law of the falling tendency of the rate of profit. Few twentieth-century Marxists were to emphasize this law, however, until the 1970s and 1980sm when a long-term decline in the post-war average rate of profit became visible to a wide spectrum of Marxist and non-Marxist economists in several advanced capitalist countries. Prior to the 1970s, the majority of Marxist theorists adhered to underconsumption or disproportionality theories to explain the etiology of capitalist crisis and decline (Shaikh 1978a). Baran and Sweezy's highly influential account of capitalist stagnation tendencies is a case in point. In *Monopoly Capital* Baran and Sweezy insisted that Marx's law was not relevant under conditions of monopoly capitalism and that a "law of the rising surplus" should be substituted for it. To establish the empirical relevance of this alleged law of monopoly capitalism, they measured the magnitude of the U.S. "economic surplus" and then calculated it as a percentage of gross national product for the years 1929–63.

Interestingly, an analysis of the data presented in Joseph Phillips' statistical appendix to *Monopoly Capital* discloses, in light of the value specifications defended above, a tendency exactly *opposite* to what Baran and Sweezy attribute to twentieth-century advanced capitalism. Baran, Sweezy and Phillips define the major components of the economic surplus as: 1) total property income, corresponding roughly to Marx's definition of surplus value as the sum of profit of enterprise, interest and rent; 2) waste in distribution, including a major part of what Marx called the costs of circulation; 3) corporate advertising, which also forms part of Marx's costs of circulation; 4) surplus employee compensation, corresponding to the income of SNUL in financial, insurance, real estate and legal firms; and 5) surplus absorbed by government, that is, tax revenues. The sum of these components rose from 46.9 percent of GNP in 1929 to 56.1 percent in 1963. Yet the trend for "total property income" considered alone was strikingly different: this fell as a percentage of GNP from 26.9 to 17.9 percent over the same period. Moreover, it is clear that the relative expansion of unproductive expenditures accounts for much of the observed decline in total property income (that is, what we would regard as *real* surplus value) as a percentage of GNP from 1929 to 1963. Thus, it was only by defining the costs of circulation and of social maintenance as components of the economic surplus that Baran and Sweezy could justify the substitution of the "law of the rising surplus" for the law of the tendency of the rate of profit to fall. Significantly, a more recent study updating this data series shows that between 1963 and 1988 the (actual) surplus percentage (inclusive of adjusted corporate profits, estimated profits of unincorporated business, rental income, net interest and the profit element of corporate officer compensation) persistently fluctuated in the 16 to 20 percent range, displaying no clearcut (upward or downward) trend over the twenty-five-year period (Dawson and Foster 1991). This tends to support the hypothesis that the expansion of SNUL in the post-war period eventually ran up against formidable structural limits and that the (profitability) crises of the 1970s and 1980s cannot be adequately explained on the basis of an underconsumptionist mode of analysis.

With the "law of the rising surplus" unable to explain the provenance of capitalist malaise (crisis *cum* stagnation) in a period of declining profitability, it was to be expected that Marx's own law would begin to attract greater interest (see, especially, Yaffe 1973; Laibman 1982; Shaikh 1978c, 1987; Moseley 1987; Dumenil, Glick and Rangel 1987 ; Chernomas 1990; Smith 1991b). Despite the renewed interest in Marx's own account of profitability crises, however, many of the empirical tests of Marx's hypotheses concerning the tendencies of capitalist accumulation were skewed by the propensity of the investigators to theoretically define and empirically measure surplus value as inclusive of SNUL. To fully appreciate this, a brief review of the main elements of Marx's law of the falling rate of profit is necessary.

Briefly, Marx's law asserts that the productivity-enhancing imperatives of the capitalist mode of production must impart to the process of capitalist accumulation a labour-saving bias, the result of which will be a diminution in the role of living labour relative to that of the physical means of production (fixed capital in particular). Since living labour is the sole source of surplus value, this trend in capital accumulation must produce a depressing effect on the rate of profit, the decisive regulator of economic growth. More technically, the theory involves the proposition that the diminution in the role of living labour will find a *value* expression such that the organic composition of capital, the ratio $C/s+v$, will rise and the rate of profit, s/C, will show a tendency to fall. Now, if aggregate social surplus value is not limited to profits, rents and interest (along with some tax revenues) but includes the wage bill of SNUL and other unproductive expenditures as well, then the organic composition of capital may not seem to be rising and the (value) rate of profit may not appear to be falling, simply because the specific weight of SNUL within advanced capitalist economies has been increasing.

My own study of the Canadian economy for the years 1947–1980 involved the calculation of such fundamental Marxian ratios as the rate of surplus value (s/v), the organic composition of capital $(C/s+v)$, and the average rate of profit (s/C) with two different measures of "aggregate surplus value" (Smith 1984, 1991b; also Smith 1994a , chapter 8). The first measure, s4, conformed to the "narrow" definition of surplus value defended in this appendix; that is, "surplus value privately appropriated" plus an estimate of current surplus value transferred to the state resulting from a real increase in the tax flow. The second measure, s5, conformed to the "expanded" definition of surplus value associated with the conventional treatment of SNUL. Accordingly, the s5 measure included all tax revenues, the after-tax wage bill of SNUL in the private sector, as well as the non-tax components of s4.

Table A2.1 contains a sample of the results of this study. Both the s4 and the s5 data series disclose a tendency for the rate of surplus value to rise, although this is far more pronounced in the s5 series than the s4. The comparative results for the organic composition of capital and the rate of profit are, however, strikingly different. The s4 series displays a marked tendency for the organic composition to rise, while the s5 series depicts long-term stability in this ratio. Further, the s4 series points to a long-term fall in the rate of profit over the thirty-four-year period, while the s5 series shows a flat secular trend, evincing a tendency to decline only in the 1970s.[5]

These empirical results demonstrate that the way that surplus value is specified is of decisive significance to any test of Marx's hypotheses. Little wonder, then, that most recent proponents of Marx's law of the falling tendency of the rate of profit have considered it felicitous to work with a narrow net measure of surplus value, even while insisting that SNUL constitutes a non-profit component of aggregate surplus value (Shaikh 1987, Moseley 1987).

A proper value specification of the income of the SNUL labour force is of critical importance to empirical work in Marxian crisis theory precisely because there has been an undeniable secular trend for the specific weight of SNUL to increase in advanced capitalist countries, at least up until recently. The empirical results from the Canadian economy reported above reflect a shift in the Canadian occupational structure that has been fairly typical

Table A2.1: Trends in the Rate of Surplus Value (s/v), the Organic Composition of Capital (C/(s+v) and the Average Rate of Profit (s/C) using two measures of Aggregate Surplus Value. Canada, Selected Years from 1947 to 1980

	s/v		C/(s+v)		s/C	
Year	s4	s5	s4	s5	s4	s/5
1947	.476	1.92	3.94	1.99	.081	.331
1950	.649	1.92	3.58	2.01	.111	.326
1953	.593	2.00	3.73	1.98	.100	.337
1956	.668	2.14	3.87	2.06	.103	.331
1959	.654	2.31	4.35	2.19	.092	.319
1962	.679	2.60	4.72	2.20	.086	.329
1965	.755	2.88	4.90	2.22	.088	.334
1968	.698	3.10	4.95	2.05	.083	.368
1971	.638	3.37	5.64	2.11	.069	.365
1974	.940	3.78	5.35	2.17	.091	.365
1977	.732	3.85	5.78	2.15	.073	.364
1980	.882	3.88	5.96	2.30	.079	.345

Source: Smith 1984; see also Smith 1991b or Smith 1994a, chapter 8.

among the most developed capitalist countries: a redistribution of wage labour away from manufacturing, mining and other unarguably productive sectors of the economy and toward the service sector; and a redistribution of wage labour within the productive sectors of the economy from productive to socially necessary unproductive tasks.

Conclusion: SNUL, Productivity and Historical Materialism

At the centre of Marx's critique of capitalism is the historical-materialist proposition that all class-antagonistic modes of production must eventually exhaust their historically specific contributions to the development of human productive capacities. At a certain stage of its development, capitalism, like the modes of production preceding it, must confront an historical-structural crisis expressed in a conflict between its forces and relations of production (Marx 1970). It is precisely in this connection that the law of the falling tendency of the rate of profit acquires its full salience.

The paradox is that capitalist social relations impart a labour-saving (and therefore productivity enhancing) bias to the development of capitalist production, even though a diminution in the role of living labour in production results in insufficient surplus-value creation relative to the capital invested. In other words, increased labour productivity resulting from labour-saving technical innovation tends to be inimical to average profitability. Crises ensue that not only create a new technical basis for accumulation but also call forth responses at the level of institutional rearrangements, bureaucratic reorganization of industry, increased government intervention in the economy and so on. Under conditions where class actors are seeking to attenuate or regulate the "undesirable effects" of the law of labour value (falling profits, economic contraction, unemployment, inflation, growing debt and so forth), these structural remedies may themselves come to play a role in defining the specific contours of capitalist crisis. In other words, profitability may fall victim to downward pressures stemming not only from a rising technical and organic composition of capital within production, but from the expanded weight of unproductive capital and SNUL in the economy as well.

Such an adulteration of Marx's law of the falling rate of profit is fully consistent with his expectation that capital's role in systematically promoting human productive capacities must eventually decline. Moreover such an adulteration is consistent with the praxis-grounded theoretical premise that human agency and class struggle are capable of producing a variety of possible institutional and labour force configurations within the broad parameters defined by the law of labour value and its profit-rate corollary. It is just these configurations, involving an expansion of the role of SNUL in advanced capitalist economies, that are now attracting increasing attention from mainstream economists of both conservative and liberal ilk. In a survey of literature on productivity growth and U.S. competitiveness, Baumol and McLennan observe:

> Although it has been a source of considerable controversy, a number of analysts have attributed a substantial role [in the American productivity slowdown] to changes in the composition of U.S. output and, particularly, to the shift of the labour force from manufacturing to the services, whose productivity growth has historically been relatively slow. Estimates of the effect of this influence [on the slowdown] range from 10 to 40 percent, and several more extreme figures have also been proposed. (1985: 9)

For non-Marxist (and some neo-Marxian) economists, of course, the Marxist proposition that increased labour productivity (as expressed in a rising organic composition of capital) may result in a falling profit rate is simply counterintuitive. Rejection of crude versions of the labour theory of value and/or uncritical acceptance of Okishio's (1961) notion that profit rates will tend to equalize at levels reached by the most technically innovative and productive capitals have led to hasty dismissals of Marx's law of the falling tendency of the average rate of profit. Three alternative explanations for the profitability crisis are frequently proffered: a rising strength of labour; deteriorating terms of international trade; and growing outlays on non-productive (especially government-funded) activities. Each of these has an evident relationship to the overall question of macro-economic productivity. A rising strength of labour at the point of production may result in declining industrial productivity (as well as in a possible "wage-push/profit squeeze"); deteriorating terms of trade, and loss of global market share, may be the result of national productivity increases smaller than those enjoyed by competitors; and increased investment in non-productive activities (or activities in which productivity growth is slower than average) may result in an output that is inadequate in relation to its labour (and other) inputs.

Notwithstanding that these phenomena have been adduced as alternatives to Marx's account of capitalist crisis, it is important to stress that none of them is entirely incompatible with it. A "rising strength of labour" and fierce competition in international trade are factors that strongly militate in favour of a rising technical/organic composition of capital, enhanced industrial productivity and a declining value rate of profit. Moreover, growth in the unproductive spheres of the economy can be a supplementary source of a valorization (profitability) crisis to the extent that it manifests itself through a disproportionate increase in the constant capital flow.

What all this points to is that both the specific weight and the rate of exploitation of the SNUL workforce matters for capital. To the extent that the SNUL workforce eclipses the productive workforce in relative size, this can only signify that enormous economic resources (as measured in value terms) are being diverted from productive to unproductive uses. And to the extent that the "productivity" and the rate of exploitation of the SNUL workforce declines relative to the productive workforce, this can only serve to slow the productivity growth of the economy, however innovative industry has become in its efforts to save on labour.

From a Marxist value-theoretical standpoint, the most salient difference between the surplus labour appropriated from SNUL workers and from productive workers is that more productive surplus labour translates into rising surplus value, while more SNUL surplus labour translates into reduced overhead costs. Every economy (whether ruled by the law of labour value or not) must, of course, be concerned with the efficient allocation of economic resources and the minimization of unnecessary overhead costs. However, only the capitalist economy requires the production of surplus value as its lifeblood. Hence, in acknowledging the truth in the proposition that increased social investment in education, health and welfare, and many other human services may constitute a non-productive burden on an anemic economic organism, Marxists must be insistent that it is only the capitalist economic organism that is dependent specifically on the production of surplus value. Further, while the expansion or contraction of production is necessarily governed by the appropriation of surplus labour under capitalist social-production rela- tions, production can indeed be governed by "the needs of socially developed human beings" given alternative (non-antagonistic) relations of production. Indeed, in a society liberated from the capitalist law of labour value, there may be no specifically social-structural obstacles to the near-total transfer of human activity from the sphere of "necessary" material production to the realm of freedom (Marx 1981b: 959).

The promise of Marx's vision of socialism is precisely a society in which "socially necessary labour time" will cease to be the measure of social wealth, and in which, as a consequence, the full potential of labour-saving technology can be realized and the free activity of human beings directed to socially useful and creative tasks. From this perspective much "socially necessary unproductive labour" under capitalism may be regarded as an alienated and adulterated prefiguration of the "free labour time" that will be at the disposal of a socialist society (Marx 1973: 705–706). To the extent that advanced capitalism allocates an increasing amount of social labour time to circulation activities (buying and selling, advertising, marketing, extending or withdrawing credit, changing titles of ownership and so forth) — time that might otherwise be used in the democratic planning and administration of a socialist economy — this can only reveal how the potential that now exists for the "many-sided development of human individuals" is systematically sacrificed on the altar of reproducing capitalist social relations. Moreover, to the extent that advanced capitalist states become less willing to support the social-maintenance labour involved in health care, education and social welfare — the paltry "programs for people" that reformist labour movements have been able to wring from a miserly social capital — this can only register as yet another index of capitalism's mounting contradictions, fundamental irrationality and boundless inhumanity.

Notes

1. A critical response to the argument contained in this article is provided by Dawson and Foster (1994). My reply to Dawson and Foster is found in Smith (1994–95).

2. Marx's most important writings on the subject of productive and unproductive labour include passages from *Theories of Surplus Value* (written between 1861 and 1863), the three volumes of *Capital* (drafted between 1863 and 1878) and *The Results of the Immediate Process of Production* (drafted between 1863 and 1866 as a possible bridging chapter between the first and second volumes of *Capital*).

3. The conventional Marxist treatment of the unproductive labour wage bill as part of social surplus value has been most frequently challenged by neo-Ricardian or neoclassical critics, who insist that the income of all wage labourers should be subsumed under variable capital. As I suggest later, the conventional conceptualization of unproductive labour is indeed susceptible to this sort of critique (which simply obviates the productive-unproductive distinction entirely) in so far as it involves a fetishistic departure from Marx's value theory.

4. For further discussion on this point, see Seymour 1972. On the concept of a functional loop, see Stinchcombe 1968: 80–100, who argues that a functionalist analysis is deficient if it is unable to a) incorporate intent (and therefore human agency) into its explanations, and b) specify the feedback mechanisms whereby structural patterns are reinforced and preserved over time.

5. A caveat is necessary here. Following the method of Mage's (1963) study, I distinguished between "flow" and "stock" expressions of constant capital and used only a stock measurement of constant capital in calculating the organic composition of capital and the rate of profit.

Bibliography

Abercrombie, Nicholas, and John Urry. 1983. *Capital, Labour and the Middle Classes*. London: Allen and Unwin.

Achcar, G. 2002. *The Clash of Barbarisms*. New York: Monthly Review Press.

Albert, Michael, and Alex Callinicos. 2003. *Movement Building 2004: Vision and Strategy*. <www.zmag,org/znet/zdebatealbertvscallinicos.htm>.

Ali, Tariq. 2002. *The Clash of Fundamentalisms*. London: Verso.

Anderson, Sara, and John Cavanagh. 2000. *The Rise of Corporate Global Power*. London: Institute for Policy Studies.

Armstrong, P., A. Glyn and J. Harrison. 1991. *Capitalism Since 1945*. Oxford: Blackwell.

Baragar, F. 2009. "Canada and the Crisis." In J. Guard and W. Antony (eds.), *Bankruptcies and Bailouts*. Halifax and Winnipeg: Fernwood Publishing.

Baran, Paul, and Paul Sweezy. 1966. *Monopoly Capital*. New York: Monthly Review Press.

Basu, K. 2009. "China and India: Idiosyncratic Paths to High Growth." *Economic and Political Weekly* XLIV: 38.

Baumol, W., and K. McLennan. 1985. "U.S. Productivity Performance and its Implications." In Baumol and McLennan (eds.), *Productivity Growth and U.S. Competitiveness*. New York and Oxford: Oxford University Press.

Blackwell, Judith C., Murray E.G. Smith and John S. Sorenson. 2003. *Culture of Prejudice: Arguments in Critical Social Science*. Peterborough: Broadview Press.

Bottomore, Tom. 1990. *The Socialist Economy: Theory and Practice*. New York and London: Guilford Press.

Braverman, Harry. 1974. *Labor and Monopoly Capital*. New York: Monthly Review Press.

Brenner, R. 1998a. "Uneven Development and the Long Downturn: The Advanced Capitalist Economies from Boom to Stagnation, 1950–1998." *New Left Review* 229.

_____. 1998b. "The Looming Crisis of World Capitalism: From Neoliberalism to Depression?" *Against the Current* 77 (November-December).

_____. 2009. "What is Good for Goldman Sachs Is Good for America: The Origins of the Current Crisis." Prologue to the Spanish translation of the author's *Economics of Global Turbulence* (Verso 2006), published by Akal.

Butovsky, J., and M.E.G. Smith. 2007. "Beyond Social Unionism: Farm Workers in Ontario and Some Lessons from Labour History." *Labour/Le Travail* 57 (Spring).

Carchedi, Guglielmo. 1977. *On the Economic Identification of Social Classes*. London and Boston: Routledge and Kegan Paul.

_____. 1987. "Class Politics, Class Consciousness, and the New Middle Class." *The Insurgent Sociologist* 14, 3.

Campbell, Ken. 2009. *Contours of the Collapse.* Unpublished manuscript.

Capitalism and Economic Crisis Website. n.d. Available at <http://www.capitalism-and-crisis.info/en/Welcome/New#Wages_and_productivity_USA>.

Chernomas, R. 1987. "Is Supply-Side Economics Rational for Capital?" *Review of Radical Political Economics* 19, 3.

_____. 1990. "Productive and Unproductive Labor and the Rate of Profit in Malthus, Ricardo and Marx." *Journal of History of Economic Thought* 12.

_____. 2009. "The Economic Crisis: Class Warfare from Reagan to Obama." In J. Guard and W. Antony (eds.), *Bankruptcies and Bailouts.* Halifax and Winnipeg: Fernwood Publishing.

Chomsky, Noam. 2004. *Hegemony or Survival.* London: Penguin.

Clawson, Dan. 1980. *Bureaucracy and the Labor Process.* New York: Monthly Review Press.

Cockshott, W. Paul, and Allin Cottrell. 1993. *Towards a New Socialism.* Nottingham: Spokesman. Available at <http://ricardo.ecn.wfu.edu/~cottrell/social-ism_book/>

Communist International. 1980 [1921]. "On Tactics." In *Theses, Resolutions and Manifestos of the First Four Congresses of the Third International.* London: Ink Links.

Dawson, M., and J.B. Foster. 1991. "The Tendency of the Surplus to Rise, 1963–1988." *Monthly Review* 43, 4.

_____. 1994. "Is There an Allocation Problem? Accounting for Unproductive Labor." *Science & Society* 58, 3 (Fall).

De Brunhoff, Suzanne. 1990. "Fictitious Capital." In J. Eatwell, M. Milgate and P. Newman (eds.), *The New Plagrave: Marxian Economics.* New York and London: W.W. Norton.

De Vroey, Michel. 1981. "Value, Production and Exchange." In Ian Steedman et al., *The Value Controversy.* London: Verso.

Deutscher, Isaac. 1973. *Marxism in Our Time.* San Francisco: Ramparts Press.

Dobb, Maurice. 1973. *Theories of Value and Distribution since Adam Smith.* Cambridge: Cambridge University Press.

Duménil, Gerard, and Dominique Lévy. 1993. *The Economics of the Profit Rate: Competition, Crises and Historical Tendencies of Capitalism.* Aldershot: Edward Elgar.

Duménil, G., M. Glick and J. Rangel. 1987. "The Rate of Profit in the United States." *Cambridge Journal of Economics* 11: 4.

Elson, D. 1979. "The Value Theory of Labour." In Diane Elson (ed.), *Value: The Representation of Labour in Capitalism.* London: CSE Books.

_____. 1988. "Market Socialism or Socialization of the Market?" *New Left Review* 85.

Fine, B. 2008. "Debating Lebowitz: Is Class Conflict the Moral and Historical Element in the Value of Labour-Power?" *Historical Materialism* 16, 3.

Fine, B., and L. Harris. 1979. *Rereading Capital.* New York: Columbia University Press.

Fischer, N. 1982. "The Ontology of Abstract Labor." *Review of Radical Political Economics* 14, 2.

Flaherty, D. 1992. "Self-Management and Socialism: Lessons from Yugoslavia." *Science & Society* 56, 1.

Foley, Duncan. 1986. *Understanding Capital: Marx's Economic Theory*. Cambridge, MA: Harvard University Press.

Foster, John Bellamy. 1986. *The Theory of Monopoly Capitalism*. New York: Monthly Review Press.

Freeman, Alan, and Guglielmo Carchedi (eds.). 1996. *Marx and Non-Equilibrium Economics*. Cheltenham, UK: Edward Elgar.

Freeman, Alan, Andrew Kliman, and Julian Wells (eds.). 2004. *The New Value Controversy and the Foundations of Economics*. Cheltenham, UK: Edward Elgar.

George, Susan. 1988. *A Fate Worse than Debt*. Harmondsworth: Penguin.

_____. 2004. *Another World is Possible if...* London: Verso.

Gerstein, Ira. 1986. "Production, Circulation and Value." In Ben Fine (ed.), *The Value Dimension*. London and New York: Routledge and Kegan Paul.

Gillman, Joseph. 1957. *The Falling Rate of Profit*. London: Dobson.

Goldfield, M., and B.D. Palmer. 2007. "Canada's Workers Movement: Uneven Developments." *Labour/Le Travail* 57 (Spring).

Gorbachev, Mikhail. 1987. *Perestroika: New Thinking for our Country and the World*. New York: Harper and Row.

Gorz, Andre. 1973. *Socialism and Revolution*. New York: Anchor.

_____. 1982. *Farewell to the Working Class: An Essay on Post-Industrial Socialism*. Boston: Pluto Press.

Hart-Landsberg, Martin, and Paul Burkett. 2005. *China and Socialism: Market Reforms and Class Struggle*. New York: Monthly Review Press.

Harvey, David. 2003. *The New Imperialism*. Oxford: Oxford University Press.

_____. 2005. *A Brief History of Neoliberalism*. Oxford and New York: Oxford University Press.

Hilferding, R. 1975. "Böhm-Bawerk's Criticism of Marx." In Paul Sweezy (ed.), *Karl Marx and the Close of his System & Böhm-Bawerk's Criticism of Marx*. London: Merlin Press

Himmelweit, S., and S. Mohun. 1981. "Real Abstractions and Anomalous Assumptions." In Ian Steedman et al., *The Value Controversy*. London: Verso

IBT (International Bolshevik Tendency). 2001. "Global Capitalism and Class Struggle." *1917—Journal of the International Bolshevik Tendency* 23. Available at <www.bolshevik.org>.

_____. 2002. "Platformism and Bolshevism." Available at <www.bolshevik.org>.

_____. 2009. "Political Revolution or Counter-Revolution — Whither China?" *1917—Journal of the International Bolshevik Tendency* 31 (April). Available at <www.bolshevik.org>.

ILO (International Labour Organization). 2001. *World Employment Report*. Geneva.

_____. 2009. *Key Indicators of the Labour Market*. Sixth edition. Geneva.

IMF (International Monetary Fund). 2009. *World Economic Outlook* October.

Kilmister, A. 1998. "Simply Wrong — How Brenner's Stripped Down View of Crisis Leads to Reformism or Reaction." *Socialist Outlook* 20.

Klein, Naomi. 2007. *The Shock Doctrine: The Rise of Disaster Capitalism*. Toronto: Knopf Canada.

Kliman, Andrew. 2007. *Reclaiming Marx's "Capital."* Lanham, MD: Lexington

Books.

Laclau, Ernesto, and Chantal Mouffe. 1985. *Hegemony and Socialist Strategy*. London: Verso.

Laibman, David. 1982. "Technical Change, the Real Wage and the Rate of Exploitation: The Falling Rate of Profit Reconsidered." Review of *Radical Political Economics* 14: 2.

_____. 1992. "Market and Plan: Socialist Structures in History and Theory." *Science & Society* 56, 1.

Le Grand, J., and S. Estrin (eds.). 1989. *Market Socialism*. Oxford: Clarendon Press.

Lebowitz, Michael. 1972. "The Increasing Cost of Circulation and the Marxian Competitive Model." *Science & Society* 36, 3.

_____. 1991. "The Significance of Marx's Missing Book on Wage-Labor." *Rethinking Marxism* 4, 2.

_____. 2003. *Beyond* Capital: *Marx's Political Economy of the Working Class*. Second edition. Basingstoke, Hampshire: Palgrave Macmillan.

Leontieff, W. 1982. "The Distribution of Work and Income." *Scientific American* September.

Lindsey, J.K. 1980. "The Conceptualization of Social Class." *Studies in Political Economy* 3.

Lipietz, Alain. 1985. *The Enchanted World*. London: Verso.

Magdoff, Harry. 1992. "Globalization — To What End?" In Ralph Miliband and Leo Panitch (eds.), *Socialist Register 1992*. London: Merlin Press.

Mage, Shane. 1963. *The Law of the Falling Tendency of the Rate of Profit: Its Place in the Marxian Theoretical System and Relevance to the U.S. Economy*. Columbia University, PhD Dissertation.

Mandel, Ernest. 1968. *Marxist Economic Theory* Volumes 1 and 2. New York: Monthly Review Press.

_____. 1975. *Late Capitalism*. London: New Left Books.

_____. 1981. "Introduction." In Karl Marx, *Capital* Volume Three. New York: Vintage.

_____. 1986. "In Defense of Socialist Planning." *New Left Review* 159.

_____. 1989. "How to Make No Sense of Marx." In R. Ware and K. Nielsen (eds.), *Analyzing Marxism*. Canadian Journal of Philosophy, Supplementary Volume 15.

_____. 1992. *Power and Money: A Marxist Theory of Bureaucracy*. London and New York: Verso.

Mandel, Ernest, and Alan Freeman (eds.). 1984. *Ricardo, Marx, Sraffa*. London: Verso.

Marx, Karl. 1953. "Die Wortform." In *Kleine Okonomische Schriften*. Berlin: Dietz Verlag.

_____. 1965. "Marx to L. Kugelmann in Hanover, July 11 1868." In Karl Marx and Frederick Engels, *Selected Correspondence*. Moscow: Progress Publishers.

_____. 1970. "Marginal Notes on the Programme of the German Workers' Party." In K. Marx and F. Engels, *Selected Works*, Volume Three. Moscow: Progress Publishers.

_____. 1973. *Grundrisse*. Harmondsworth, Middlesex: Penguin Books.

_____. 1975. *Theories of Surplus Value*, Part III. Moscow: Progress.

_____. 1977 [1867]. *Capital*, Volume One. New York: Vintage.

_____. 1978a. *Theories of Surplus Value*, Part I. Moscow: Progress.

_____. 1978b. *Capital*, III. Moscow: Progress Publishers.

_____. 1981a. *Capital*, Volume Two, New York: Vintage.

_____. 1981b. *Capital*, Volume Three, New York: Vintage.

_____. 1989. *Readings from Karl Marx*, (ed. Derek Sayer). London and New York: Routledge.

Marx, Karl, and Frederick Engels. 1969 [1845]. *The German Ideology.* In Marx and Engels, *Selected Works*, Volome 1, Moscow: Progress Publishers.

_____. 1998 [1848]. *The Communist Manifesto*. New York: Monthly Review Press.

Marxsite. n.d. <http://marxsite.com/Charles%20Post%20crisis%20theory. html>.

McNally, David. 1993. *Against the Market: Political Economy, Market Socialism and the Marxist Critique.* London and New York: Verso.

_____. 2009a. "Global Finance, the Current Crisis and Challenges to the Dollar." In *Financial Meltdown: Canada, the Economic Crisis and Political Struggle.* Toronto: Socialist Interventions Pamphlet Series.

_____. 2009b. "Inequality, the Profit System and Global Crisis." In J. Guard and W. Antony (eds.), *Bankruptcies and Bailouts*. Halifax and Winnipeg: Fernwood Publishing.

Meek, Ronald. 1956. *Studies in the Labor Theory of Value*, Second edition. New York: Monthly Review Press.

Miller, Riel. 1984. "A Comment on Productive and Unproductive Labour." *Studies in Political Economy* 14.

Moreau, F. 1991. "The Condition of the Working Class under Capitalism Today: The Mexican Case." *Socialist Alternatives* 1:1 (Fall).

Moseley, Fred. 1987. "Marx's Crisis Theory and the Postwar Economy." In R. Cherry et al. (eds.), *The Imperilled Economy*. New York: Union for Radical Political Economics.

_____. 1991. *The Falling Rate of Profit in the Postwar United States Economy*. New York: St. Martin's Press.

_____. 1993. "Marx's Logical Method and the 'Transformation Problem'." In Fred Moseley *Marx's Method in* Capital*: A Reexamination*. Atlantic Highlands: Humanities Press.

_____. 2009. "The U.S. Economic Crisis: Causes and Solutions." *International Socialist Review* 64 (March–April). Available at <http://www.isreview.org/issues/64/feat-moseley.shtml>.

Moseley, Fred (ed.). 1993. *Marx's Method in* Capital*: A Reexamination*. Atlantic Highlands: Humanities Press.

Nove, Alec. 1983. *The Economics of Feasible Socialism*. London: George Allen and Unwin.

_____. 1987. "Markets and Socialism." *New Left Review* 161.

Okishio, N. 1961. "Technical Change and the Rate of Profit." *Kobe University Economic Review* 7.

Ollman, Bertell (ed.). 1998. *Market Socialism and the Debate among Socialists.* New York and London: Routledge.

Palmer, Bryan D. 2007. *James P. Cannon and the Origins of the American Revolutionary Left, 1890–1928*. Urbana and Chicago: University of Illinois Press.

Petras, James, and Henry Veltmeyer. 2001. *Globalization Unmasked: Imperialism in the*

21st Century. Halifax: Fernwood Publishing; London: Zed Books.

Poulantzas, Nicos. 1978. *Classes in Contemporary Capitalism*. London: Verso.

Rinehart, James. 2006. *The Tyranny of Work*. Toronto: Thomson-Nelson.

Rubin, I.I. 1973. *Essays on Marx's Theory of Value*. Montreal: Black Rose.

Samary, C. 1991. "To Live Better and More Freely: Of Ends and Means." *Socialist Alternatives* 1, 1.

Samuelson, Paul. 1968. *Economics: An Introductory Analysis*, Second Canadian edition (with Anthony Scott). Toronto: McGraw-Hill.

Seymour, J. 1972. "Myth of Neo-Capitalism." *RCY Newsletter*.

Shaikh, Anwar. 1977. "Marx's Theory of Value and the 'Transformation Problem'." In J. Schwartz (ed.), *The Subtle Anatomy of Capitalism*. Santa Monica: Goodyear Publishing.

_____. 1978a. "An Introduction to the History of Crisis Theories." In *U.S. Capitalism in Crisis*. New York: Union for Radical Political Economics.

_____. 1978b. "National Income Accounts and Marxian Categories." Mimeo. New York: New School for Social Research.

_____. 1978c. "Political Economy and Capitalism: Notes on Dobb's Theory of Crisis." *Cambridge Journal of Economics*, June.

_____. 1981. "The Poverty of Algebra." In Ian Steedman et al., *The Value Controversy*. London: Verso.

_____. 1987. "The Falling Rate of Profit and the Economic Crisis in the U.S." In R. Cherry et al. (eds.), *The Imperilled Economy*. New York: Union for Radical Political Economics.

_____. 1989. "The Current Economic Crisis: Causes and Implications." <http://homepage.newschool.edu/~AShaikh/The%20current%20economic%20crisis.pdf>.

_____. 1990. "Abstract and Concrete Labour." In J. Eatwell, M. Milgate and P. Newman (eds.), *The New Plagrave: Marxian Economics*. New York and London: W.W. Norton.

Shaikh, Anwar, and Ahmet E. Tonak. 1994. *Measuring the Wealth of Nations: The Political Economy of National Accounts*. Cambridge: Cambridge University Press.

Smith, Murray E.G. 1984. *The Falling Rate of Profit*. M.A. Thesis, Department of Sociology, University of Manitoba.

_____. 1989. *The Value Controversy and Social Theory: An Inquiry into Marx's "Labour Theory of Value."* Ph.D. dissertation, University of British Columbia.

_____. 1991a. "Understanding Marx's Theory of Value: An Assessment of a Controversy." *Canadian Review of Sociology and Anthropology* 28, 3.

_____. 1991b. "Respecifying Marx's Value Categories: A Theoretical and Empirical Reconsideration of the 'Law of the Falling Rate of Profit'." *Studies in Political Economy* 35.

_____. 1993. "Productivity, Valorization and Crisis: Socially Necessary Unproductive Labour in Contemporary Capitalism." *Science & Society* 57, 3.

_____. 1994a. *Invisible Leviathan: The Marxist Critique of Market Despotism beyond Postmodernism*. Toronto: University of Toronto Press.

_____. 1994b. "Alienation, Exploitation and Abstract Labour: A Humanist Defense of Marx's Theory of Value." *Review of Radical Political Economics* 26, 1.

_____. 1994–95. "Unproductive Labor and Profit Rate Trends: A Rejoinder." *Science*

& Society 58, 4.

_____. 1996–97. "Revisiting Trotsky: Reflections on the Stalinist Debacle and Trotskyism as Alternative." *Rethinking Marxism* 9, 3.

_____. 1997. "Rethinking 'The Middle Class': Ideological Constructions and Contradictory Structural Locations." *Brock Review* 6, 1/2.

_____. 1999. "The Necessity of Value Theory." *Historical Materialism* 4.

_____. 2000. "Political Economy and the Canadian Working Class: Marxism or Nationalist Reformism?" *Labour/Le Travail* 46.

_____. 2008. "Self-Employment." In William Darity, Jr. (ed.), *International Encyclopedia of the Social Sciences.* Second edition. Detroit: MacMillan Reference.

_____. 2009. "Against Dualism: Marxism and the Necessity of Dialectical Monism." *Science & Society* 73, 3 (July).

Smith, M.E.G., and K.W. Taylor. 1996. "Profitability Crisis and the Erosion of Popular Prosperity: The Canadian Economy, 1947–1991." *Studies in Political Economy* 49.

Smith, Tony. 2000. *Technology and Capital in the Age of Lean Production.* Albany: State University of New York Press.

Sohn-Rethel, Alfred. 1978. *Intellectual and Manual Labour: A Critique of Epistemology.* London and Basingstoke: Macmillan.

Soros, George 1997. "Avoiding a Breakdown." *Financial Times* December 31.

Spartacist. 1988. *"Market Socialism" in Eastern Europe.* New York: Spartacist Publishing.

_____. 2001. *Marxism versus Anarchism.* New York: Spartacist Publishing.

Sraffa, Piero. 1960. *Production of Commodities by Means of Commodities.* Cambridge, U.K.: Cambridge University Press.

Statistics Canada. 1987. *Manufacturing Industries of Canada.* Catalogue 31-203 Annual.

_____. 1989. *National Income and Expenditure Accounts.* Catalogues 13-531, occasional, and 13-201, annual.

Steedman, Ian. 1977. *Marx After Sraffa.* London: New Left Books.

Stinchcombe, Arthur. 1968. *Constructing Social Theories.* Baltimore, MD: Johns Hopkins University Press.

Sweezy, Paul. 1968 [1942]. *The Theory of Capitalist Development.* New York: Monthly Review Press.

Tarbuck, K. 1983. "Marx: Productive and Unproductive Labour." *Studies in Political Economy* 12.

Thompson, Paul. 1989. *The Nature of Work.* Basingstoke and London: Macmillan.

Trepper, Leopold. 1977. *The Great Game.* New York: McGraw-Hill.

Trotsky, Leon. 1970a [1937]. *The Revolution Betrayed.* New York: Pathfinder.

_____. 1970b [1939–40]. *In Defense of Marxism.* New York: Pathfinder.

_____. 1973a [1938]. *The Transitional Program for Socialist Revolution.* New York: Pathfinder.

_____. 1973b. *Writings of Leon Trotsky 1932.* New York: Pathfinder.

_____. 1998 [1938]. *The Transitional Program.* London-Toronto: Bolshevik Publications.

UNDP (United Nations Development Program). 1996. *Human Development Report.* New York.

URPE (Union for Radical Political Economics). 1992. "The Future of Socialism."

Review of Radical Political Economics 24, 3–4.

von Bortkiewicz, L. 1975 (1907). "On the Correction of Marx's Fundamental Theoretical Construction in the Third Volume of Capital." In P. Sweezy (ed.), *Karl Marx and the Close of His System & Böhm-Bawerk's Criticism of Marx*. London: Merlin Press.

Webber, Michael, and David Rigby. 1996. *The Golden Age Illusion: Rethinking Postwar Capitalism*. New York: Guilford Press.

Weil, R. 1995. "Contradictory Class Definitions: Petty Bourgeoisie and the 'Classes' of Erik Olin Wright." *Critical Sociology* 21, 3.

Wood, Ellen Meiksins. 1986. *The Retreat from Class: A New "True" Socialism*. London: Verso.

Workman, Thom. 2009. *If You're In My Way, I'm Walking: The Assault on Working People since 1970*. Halifax and Winnipeg: Fernwood Publishing.

Wright, Erik Olin. 1978. *Class, Crisis and the State*. London: Verso.

Yaffe, D. 1973. "The Marxian Theory of Crisis, Capital and the State." *Economy and Society* 11, 2.

Zakaria, Fareed. 2009. "The Capitalist Manifesto: Greed Is Good (To a Point)." *Newsweek*, June 13. <http://www.newsweek.com/id/201935>.

Index

De Brunhoff, Suzanne, 26
debt, 2, 7, 9, 16, 20, 23, 73, 104, 127, 163
deduction from surplus value, 69, 88, 152-153
deformed workers state –19, 29
degenerated workers state, 29, 110, 115
Deng Xiaoping, 17, 19
domestic labour, 26, 46, 114, 148
ecology; ecological sustainability, 25, 44, 118
embodied labour, 142
Engels, Frederick, 32-33, 60, 122
equalization of profit rates, 48, 104, 139
Erfurt Programme, 107, 126
European Union, 62, 64
Eurozone, 1
exploitation; relations of exploitation, xi, 3, 10, 12, 16, 18, 24, 26, 28, 32, 39, 40, 43-46, 48, 52- 56, 59, 61, 69, 79, 95-97, 119, 127, 130, 137, 139, 149, 164-165
feudalism, 37-38, 148
fictitious capital, 7, 12, 15-16, 26, 127
finance; financial capital; financialization, ix-x, 1-2, 6-12, 15-16, 18-23, 25-28, 34, 39-40, 47- 48, 50-61, 63, 65, 84-85, 94-95, 99, 127, 149, 150, 159-160
forces of production, 32, 37, 52, 57-58, 67, 90, 119, 122
formal equality (relations of), 32
Fourth International, 107, 135
France, 10, 105, 127
Fukuyama, Francis, 117
fundamentalist crisis and value theory, 74, 76, 80-81, 83-84, 86, 142-146
Gates, Bill, 33-34
Geithner, Tim, 36
George, Susan, 129-131
Germany, 10, 21-22, 71-73, 76
Gillman, Joseph, 151-152
global social-justice movement, 118
Gorbachev, Mikhail, 110-111
Gorz, Andre, 107, 114

Gotha Programme, 4, 67
Great Depression, 1, 23, 66, 74, 127
Greenspan, Alan, 15, 16
growth rates, 1, 10, 11, 16-18, 29, 110
Harvey, David, 28, 39
Heyman, Jack, 133
Hilferding, Rudolf, 39, 41, 75
historical structural crisis of capitalism, x, 57, 59, 94, 163
housing; housing market, 2, 7, 20, 30, 50
Human Development Index, 124
Hungary, 1
Iceland, 1
imperialism, 59, 73, 75, 109,
independent socialists, 118, 126-127, 131-132
indicators of development, 1987, 124
India, 15, 61, 119, 124,
inflation, 8, 16, 23, 65, 108, 139, 163
Institute for Policy Studies, 62
International Bolshevik Tendency (IBT), 136
International Longshore and Warehouse Union (ILWU), 133
International Monetary Fund (IMF), 1
international trade, 1, 69, 164
Invisible Leviathan, x, xi, 3, 4, 69, 70, 90
Italy, 10, 105, 127
Japan, 1, 10, 16, 19, 21-23, 62, 71-74, 76
Keynes, John Maynard; Keynesianism, 8, 22, 23, 26 60, 65, 73, 76
Khrushchev, Nikita, 19, 109
Klein, Naomi, 26
Korea (North), 124
Korea (South), 16
labour movement, 8, 14-15, 18, 25, 36, 55, 59, 93, 98, 109, 125, 132, 136, 166
Labour Party, 133
labour value; law of labour value, xi, 26, 31, 4, 49, 50, 68, 71, 78, 84, 120, 137, 139, 141, 143, 163, 165
law of the falling tendency of the rate of profit, xi, 24, 41, 51, 56, 57, 66, 67, 71, 79, 94, 151, 159, 162, 163